Colloquial
Dutch

The Colloquial Series

Series Adviser: Gary King

The following languages are available in the Colloquial series:

Albanian	Italian
Amharic	Japanese
Arabic (Levantine)	Korean
Arabic of Egypt	Latvian
Arabic of the Gulf and	Lithuanian
Saudi Arabia	Malay
Basque	Norwegian
Bulgarian	Panjabi
* Cambodian	Persian
* Cantonese	Polish
†* Chinese	† Portuguese
Croatian and Serbian	Portuguese of Brazil
Czech	Romanian
Danish	* Russian
Dutch	Slovak
English	Slovene
Estonian	Somali
Finnish	†* Spanish
† French	Spanish of Latin America
† German	Swedish
* Greek	* Thai
Gujarati	Turkish
Hindi	Ukrainian
Hungarian	* Vietnamese
Indonesian	Welsh

Accompanying cassette(s) are available for the above titles.
*Accompanying CDs are also available.
†CD-ROMs are also available. (German available autumn 1998)

Colloquial
Dutch

The Complete Course for Beginners

Bruce Donaldson

London and New York

First published 1996
by Routledge
11 New Fetter Lane, London EC4P 4EE

Simultaneously published in the USA and Canada
by Routledge
29 West 35th Street, New York, NY 10001

Reprinted 1998 and 1999

© 1996 Bruce Donaldson

Illustrations on pages 136–7, 211 and 219 by Matthew Crabbe

Typeset in Times Ten by Florencetype Ltd, Stoodleigh, Devon

Printed and bound in England by Clays Ltd, St Ives PLC

The author has asserted his moral rights in accordance with Section 77
of the Copyright, Designs and Patents Act 1988

British Library Cataloguing in Publication Data
A catalogue record for this book is available from the British Library

Library of Congress Cataloguing in Publication Data
  Donaldson, B.C. (Bruce C.), (1948–
    Colloquial Dutch : a complete language course / Bruce Donaldson.
      p. cm. – (Colloquial series)
    1. Dutch language – Grammar. 2. Dutch language – Textbooks for
  foreign speakers – English. I. Title.
  PF112.D59 1996
  439.3'182421—dc20   95–35857
                                                            CIP

ISBN 0–415–13086–7 (book)
ISBN 0–415–13087–5 (cassettes)
ISBN 0–415–13088–3 (book and cassettes course)

Contents

About this book

Where is Dutch spoken and who is it spoken by?

The official name of the country we generally know as Holland is the Kingdom of the Netherlands, **het Koninkrijk der Nederlanden**. The everyday official term is **Nederland**, but colloquially many people living in the west of the country refer to it as **Holland** (see page 24). The country, which is only 42,000 square kilometres in size, has some 15,000,000 inhabitants.

In addition, the northern half of Belgium, known as Flanders (**Vlaanderen**), also speaks Dutch while the southern half, known as Wallonia (**Wallonië**), speaks French. Of the approximately 10 million inhabitants of the Kingdom of Belgium (**het Koninkrijk België**) 58 per cent are Flemings who speak Dutch as their mother tongue. The Netherlands and Belgium, together with Luxemburg, are known collectively as the Low Countries (**de Lage Landen**), which also happens to be the literal meaning of 'The Netherlands'.

In the five islands of the Dutch Antilles (**de Nederlandse Antillen**) and on the island of Aruba, which are constitutionally part of the Netherlands and whose combined population numbers some 200,000, Dutch is an official language, although it is not necessarily the mother tongue of the majority of the population.

Dutch is also the official language of the former Dutch colony of Surinam (**Suriname**), which obtained independence from the Netherlands in 1975. Although many languages are spoken there, affairs of state and education are conducted in Dutch. The tens of thousands of **Surinamers** who have settled in the Netherlands since the 1970s speak Dutch more or less as their mother tongue, or at least as proficiently as their mother tongue, which is also the case with the thousands of people of Indonesian descent who left for the Netherlands when the Dutch East Indies gained independence after World War II.

Many tens of thousands of Dutch people left the country of their birth after World War II to emigrate to North America, Australia, South Africa and New Zealand. The number of native-speakers of Dutch is estimated to be somewhere in excess of 21 million and Dutch is thus not quite the 'minor' language it is sometimes purported to be.

Standard Dutch/ABN

Standard Dutch is most usually referred to by the abbreviation **ABN**, short for **Algemeen Beschaafd Nederlands** (General Cultivated Dutch). **ABN** is thus the Dutch equivalent of 'King's English' or 'RP' or whatever term you use to designate standard English. This abbreviation is used from time to time in this book.

Where an asterisk precedes a Dutch construction, e.g. *op het, this indicates that what follows is ungrammatical, i.e. a construction that is not possible.

Flemish usage

The differences between the Dutch and Belgian varieties of the language are minimal, at least at an official level – at the level of dialect they can be quite substantial, even to the point of some Belgian dialects being incomprehensible to a Dutch person, but this also applies to certain dialects spoken in the Netherlands. There is an official body, **De Nederlandse Taalunie**, based in The Hague, which is charged among other things with keeping the official Dutch language uniform in the two countries in which it is spoken. Generally speaking, the northern norm has gradually asserted itself in Flanders and although Flemish usage, even at the official level, varies slightly from that of the north (e.g. certain words and variations in word order sometimes called **Algemeen Zuidnederlands** or simply **Zuidnederlands**), this constitutes no impediment to mutual comprehension. Consequently the Dutch presented to you in this book is based solely on **ABN** as spoken in the Netherlands.

Culture points

Every lesson contains a section entitled 'Culture point' which attempts to give some feeling for the cultural differences of the Netherlands and is often of relevance to the content of the chapter. Although the Netherlands and Flanders form a linguistic entity, the cultural differences between the two peoples are enormous, this being the result of centuries of political separation and the understandably overwhelming influence of French culture on Flanders. Generally speaking, the culture points relate only to the Netherlands – to have devoted equal time and space to both cultures would have been unwieldy.

I have been heavily involved with the Dutch language for twenty-five years and have a great love of the language and admiration for the achievements of the Dutch nation, as well as a soft spot for the Flemish people, ever generous and modest. I hope therefore that the reader will forgive me when from time to time in the culture points I have a dig at the Dutch. The remarks are not meant to be malicious, merely entertaining; they may on occasion tend to hyperbole, but nevertheless there is a grain of truth in all of them, as I am sure you will find other foreigners will confirm (but perhaps not the Dutch).

Getting the Dutch to speak Dutch

Learning Dutch is a fascinating experience, all the more so if you know German, but even if English is the only other language you know, you will find much in Dutch that will be familiar to you as the languages are historically quite closely related. Indeed, had the Normans never invaded England, the two languages might well have been mutually intelligible. Learning a foreign language is never easy, not even one as close to English as Dutch, but there are certainly many languages that English-speaking people find much harder to learn than Dutch. Don't let yourself get discouraged. Success in foreign language learning comes from devotion and perseverance. The rewards at the end are worth it. You must make use of every opportunity to hear, read, write and speak it. Don't worry about making mistakes; if you wait until you can express yourself perfectly before ever opening your mouth, that day will never come – fluency always precedes correctness.

One of the traditional grumbles of English-speaking learners of Dutch is that the Dutch are loath to speak Dutch to them, their own linguistic ability being quite remarkable, but also an inevitable consequence of nobody but the Dutch and Flemings being able to speak Dutch, which is hardly the case with the French and the Germans, for example. You may need to plead your case with the Dutch to speak Dutch to you. Even your attempts to do so, let alone final success in mastering their language, will earn you their instant admiration, even if they may think you are a little quaint for wanting to do so. Much has been written on their lack of linguistic pride, which is an allegation that certainly could not be directed at the Flemings, but then they have French-speaking compatriots to contend with.

This book covers all the essentials of Dutch grammar and presents them in a form suitable for self-study or class use. Inevitably there are many finer points of grammar not covered in a book of this size. Those who have worked through this book and feel inspired to learn further are advised to acquire *Dutch: A comprehensive grammar*, written by the same author and also published by Routledge.

Any comments from readers for the improvement of future editions will be gratefully received. Please write to me at the Department of Germanic Studies and Russian, University of Melbourne, Parkville, Victoria, Australia 3052 or send an e-mail to <b.donaldson@language.unimelb.edu.au>.

Acknowledgements

I wish to thank Eve Oakley for casting her native-speaker eye over the completed manuscript, Helen Cain for her contribution in compiling the glossaries and Anke de Vries for providing me with the realia scattered through this book.

Introduction

The pronunciation of Dutch

Possibly the most difficult aspect of learning Dutch is the pronunciation and unfortunately that is where you have to start. Don't be discouraged by sounds that you may feel you will never be able to get your tongue around. With exposure to the language your accent will improve with time. The Dutch themselves think that mastering the **g/ch** sound is the greatest challenge the pronunciation of their language confronts the learner with and they constantly test foreigners' articulation skills by asking them to pronounce the place name **Scheveningen**. Anyone who has ever had a fly stuck in their throat can articulate a **g/ch**; the Dutch **r** sound, on the other hand, can be quite tricky for English speakers. But in general one short vowel, some of the long vowels and especially the diphthongs are what you will most probably find the greatest challenge, e.g. **put**; **brood, muur; lijden, huis**. Perfection comes with time and practice. Simply persevere.

It is not easy to give a true indication of the sounds of Dutch in writing without resorting to phonetic symbols, which most readers will presumably not be acquainted with. Thus where the following Dutch sounds are compared to those in English words, these merely represent an approximation of their pronunciation. Don't worry about what the Dutch sample words mean, just practise the sounds.

Vowels 🔲

Short vowels

a This is a very short sound not unlike the vowel in English *but*, e.g. **bal, kat, zat, mat, rat, plak**.

e Generally speaking, this vowel does not differ greatly from that in *pet* but it can tend towards that in *pat*,[1] e.g. **bed, zet, trekken, vet, met**.

i This vowel is identical to that in *lit*, e.g. **zit, rits, kil, pit, pil**.

o This vowel is similar to that in *rot*. In the speech of some, but only in certain words, it tends to sound like the vowel in *ought* but pronounced very short. The non-native-speaker can ignore this distinction, e.g. **pot, hond, kok, rots, strop, vos**.

u This is the most difficult of the short vowels as it has no equivalent in English. It is not unlike an English *er* sound as in *heard* and *curse* but is shorter, e.g. **put, bus, mus, suf, pick-up**.

Half-long vowels

The three vowels dealt with here are all pronounced longer when an **r** follows.

eu This sound is pronounced with clear rounding of the lips and is similar to that in English *heard*. This is very much only an approximate description of the sound. Listen closely to how the Dutch pronounce it, e.g. **heus, leunen, steunen; deur, geur, kleur, zeuren**.

ie This is identical to the sound in *peek*, e.g. **dief, fiets, hielp, Pieter; dier, mier, vieren**.

oe This vowel is more or less the same as that in *put*, e.g. **boek, zoek, moeder, poes, zoet; boer, voeren**.

Long vowels

Note that the long vowels are written double in closed syllables and single in open syllables, which is one of the basic rules of Dutch spelling.

aa This vowel is similar to that in *father* and is pronounced distinctly long, e.g. **laat, maat, raaf, zaal; manen, vader, varen**.

ee This is a long, pure *ay* sound as in *lay* but avoiding any tendency

---

1 For this reason the vowels in *pet* and *pat* and *leg* and *lack* are often indistinguishable to Dutch speakers. Conversely, if a Dutchman introduces himself as **Henk**, an English speaker may well assume it is written **Hank**. For the same reason the very common English loanwords **tram, flat** and **tank**, for example, are pronounced and sometimes even written **trem, flet** and **tenk**.

to diphthongise, e.g. **leed, leef, meel, peer, teen; keren, peren, zeven.**

oo This is a long, pure *oh* sound, more or less as in *wrote* but is a little shorter and without any diphthongisation. This is very much only an approximate description of the sound. Listen closely to how the Dutch pronounce it, e.g. **brood, roos, zool, zoon; broden, lopen, rozen, toren.**

uu This is the same sound as in French *pur* or German *Tür*, e.g. **fuut, minuut; muren, zuur, puur.**

Diphthongs

auw, ou(w) This sound, which is similar to that in English *house*, is written for historical reasons either **auw, ou** or **ouw.** Where another syllable follows, the **w** is pronounced as an English *w*, e.g. **blauw, lauw, miauw, rauw; blauwe, bouwen, vouwen.** The combination **oude** is colloquially pronounced **ouwe**, e.g. **houden, oude, schouder.**

ei/ij This sound is written for historical reasons in two ways. It is a long diphthong similar to that in *lay* in certain types of English (e.g. Cockney, Australian), but it must not be allowed to become an *i* sound as in *fight*, e.g. **ei, bereid, leiden, weide; bij, ijzer, lijden.** The combination **ijde** is colloquially pronounced **ije**, e.g. **rijden, snijden.** In the adjectival ending **-lijk** the vowel is pronounced like the *er* in *father*, e.g. **dagelijks, gemakkelijke, tijdelijk.**

ui This is possibly the hardest sound to master. It is similar to the vowel in *heard* but is pronounced with rounded lips. Listen closely to the way the Dutch pronounce it, e.g. **huis, kruit, muis, vuist.**

Double vowels

With all of those that end in **w**, if another syllable with an **e** follows, the **w** is pronounced like an English *w*.

aai Pronounce **aa + ie**, e.g. **kraai, saai, haaien, maaien.** In practice monosyllabic words like **kraai** and **saai** are scarcely distinguishable from the *i* sound in *fight* but with an **-en** ending, as in **maaien**, there are three distinct vowel sounds, i.e. **maa + ie + en.**

eeuw Pronounce **ee** + **oe**, e.g. **leeuw, meeuw, sneeuwen.**
ieuw Pronounce **ie** + **oe**, e.g. **hieuw, nieuw.**
oei Pronounce **oe** + **ie**, e.g. **koeien, boei, snoei. Goede** 'good' is occasionally written and always pronounced **goeie**, but in this case the pronunciation is more **oe** + **je**.
ooi Pronounce **oo** + **ie**, e.g. **mooi, hooi, vlooien, looien.** Colloquially the combination **ode** is pronounced **ooie**, e.g. **rode, dode.**
uw Pronounce **uu** + **oe**, e.g. **ruw, sluw, uw.** If such words have an **e** ending, the combination is pronounced **uu** + **e**, e.g. **ruwe, sluwe, uwe.**

Consonants 🔲

b There is little or no distinction between an English and a Dutch **b**, e.g. **bal, bier, boek; hebben, webben.** At the end of a word a **b** is pronounced as a **p**, e.g. **heb, web.**
c This letter is only used in foreign words and can correspond, as in English, to either an **s** or a **k** sound, e.g. **cent, circa; accoord, consequent.**
ch This letter combination is pronounced like the 'ch' in Scottish *loch*. It is certainly much harsher, i.e. more guttural, than the sound in German *ich* but commonly even more guttural than that in German *ach*. In indigenous words it only occurs after a vowel, e.g. **chaos, kachel, lach.**
d There is little or no distinction between an English and a Dutch **d**, e.g. **den, doen, door, dier, deur; bedden, doden.** At the end of a word a **d** is pronounced as a **t**, e.g. **bed, dood, wed, pad.**
f There is no distinction between an English and a Dutch **f**, e.g. **Fries, fiets, fris; blaffen; laf.**
g This is the same sound as that written **ch** but unlike **ch** it occurs at the beginning of words, e.g. **gaan, gat, goot, gieten.**
h There is no distinction between an English and a Dutch **h**, e.g. **hond, haan, hut.**
j This letter is pronounced as an English *y*, e.g. **jaar, juk, jenever.**
k This letter is pronounced like *k* in English but without aspiration,[2] e.g. **kat, kar, koor, kier; boeken, lakken; rok, vak.**

---

2 Aspiration is the term given to the 'breathiness' with which English *k*, *p* and *t* are pronounced. Compare English *cat*, *pot* and *table* with Dutch **kat**, **pot** and **tafel**. By putting your hand to your mouth as you pronounce these six words you should feel air being blasted onto it when you pronounce the English words, but it should

l   A Dutch **l** is said to be 'thicker' than in English, particularly after a vowel, e.g. **liep, lint, lopen; bellen, zullen; wel, zal.**

m   There is no distinction between an English and a Dutch **m**, e.g. **maan, man, mat; lammeren; kam.**

n   There is no distinction between an English and a Dutch **n**, e.g. **nee, niet, noot; bonen; ben.**

ng   This combination is always pronounced as in *singer*, never as in *finger*, e.g. **honger, vinger, zingen; ging, zong.**

p   This letter is pronounced like *p* in English but without aspiration, e.g. **Piet, pet, pan, poep; lappen; krap.**

qu   This combination is pronounced as if it were written **kw** (i.e. as an English *kv*), as indeed it often is in avant-garde publications, e.g. **qua, consequent/konsekwent.**

r   A Dutch **r** is difficult for English speakers to pronounce. First, it must always be pronounced even at the end of words. There are basically two acceptable pronunciations of the sound. You can choose between a rolled *r*, trilling the tip of your tongue against your teeth, as in Italian, or you can opt for a throaty *r*, not unlike the *r* usually heard in German but certainly not as rasping as a French *r*. Choose whichever *r* you find easier to pronounce, but be consistent. It is usually easiest to pronounce, and thus practise, *r* when immediately followed by a vowel; final *r* is the hardest to master, e.g. **Rus, riet, rood; brood, draad, praat; kar, ver, word; baard, woord, leert; duur, puur, mier, broer, koor, raar; vader, moeder, poeder, verder.**

s   You will get away with pronouncing **s** as in English but if you listen closely to the way the Dutch pronounce this sound, it has a slight hissed quality to it, e.g. **sok, suiker; kussen, Brussel; kus, lus.**

sj   This letter combination is the way the Dutch render *sh* in their orthography. At the beginning and end of words it occurs only in loanwords and in indigenous Dutch words it only occurs where the diminutive ending **-je** is added to a word ending in s, e.g. **sjaal, sjouwen; huisje, muisje; hasj.**

sch   This should be read as **s** + **ch**. Although that combination is not difficult if you can manage a Dutch **ch**, in combination with **r** it can be harder to get your tongue around, e.g. **schouw,**

---

be absent when you utter the Dutch words. It is difficult for English speakers to eradicate this from their Dutch. Continuing to aspirate these sounds will be no impediment to Dutch people understanding you, but it will be an ever-present reminder to them that you are not a native speaker.

school, schoen, schrijven. For historical reasons many foreign adjectives end in **-isch,** which is pronounced as if spelt **-ies,** e.g. **historisch, logisch, psychologisch.**

t This letter is pronounced like *t* in English but without aspiration, e.g. **tafel, tellen, tien, tol, trein, trekken; boter, ratten; gat, grot.** For historical reasons a few words still begin with **th** but they should be read as if they were written with a simple **t,** e.g. **thans, thee, thuis.**

tj This letter combination is the closest the Dutch come in their orthography to rendering the English sound *ch*. Like **sj, tj** only occurs when the diminutive ending **-je** is added to a word ending in **t.** You should strive to pronounce it as **t + j** and not as an English *ch*, e.g. **katje, matje, netjes.**

v In theory, as well as in certain parts of the Netherlands (notably the south), a distinction is made between **f** and **v** at the beginning of a word; **v** is pronounced by starting with a **v** sound and letting it turn into an **f** sound. This is hard to mimic but fortunately not necessary. In the west of the Netherlands virtually everybody pronounces an initial **v** as an **f,** and after a vowel it is to all intent and purposes indistinguishable from an English *v*, e.g. **vader, val, vijf, vrij; even, raven, beloven, schrijven.**

w This letter is pronounced as an English *v*. As a Dutch **v** is pronounced **f,** there is no confusion between **w** and **v,** e.g. **water, weten, wie, wonen; kwaad, twee, twijfel, zweren.** In the following words, where **w** belongs to the stem of the word and an **-e** or **-en** ending has been added, **w** is pronounced as in English, e.g. **blauwe, nieuwe, meeuwen, vouwen.**

z This letter is pronounced as in English. A common tendency in the west of the country is to pronounce **z** at the beginning of a word as an **s.** Do not copy the practice as it is socially stigmatised, e.g. **zes, zeven, zoen, zuster; Zweden, Zwolle, zweten, zwaard.**

Other idiosyncrasies of the pronunciation of Dutch ▣

1 **E** in unstressed syllables is pronounced as the vowel in the first syllable of English *about* or the last syllable of *father*, e.g. **beloven, geloven, verstaan, vader.**

2 The same weak colourless vowel, called schwa by linguists, is also heard in the adjectival endings **-ig** and **-lijk**, e.g. **gelukkig**, **prettig, vriendelijk, vrolijk**.

3 In the exceedingly common ending **-en**, which contains the vowel referred to in point 1, the **n** is usually dropped in natural speech. Thus **open, praten, mannen** and **vrouwen** are pronounced in practice **ope, prate, manne** and **vrouwe**.

4 The consonant combinations **lk, lm, rg, rk** and **rm** are commonly broken up by inserting a schwa between them, i.e. **melk, zulke, film, berg, kerk, kurk** and **scherm** can be pronounced **melek, zuleke, filem, bereg, kerek, kurek** and **scherem**. Some people do the same with *film* in English but whereas this is stigmatised in English, it is not in Dutch.

Stress

The general rule is that Dutch words carry the main stress on the first syllable but some don't; many foreign words (often borrowed from French) stress a later syllable, and the Dutch prefixes **be-, ge-, her-, ont-** and **ver-** never take the stress. Practise the pronunciation of the following words, concentrating on getting the stress right. The stressed syllables are the ones following the stress mark:

'Engelsman	'leraar	secreta'resse	Van den 'Berg
Amster'dam	waa'rom	be'looft	ge'loven
ver'talen	her'halen	per'ron	'ziekenhuis
ont'moeten	inge'nieur	'antwoorden	'middelbaar

Dutch spelling

Dutch spelling is more or less 'phonetic' and is thus easy once one has mastered a few hard-and-fast rules which clarify the changes that often take place when one (1) makes a noun plural, (2) inflects an adjective or (3) conjugates a verb. You will meet these grammatical concepts as you work your way through the book but here is a general summary of the principles of Dutch spelling.

1 Let us first deal with nouns. The following three words illustrate the changes that can occur: **aap – apen** 'monkeys', **noot – noten** 'nuts', **muur – muren** 'walls'; **duif – duiven** 'doves', **huis – huizen** 'houses'.

2 The same applies to adjectives when the **-e** ending is added: **kaal** – **kale** 'bald', **bloot** – **blote** 'naked', **puur** – **pure** 'pure'; **lief** – **lieve** 'dear', **vies** – **vieze** 'dirty'.

3 And the same occurs in reverse when conjugating verbs: **praten** – **ik praat** 'to talk', **horen** – **ik hoor** 'to hear'; **leven** – **ik leef** 'to live', **verhuizen** – **ik verhuis** 'to shift'.

The reasons for these spelling changes are:

> **Huis, vies** and **verhuis** change to **huizen, vieze** and **verhuizen** because with the addition of the **-e(n)** ending, the **s** is pronounced **z** and any such change in pronunciation is shown in the spelling. The same applies to **duif, lief** and **leef** changing to **duiven, lieve** and **leven**. The **f** becomes a **v** as it now occurs between two vowels.
>
> **Noot, bloot** and **hoor** changing to **noten, blote** and **horen** can be explained as follows: the double **o** (or double **a, e** or **u**) signifies a long vowel. To write **nooten, bloote** and **hooren** would be unnecessary because any **a, e, o** or **u** followed by a single consonant plus a vowel is automatically long and a 'phonetic' spelling system does not tolerate redundant letters.

One further spelling point to watch is the following. Although two consonants are required when there are two syllables, to indicate that the preceding vowel is short, only one consonant is required when there is one syllable:

1 nouns: **kat** – **katten** 'cats', **pot** – **potten** 'pots', **bed** – **bedden** 'beds'

2 adjectives: **dik** – **dikke** 'fat', **nat** – **natte** 'wet'

3 verbs: **blaf** – **blaffen** 'to bark', **zit** – **zitten** 'to sit', **kus** – **kussen** 'to kiss'

The alphabet 🔲

The letters of the alphabet are pronounced as indicated on page 9 (read the words in the second column as Dutch words).

a	a	n	en
b	bee	o	o
c	see	p	pee
d	dee	q	ku
e	e	r	er
f	ef	s	es
g	gee	t	tee
h	ha	u	u
i	ie	v	fee
j	jee	w	wee
k	ka	x	iks
l	el	y	ij *or* ie grec *or* ipsilon
m	em	z	zet

1 Piet en Pauline en hun kinderen

Piet and Pauline and their children

In this lesson you will learn about:

- personal pronouns
- expressing nationality and occupation
- the present tense of verbs
- saying 'please' and 'thank you'
- beginning a conversation
- asking 'how are you?'
- saying 'goodbye'

Reading text 🔲

You will find many Dutch words easily recognisable. See if you can make sense of the following text, in which a Dutchman, Piet, talks about himself and his family. Don't worry about understanding every word, just the general sense. If you're really stuck, there's a translation in the key at the back of the book. Here are some of the words.

Vocabulary

ik heet	I'm called, my name is
woon	live
getrouwd	married
Nederlands	Dutch
een leraar	a teacher
middelbare	secondary
maar	but
gaat	goes, travels

bij	at, in
een reisbureau	a travel agency

Piet talks about his family

Ik heet Piet en ik woon in Amsterdam. Ik ben getrouwd met Pauline. Zij is Engels, maar ze spreekt Nederlands. Ik ben leraar op een middelbare school in Amsterdam maar Pauline werkt in Den Haag. Ze gaat elke dag met de trein naar haar werk. Zij is secretaresse bij een reisbureau. Wij hebben twee kinderen, een zoon en een dochter. Hij heet Marius en zij heet Charlotte.

Language points

Personal pronouns as subjects

Personal subject pronoun: He is a teacher.

Singular		Plural	
ik	I	**wij/we**	we
jij/je	you	**jullie**	you
u	you	**u**	you
hij	he	**zij/ze**	they
zij/ze	she		
het	it		

Where two forms are given, e.g. **jij/je**, **zij/ze** and **wij/we**, the former is the emphatic form and the latter the unemphatic form; compare English *you/ya*, but Dutch makes this distinction in writing too. Notice how **zij** and **ze** alternate in the reading text above.

In both the singular and the plural, Dutch has two words for 'you'. **Jij/jullie** are more familiar than **u**, which is only used towards adult strangers as well as people one needs to show respect towards, e.g. grandparents, your boss. Generally speaking, anyone you call by their first name is addressed as **jij** (and **jullie** if there is more than one person), and anyone you call by their surname, is addressed as **u**, e.g.

Piet, waar woon jij?
Waar woont u, meneer Van den Berg?
Waar wonen jullie? (*addressed to both Piet and Pauline*)

The plural of **u** remains **u**, with the same form of the verb (i.e. singular), e.g. **Waar woont u, meneer en mevrouw Van den Berg?**

Exercise 1

Find the personal pronouns in the reading text above and underline them. Check in the key that you have them all.

Exercise 2

Using the vocabulary at the back of the book, write down the words that would complete the table below. Note that all these words are written with capital letters, as in English.

Country	Inhabitant (male)	Language/nationality
–	Duitser	–
–	Engelsman	–
Frankrijk	–	–
–	–	Nederlands
–	–	Zweeds
België	–	–

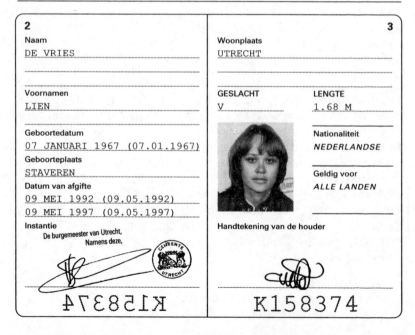

2			3
Naam		Woonplaats	
DE VRIES		UTRECHT	

Voornamen		GESLACHT	LENGTE
LIEN		V	1.68 M

Geboortedatum
07 JANUARI 1967 (07.01.1967)
Geboorteplaats
STAVEREN
Datum van afgifte
09 MEI 1992 (09.05.1992)
09 MEI 1997 (09.05.1997)
Instantie
De burgemeester van Utrecht,
Namens deze,

Nationaliteit
NEDERLANDSE

Geldig voor
ALLE LANDEN

Handtekening van de houder

K158374

Exercise 3

Reading the text below and referring to the glossary at the back of the book, fill in the missing details on Otto's 'ID-card'.

```
                         Voornaam      .........................................
                         Familienaam   .........................................
                         Leeftijd      .........................................
                         Lengte        .........................................
                         Nationaliteit .........................................

Beroep      .........................................
Ogen        .........................................
Haar        .........................................

Adres       Europaweg 5 .........................................
            Hamburg     .........................................
            Bondsrepubliek Duitsland .........
```

Otto Schmidt is dertig jaar oud. Hij is bakker. Hij is 1.86 m[1] lang en heeft blauwe ogen en lichtbruin haar. Hij is Duitser en hij woont in Duitsland.

The present tense of zijn

Present tense of 'to be': I *am* a Dutchman, He *is* a teacher.

The present tense of the irregular verb **zijn** 'to be' is as follows:

ik ben	I am	**wij zijn**	we are
jij/u bent	you are	**jullie zijn**	you are
hij/zij/het is	he/she/it is	**zij zijn**	they are

---

1 Read as **één meter zesentachtig**.

Expressing nationality and profession

Words expressing a person's nationality or profession, when standing alone, carry no article, for example:

Hij is Nederlander.	He is a Dutchman.
Hij is leraar.	He is a teacher.
Zij is Nederlandse.	She is a Dutch woman.
Zij is secretaresse.	She is a secretary.

It is also possible to express nationality with adjectives, as in English, e.g. **Hij/zij is Nederlands** 'He/she is Dutch'. The female of most nationalities is formed by adding **-e** to the adjective, as illustrated. Most professions also have a separate feminine form, e.g. **leraar/lerares**.

When a nationality or profession does not stand alone but is preceded by an adjective, the article **een** is used, e.g. **Hij is een goede leraar** 'He is a good teacher'.

Exercise 4

```
                              Voornaam      Lisa
                              Familienaam      Houghton
                              Leeftijd    31
                              Lengte    1.70  m
                              Nationaliteit    Engels

Beroep    lerares
Ogen    groen
Haar    zwart

Adres    Damstraat 10
         3822  RD  Amsterdam²
         Nederland
```

Write a paragraph or two about Lisa, similar to the one about Otto Schmidt on page 13.

---

2 Dutch postal codes all consist of four digits followed by a space and two capital letters and are placed before the name of the town or village.

Culture point

The concepts of **ten noorden/zuiden van de grote rivieren** 'north/south of the great rivers' pervades many aspects of Dutch society. The Rhine (**de Rijn**), which becomes the Lek south of Utrecht, the Waal (**de Waal**) and the Meuse (**de Maas**) flow through the middle of the Netherlands from east to west (see map on page 22). They form a cultural and linguistic divide: south of the rivers is overwhelmingly Catholic, traditionally less economically developed and considered by northerners to be more happy-go-lucky with less of a work ethic; the stereotype of a northerner in southern eyes is an austere Protestant who doesn't know how to have a good time. The most distinctive regional variation a learner of Dutch will soon be confronted with is that between the north (standard Dutch pronunciation and usage being based on the dialects of North and South Holland) and the provinces of Brabant and Limburg, which both lie south of the rivers. A sure give-away of a southerner, and one that causes mild derision in the north, is the softer pronunciation of **ch/g**, called **de zachte g** 'the soft g', as well as a tendency to trill your **r**'s in your throat. The Dutch have a verb to describe this speech habit: **Hij brouwt**, which translates somewhat loosely as 'He rolls his **r**'s in his throat in a way which I as a northerner don't (and thank God I don't suffer from the same affliction)'.

The present tense

Present tense of a verb: Joop *works* in Utrecht.

All Dutch verbs take the following endings in the present tense:

ik werk	I work	**wij werken**	we work
jij/u werkt	you work	**jullie werken**	you work
hij/zij/het werkt	he/she/it works	**zij werken**	they work

The stem of a verb

Verbs in the vocabulary lists will appear in the infinitive, which in Dutch almost always ends in **-en**:

Infinitive	*Infinitive*
werken	to work

By removing the **-en** from the infinitive you get the basic core of the verb, a form of the verb which is called the *stem*, to which different endings are added:

Infinitive	*Stem*
werken	**werk**

How to construct the present tense

The **ik** form of the verb is always the same as the stem, the **jij/u** and the **hij/zij/het** form is the stem plus **-t** and all persons of the plural are identical to the infinitive.

Sometimes spelling changes occur when forming the stem of a verb from its infinitive:

1 Where the stem of the verb contains a long **a**, **e**, **o** or **u**, this vowel is doubled, according to the rules of Dutch spelling, after removal of the **-en** ending of the infinitive in order to indicate the length of the vowel, e.g. **praten** 'to talk', **ik praat** 'I talk', **jij praat** 'you talk', etc. Similarly **spreken** 'to speak', **ik spreek** 'I speak', **jij spreekt** 'you speak', etc.; **wonen** 'to live', **ik woon** 'I live', **jij woont** 'you live', etc.; **huren** 'to rent', **ik huur** 'I rent', **jij huurt** 'you rent', etc.

2 Where the vowel of the stem is short, as indicated by a double consonant after it in the infinitive, the stem is written with only one consonant; two consonants are seen as superfluous, e.g. **bakken** 'to bake', **ik bak** 'I bake', **jij bakt** 'you bake', etc.; **rennen** 'to run', **ik ren** 'I run', **jij rent** 'you run', etc.

3 Verbs whose stem would seem to end in **v** or **z** after the removal of the **-en** ending, write their stem with **f** and **s** respectively to reflect the way they are pronounced, e.g. **schrijven** 'to write', **ik schrijf** 'I write', **jij schrijft** 'you write', etc.; **reizen** 'to travel', **ik reis** 'I travel', **jij reist** 'you travel', etc.; **verven** 'to paint', **ik verf** 'I paint', **jij verft** 'you paint', etc.

4 In some verbs it is necessary to combine the spelling changes outlined under points 1 and 3, e.g. **lezen** 'to read', **ik lees** 'I read',

jij leest 'you read', etc.; **leven** 'to live/be alive', **ik leef** 'I live', **jij leeft** 'you live', etc.; **blozen** 'to blush', **ik bloos** 'I blush', **jij bloost** 'you blush', etc.

Note: A verb whose stem ends in **t** does not add another **t**, whereas stems that end in **d**, do add a **t** although the **-dt** ending is pronounced simply as **t**, e.g. **zitten** 'to sit', **ik zit** 'I sit', **jij zit** 'you sit', etc. (see also **praten** above); **vinden** 'to find', **ik vind** 'I find', **jij vindt** 'you find', etc.

It is important for other tenses of the verb that you get used to forming and building on to the stem of the verb.

There is only one really irregular verb in the present and that is **zijn** 'to be', which you are already acquainted with. Otherwise there are only two other verbs that show slight irregularities in the present. They are **hebben** 'to have' and **komen** 'to come'. Their forms are as follows:

hebben		*komen*	
ik heb	wij hebben	ik kom	wij komen
jij hebt	jullie hebben	jij komt	jullie komen
hij heeft	zij hebben	hij komt	zij komen

Note that the **u** form of **hebben** can be either **u hebt** or **u heeft**.

We have seen that all Dutch verbs so far, with the exception of **zijn**, end in **-en**. There are in fact five other so-called monosyllabic verbs which show only a slight irregularity in their forms:

doen 'to do'	*gaan* 'to go'	*slaan* 'to hit'	*staan* 'to stand'	*zien* 'to see'
ik doe	ik ga	ik sla	ik sta	ik zie
jij doet	jij gaat	jij slaat	jij staat	jij ziet
hij doet	hij gaat	hij slaat	hij staat	hij ziet
wij doen	wij gaan	wij slaan	wij staan	wij zien *etc.*

Stems containing the diphthongs **ij** or **ou** followed by a **d** often drop the **d** of the stem in the first person singular, e.g.

Ik snij het brood. I'm cutting the bread. (infinitive **snijden**)
Ik rij nu naar huis. I'm driving home now. (infinitive **rijden**)
Ik hou van jou. I love you. (infinitive **houden**)

This only occurs with very common verbs, as illustrated; thus not, for example, in the following: **ik lijd** 'I suffer' (infin. **lijden**), **ik vermijd** 'I avoid' (infin. **vermijden**).

Note: Unlike English, Dutch does not distinguish between the present simple tense ('I live') and the present progressive tense ('I am living'). Dutch has only the present simple tense, and so the translation of both verbal forms is **ik woon**.

Exercise 5

Translate the following into English, then cover over the Dutch text and translate your English translation back into Dutch, comparing your own Dutch version with the original text.

Piet is leraar. Hij is Nederlander en hij is getrouwd met Pauline. Pauline is Engelse. Zij is secretaresse en zij werkt in Den Haag. Ze spreekt Engels en Nederlands.

Exercise 6

Find all the verbs in the reading text on page 11 and circle them. Check them against the key in the back of the book.

Exercise 7

Write down the infinitive, the stem and the third person singular (i.e. the **hij** form) of the Dutch for the following verbs. Use the vocabulary list at the end of the book.

to walk	to answer	to sew
to translate	to ask	to promise

Exercise 8

Translate the following short sentences into Dutch:

She is sewing.	They are walking.
I live in London.	She has a son and a daughter.
He is translating a book.	They are living in England.
I ask something.	You (singular) promise.

Dialogue

Piet meets an old friend in the street

PIET: Ben[3] jij het, Jaap? Hoi!
JAAP: Hallo, Piet. Het is leuk om je weer te zien.

---

3 The dropping of **t** from this form of the verb is explained on page 48.

PIET: Hoe gaat het (met jou)?
JAAP: Niet slecht. En (hoe gaat het) met jou?
PIET: Prima, hoor!⁴
JAAP: Woon jij hier in Amsterdam?
PIET: Ja!
JAAP: Ik werk nu als ingenieur in Amsterdam. Wat doe jij?
PIET: Ik ben leraar op een middelbare school hier in Amsterdam.

PIET: *Is that you, Jaap? Hi!*
JAAP: *Hello, Piet. It's nice to see you again.*
PIET: *How are you?*
JAAP: *Not bad. And how are you?*
PIET: *Great!*
JAAP: *Do you live here in Amsterdam?*
PIET: *Yes!*
JAAP: *I'm working as an engineer in Amsterdam. What do you do?*
PIET: *I'm a teacher at a secondary school here in Amsterdam.*

Language points

Saying 'please' and 'thank you'

There are several ways of expressing 'thank you' in Dutch:

dank je wel or **dank u wel**	thank you very much (most common)
dank je or **dank u**	thanks
bedankt	thanks
heel erg bedankt	thanks a lot
dank u zeer	thank you very much (formal)
ik dank u	thank you (formal)

Note that in using either of the first two alternatives, the form required depends on whether one is on a **jij** or an **u** footing with the person being addressed; (**heel erg**) **bedankt** avoids this complication. The same applies to the expressions for 'please', **alsjeblieft** or **alstublieft** (literally 'if it pleases you').

The English use of *please* and *thank you* does not always correspond with the use of the Dutch equivalents of these expressions.

---

4 **Hoor** is an intensifier, most commonly used in retorts, particularly after **ja** and **nee**. It has no direct equivalent in English. You will find it used in many of the dialogues in this book. Observe how it is used to get a feeling for it.

When asked if one wants a cup of coffee, one can say in English either *Yes, please* or *Thank you*. In the Netherlands the retort **Dank je/u** to the question **Wil je/wilt u een kopje koffie?** is the equivalent of *No, thank you*. If wishing to reply in the affirmative, one must answer (**Ja,**) **alsjeblieft/alstublieft** or alternatively (**Ja,**) **graag**. **Graag** can only render 'please' in reply to a question, and is not appropriate in the following context for example: **Geef mij alsjeblieft een kopje thee** 'Please give me a cup of tea'. Note the position of **alsjeblieft** in the sentence; in Dutch it can stand either in the middle of the statement (as illustrated) or at the end, not at the beginning as in English.

How to begin a conversation

Obviously the choice of words and phrases is enormous, but here are a few of the more common greetings:

Formal/neutral		*Informal*	
Goeie morgen!	Good morning!	**Hallo!**	Hello!
Goeie middag!	Good afternoon!	**Hoi!**	Hi!
Goeien avond!	Good evening!	**Hai/Hi!**	Hi!

Asking and answering 'How are you?'

Hoe gaat het?	How are things? How are you?
(Heel) goed/prima/uitstekend.	(Very) well/fine/great.
Niet slecht.	Not bad.
Het gaat (heel) goed/prima/ uitstekend.	All's well. I'm fine.
Het gaat (heel) slecht.	Things are going badly.
Hoe gaat het met jou/u/jullie?	How are you?
Hoe gaat het met jou en Pauline/met jullie?	How are things with you and Pauline/the two of you?
Gaat het goed met Pauline?	How's Pauline?
Het gaat goed met haar.	She's okay.

Exercise 9

Write the following dialogue in Dutch.

You run into an old friend one morning

YOU: Greet your friend.
FRIEND: Returns your greetings.

YOU:	Say it's nice to see him. Ask how he is.
FRIEND:	Says he's not too well. Asks how things are with you.
YOU:	Say that things are fine.
FRIEND:	Asks how Pauline is.
YOU:	Say she's fine.
FRIEND:	Asks how your wife is.
YOU:	Say she is also fine. She is in The Hague.

Culture point

The Dutch always shake hands when meeting someone for the first time as well as when bumping into or visiting acquaintances. Both men and women shake hands with women and it is not uncommon to shake hands with children too, unlike in Anglo-Saxon societies. You will give affront if you do not instantly put your hand out to anybody when greeting them. With closer acquaintances and relatives it is usual for at least two, but often three, kisses to be given on alternate cheeks while shaking hands. Women do this to other women and men to women, but not men to other men as is the custom in some countries. There was a time when three kisses were considered a southern Dutch tradition (i.e. Catholic) but the custom seems to be gaining ground north of the rivers, a predominantly Protestant area.

Saying 'goodbye'

Tot ziens!	Goodbye! (literally 'till we see each other again')
Dáág! or **Doei!**	Bye! See you!
Tot morgen/vanavond/straks!	See you tomorrow/tonight/later!
Tot maandag/dinsdag!	See you Monday/Tuesday, etc.

Expressions such as **tot morgen/vanavond/maandag**, but even **tot ziens** too, are commonly followed by **dáág** as well for good measure, e.g. **Tot ziens Maarten, tot morgen. Dáág!** 'Goodbye Maarten. See you tomorrow, bye!'

'Good night' is expressed either by **welterusten** or **tot ziens/dáág** depending on the situation. When saying good night to someone who is on their way to bed, the former expression is used, whereas when leaving someone else's home or parting from friends after an evening out, you say **tot ziens** or **dáág** where in English we would say *good night*.

Noordzee

Groningen
Leeuwarden • Groningen
Friesland • Assen
Drenthe

Noord-Holland
Lelystad • Zwolle
Haarlem • Flevoland
Amsterdam Overijssel
Leiden • Utrecht Gelderland
's-Gravenhage Utrecht Arnhem
Utrecht
Lek Waal
Zuid-Holland

IJssel

's-Hertogenbosch
Zeeland Tilburg • Noord-Brabant
Middelburg •
Antwerpen Limburg
Brugge • Antwerpen Limburg
Gent
West- Oost- Hasselt Maastricht
Vlaanderen Vlaanderen Brussel
Brabant Luik DUITSLAND
Henegouwen Luik
Bergen • Namen
Namen
Luxemburg

FRANKRIJK
Schelde Maas

LUXEM-
Aarlen • BURG

Rijn

2 Nederland en België

The Netherlands and Belgium

In this lesson you will learn about:

- points of the compass
- gender of nouns
- nouns and their articles in the singular
- word order in simple sentences
- how to make simple sentences negative
- the negative **geen** 'not a, not any, no'
- numerals
- Dutch money

Reading text

See if you can make sense of the following text, using only the map and the few words given here:

liggen	to lie
de hoofdstad	the capital city
de inwoner	inhabitant
de zetel	the seat (figurative meaning only)
de regering	the government
belangrijk	important
landelijk	rural

The provinces of North and South Holland

In de provincie Noord-Holland ligt de hoofdstad van Nederland, Amsterdam. Amsterdam heeft meer dan één miljoen inwoners. Ten westen van Amsterdam ligt Haarlem, de hoofdstad van de provincie. Ten zuiden van Haarlem, in de provincie Zuid-Holland, ligt Den Haag,[1] de zetel van de regering. In de meeste landen is de hoofdstad ook de zetel van de regering, maar niet in Nederland. Het westen van Nederland is economisch het belangrijkste deel van het land. Het zuiden, noorden en oosten van het land zijn landelijker.

Language points

Points of the compass

The points of the compass are:

het noorden	the north	**het westen**	the west
het zuiden	the south	**het oosten**	the east

They are used in phrases like:

ten noorden van etc.	north of/to the north of, etc.
het noorden van Nederland	the north of the Netherlands

But when used in compounds, a shorter form without the **-en** ending is used, e.g. **Noord-Holland, de Noordpool, het noord-westen**. Note, however, **de noordenwind, westenwind** 'the northerly wind, westerly wind', etc.

Noordelijk, zuidelijk, westelijk and **oostelijk** express 'northern', 'southern', etc., e.g. **het westelijke deel van Nederland** 'the western part of the Netherlands'.

Culture point

As you will already have noticed, the term 'Holland' has a different meaning in Dutch. The Dutch generally refer to their country as **Nederland** (a singular noun not preceded by 'the') and, strictly speaking, **Holland** refers only to the two western coastal provinces that form the economic hub of the country. It is not uncommon for people living in the west of the country to refer to the country as a whole as **Holland**, the language as **Hollands** and themselves as **Hollanders**, but those living in other parts of the country take offence at this and this practice has no official status.

---

1 The official name of The Hague is **'s-Gravenhage** but this is usually only written (i.e. on signs and envelopes), not said.

Exercise 1

Referring to the map on p. 22, write some sentences about the
following large cities stating what province they are in and whether
they are in the north, south, east or west of the country. For one
of the towns the most appropriate expression is **in het midden van**
'in the middle of' – which one? Note that the verb **liggen** 'to lie,
be situated' is used here (see page 180).

> *Example:* Maastricht
> Maastricht ligt in de provincie Limburg, in het
> zuiden/zuidoosten van Nederland.

1 Groningen   4 Utrecht
2 Zwolle   5 Middelburg
3 Leiden   6 Tilburg

Dialogue 1 ▣

Piet is asking his class some questions about geography

PIET: Waar ligt Nederland?
JAAP: Het ligt in het westen van Europa.
PIET: Wat is Amsterdam?
JAAP: Het is de hoofdstad van het land.
PIET: Wat is Den Haag?
JAAP: Het is de zetel van de regering en de hoofdstad van
Zuid-Holland.
PIET: Ja, goed. En wat is de hoofdstad van Noord-Holland?
JAAP: Dat is Haarlem.

PIET: *Where are the Netherlands?*
JAAP: *In the west of Europe.*
PIET: *What is Amsterdam?*
JAAP: *It is the capital of the Netherlands.*
PIET: *What is The Hague?*
JAAP: *It is the seat of government and the capital of South Holland.*
PIET: *Yes, correct. And what is the capital of North Holland?*
JAAP: *That is Haarlem.*

Reading text 🔲

Vocabulary

men	one
Nederlandstalig	Dutch-speaking
het koninkrijk	the kingdom
want	because
tweetalig	bilingual
de grens	the border
de haven	harbour, port
ongeveer	approximately, about
de Waal	the Walloon

The Dutch-speaking provinces of Belgium

In het noorden van België spreekt men Nederlands en in het zuiden Frans. De Nederlandstalige provincies van het Koninkrijk België zijn (van west naar oost) West-Vlaanderen, Oost-Vlaanderen, Antwerpen, Brabant en Limburg. Brussel, de hoofdstad van het land, ligt in Brabant maar heeft een speciale status want het is een tweetalige stad. Antwerpen, ten noorden van Brussel niet ver van de Nederlandse grens, is een belangrijke havenstad. Er zijn tien miljoen Belgen. Ongeveer zes miljoen zijn Vlamingen. De andere vier miljoen zijn Walen.

Culture point

Just as many Dutch people refer to their language as **Hollands**, Flemings nearly always call the Dutch they speak **Vlaams** (Flemish). This has led to the erroneous impression among foreigners that Flemish is a separate language. Most Flemings do also speak one or other dialect of Dutch but their standard language is Dutch. This Dutch, sometimes referred to as **Zuidnederlands**, is as close to the Dutch of Holland as American English is to British English; you can hear from the first syllable whether the person you are talking to is Flemish or not, but this is no impediment at all to comprehension. The Flemish have fought a long, hard battle for the equality of their language with French and are gradually winning, thanks to the new-found economic might of Flanders (**Vlaanderen**), as they call the Dutch-speaking provinces of their country collectively.

Language points

The gender of nouns

Nouns: My *son* is a *teacher.*

Nouns have two genders in Dutch, common gender and neuter:

Common gender		*Neuter*	
de stad	the city, town	**het land**	the country
de inwoner	the inhabitant	**het kind**	the child

You cannot usually predict the gender of nouns, but most are common gender.

Nouns and their articles in the singular

Definite article: *The* woman has a daughter.
Indefinite article: The woman has *a* daughter.

1 The *definite articles* are **de** for common gender and **het** for neuter nouns. You should always learn each noun together with its definite article, i.e. don't simply learn that **vrouw** is 'woman' and **huis** is 'house' but that **de vrouw** is 'the woman' and **het huis** is 'the house'. In the vocabulary lists gender will be indicated in this way: **stad** (c), **huis** (n).
2 The indefinite article for nouns of both genders is **een**, pronounced but never written **'n**. This word also means 'one', in which case it is normally written **één** and pronounced the way it is spelt:

Common gender		*Neuter*	
een vrouw	a woman, wife	**een land**	a country
een stad	a city, town	**een kind**	a child

There will be more about nouns and articles in lesson 3.

Exercise 2

Now it is your turn to answer geographical questions following the pattern of the dialogue above. If you don't know the answer to a question, the answer is **Ik weet het niet** or **Dat weet ik niet**, the Dutch equivalent of 'I don't know'.

1 Wat is Leiden?	6 Wat is Brussel?
2 Wat is Den Haag?	7 Wat is Londen?
3 Wat is Noord-Holland?	8 Wat is Parijs?
4 Wat is Berlijn?	9 Wat is Nederland?
5 Wat is Kopenhagen?	10 Waar ligt België?

Exercise 3

Translate the nouns in parentheses, remembering to get the gender right.

(1 The man) in (2 the kitchen) is (3 the father) of (4 the child). She lives next door to (5 a teacher).

I don't know where (6 the woman) works.

(7 The house) is for sale. Belgium is (8 a country) to the south of the Netherlands.

(9 The school) is at (10 the end) of (11 the street).

Exercise 4

Looking up the words you don't yet know in the back of the book, decide which word is the odd one out in each of these groups:

1 Nederlander, Zweed, Frans, Belg, Duitser
2 de moeder, de vader, de dochter, de oom, de zoon
3 het bord, de school, het huis, de kerk, de bank
4 de vork, de lepel, het mes, het zout

Dialogue 2 ▣

Having a cup of coffee at Ineke's

LIEN: Morgen,[2] Ineke. Ik ben op weg naar de supermarkt en was in de buurt.

INEKE: Leuk. Kom binnen! Ga zitten! Kopje koffie?

LIEN: Ja, graag. Maar ik blijf niet lang, hoor.

INEKE: Gebruik je melk en suiker in je koffie?

LIEN: Een wolkje melk maar geen suiker, dank je.

INEKE: Heb je zin in een koekje? (*takes the lid off the biscuit tin, offers a biscuit, and replaces the lid*)

---

2 As in English, the **goeie** is often omitted from such greetings in colloquial speech.

LIEN: Waarom niet? (*bites into it*) Wat een lekker koekje, zeg!
INEKE: Ja, hè? Ik koop ze bij de warme bakker om de hoek.

LIEN: *Morning, Ineke. I'm on my way to the supermarket and was in the neighbourhood.*
INEKE: *Great. Come in! Sit down! Cup of coffee?*
LIEN: *Yes, please. But I won't stay long, you know.*
INEKE: *Do you take milk and sugar in your coffee?*
LIEN: *A dash of milk, but no sugar, thanks.*
INEKE: *Do you feel like a biscuit?*
LIEN: *Why not? What a delicious biscuit!*
INEKE: *Yeah, eh? I buy them at the pastry shop around the corner.*

Culture point

Coffee drinking is an all-important ritual in Holland. You are not normally offered the choice of tea or coffee, except perhaps in the afternoon, when tea is sometimes served in place of coffee. Coffee, which the Dutch make very strong, is always served in very small cups (and even then often not particularly full). Milk (always **koffiemelk**, a thick, slightly sweet substance) and sugar are usually added by the host or hostess and you are offered one biscuit with each cup of coffee. Once you have taken a biscuit from the biscuit barrel (**de koekje-strommel**), it is removed from your reach – a second biscuit is only offered if you consume a second cup of coffee. Coffee is drunk with breakfast, mid-morning (the main **koffietijd**), late afternoon and mid-evening. The drinking of coffee is an integral part of what the Dutch call **gezelligheid** (cosy, friendly atmosphere). There are two expressions in Dutch which aptly describe the custom: **Het is altijd koffietijd** 'It's always time for coffee' and **Gezelligheid kent geen tijd** 'No time limit should be put on *gezelligheid*'.

WAARDE
4 PUNTEN

Spaar deze punten verpakt bij
DOUWE EGBERTS
koffie, thee
en Móccona, voor
theekoppen,
theeglazen en
andere waardevolle
geschenken.
Vraag geschenkenlijst aan.
DOUWE EGBERTS
Afd. Geschenken, Utrecht
Postbus 2076

106

Dialogue 3 📼

A colleague is talking to Piet at school

COLLEGA:	Spreek je behalve Nederlands en Engels nog een andere taal?
PIET:	Ja, gelukkig spreek ik ook nog Duits.
COLLEGA:	Ik spreek helaas geen Duits, maar ik versta het. En je vrouw?
PIET:	Pauline? Zij spreekt een heleboel talen.
COLLEAGUE:	*Do you speak any other language apart from Dutch and English?*
PIET:	*Yes, fortunately I also speak German.*
COLLEAGUE:	*Unfortunately I don't speak German, but I understand it. And your wife?*
PIET:	*Pauline? She speaks a lot of languages!*

Language points

Word order in simple sentences

Subject: *Lien* takes milk in her coffee.
Verb: Lien *takes* milk in her coffee.

Normal word order in a Dutch simple sentence is first the subject and immediately after it the finite verb (a finite verb is a verb in the present tense, past tense or imperative):

Lien gebruikt melk in haar   Lien takes milk in her coffee.
  koffie.
Zij spreekt Nederlands.   She speaks Dutch.

Lien and **zij** are the subjects in these two sentences, while **gebruikt** and **spreekt** are the finite verbs.
A schematic view of these two sentences would look like this:

F	V	N	REST
Lien	gebruikt		melk in haar koffie.
Zij	spreekt		Nederlands.

F stands for Front, and this position is occupied by any word or group of words that comes to the front of the sentence. As we have seen, this is often the subject. Finite verbs have their place under V (verb). If any word or phrase other than the subject is fronted (moved to the front, which is often done for emphasis), the subject stands under N (for nominal – always a noun or pronoun), and comes immediately after the verb. This all-pervasive feature of Dutch where the subject ends up to the right of the verb, which must always be the second idea in the sentence, is called *inverted word order* or *inversion*.

Gelukkig spreek ik Duits.   Fortunately I speak German.

F	V	N	REST
Gelukkig	spreek	ik	Duits *or*
Ik	spreek	–	gelukkig Duits.

There was an example of this variation in word order in exercise 2, where **dat**, unlike **het** (lit. 'it'), is emphasised and thus stands at the beginning of the sentence:

F	V	N	REST
Ik	weet	–	het niet.
Dat	weet	ik	niet.

Exercise 5

Move the word or phrase (constituting one idea) in italics to the front, re-arranging the word order of the sentence as necessary.

1 Ik ben *helaas* leraar.
2 Wij wonen *hier.*
3 Ik ken *Engeland* niet.
4 Pauline gaat *elke dag* naar Den Haag.
5 Ineke zet *nu* koffie.

Dialogue 4 🔘

Piet is approached by another colleague during the lunch break

COLLEGA: Heb je een vuurtje?
PIET: Nee, vanaf vandaag rook ik niet meer.
COLLEGA: Wat hoor ik? Echt waar?
PIET: Ja, echt waar! Ik heb mijn laatste sigaret gerookt.
COLLEGA: Waarom?
PIET: Ik verdien niet genoeg geld.

COLLEAGUE: *Have you got a light?*
PIET: *No, from today I'm no longer smoking.*
COLLEAGUE: *What's that I'm hearing? Really?*
PIET: *Yes, really. I have smoked my last cigarette.*
COLLEAGUE: *Why?*
PIET: *I don't earn enough money.*

Language points

How to make a simple sentence negative

A negated sentence: I *don't* earn enough money.

To negate a simple sentence, Dutch inserts the negative word (for instance **niet** 'not' or **nooit** 'never') in column NE, immediately after the subject–verb group, no matter whether the word order is normal or inverted. Dutch has no equivalent to the English use of 'do' in negative sentences.

Normal word order + negation:
Ik verdien niet genoeg.

F	V	N	NE	OTHER
Ik	verdien	–	niet	genoeg.

Inverted word order + negation:
Vanaf vandaag rook ik niet meer.

F	V	N	NE	OTHER
Vanaf vandaag	rook	ik	niet	meer.

There is more to negating sentences than described here. The matter is dealt with in more detail in lessons 15 and 16.

Exercise 6

Insert **niet** in the following sentences:

1 Onze zoon is ziek.
2 Gelukkig woon ik in Rusland.
3 Ze rijden elke dag naar Leiden.
4 Morgen ga ik met de tram.

The negative geen 'not a, not any, no'

Although 'not' is rendered by **niet** in Dutch, as we have seen, 'not a', 'not any' or 'no' meaning 'not any' are expressed by **geen**:

I do *not* speak *any* German.	**Ik spreek *geen* Duits.**
I speak *no* German.	**Ik spreek *geen* Duits.**
Piet has*n't any* money.	**Piet heeft *geen* geld.**
Piet has *no* money.	**Piet heeft *geen* geld.**
Pauline has*n't* got *a* car.	**Pauline heeft *geen* auto.**

Exercise 7

Negate the following sentences using either **niet** or **geen** where appropriate:

1 Mijn collega heeft een leuke vrouw.
2 Hij woont in dit land.
3 Zij werkt in een ander land.
4 Het huis heeft een zolder.
5 Ik heb een tweede fiets.

Numerals ▢

0	nul	10	tien
1	een	11	elf
2	twee	12	twaalf
3	drie	13	dertien
4	vier	14	veertien
5	vijf	15	vijftien
6	zes	16	zestien
7	zeven	17	zeventien
8	acht	18	achttien
9	negen	19	negentien
20	twintig	70	zeventig
30	dertig	80	tachtig
40	veertig	90	negentig
50	vijftig	100	honderd
60	zestig	1,000	duizend
21	eenentwintig	31	eenendertig
22	tweeëntwintig	32	tweeëndertig
23	drieëntwintig	33	drieëndertig
24	vierentwintig etc.	34	vierendertig *etc.*

Note 1: **Een** means both 'a' and 'one' and in the latter meaning is written **één** wherever ambiguity might occur, e.g. **Ik heb een kind** 'I have a child', **Ik heb één kind** 'I have one child'.

Note 2: Dutch puts units before tens, linking them with **en** rather like the old-fashioned English *four-and-twenty*. A diæresis (**een trema**, i.e. two dots on the **e**) is used after **twee** and **drie** to help the eye read the **twee/drie** and the following **en** as separate words.

Note 3: **Honderd** and **duizend** render both 'a hundred' and 'a thousand' and 'one hundred' and 'one thousand'.

Note 4: If numerals are ever written out in full, which is as rare in Dutch as in English, they are written as follows:

    tweehonderd negenentachtig   289
    drieduizend vijfhonderd tien   3510
    een miljoen vierenzeventigduizend driehonderd twintig   1.074.320[3]

Note that where English uses 'and' between the numerals, Dutch does not.

---

3 Note the use of full stops here where English uses commas. The Dutch use a comma where English uses a decimal point; in other words the Dutch convention is the reverse of ours, e.g. **1.145,05** '1,145.05' and a temperature of '15.7 degrees' is read as **vijftien komma zeven graden**.

Exercise 8

Translate the following numbers:

1 vijfenzestig	5 drieëntachtig
2 negenenveertig	6 vijfenvijftig
3 tweeënnegentig	7 achtenzeventig
4 eenenveertig	8 zevenendertig

If you have the recording, listen to how the numbers are pronounced and try to pronounce them yourself. Then learn as many by heart as you can manage.

Dialogues 5 and 6 ▣

An American tourist walks into a bank in the Netherlands

TOERIST:	Kan ik een paar Amerikaanse dollar wisselen?
BANKBEDIENDE:	Ja, meneer, hoeveel?
TOERIST:	Honderd.
BANKBEDIENDE:	Ja, dat kan, meneer.
TOERIST:	Wat is de (wissel)koers vandaag?
BANKBEDIENDE:	Dat weet ik niet. Laat me even kijken.

TOURIST:	*Can I change some American dollars?*
BANK TELLER:	*Yes, sir, how many?*
TOURIST:	*A hundred.*
BANK TELLER:	*Yes, that's possible, sir.*
TOURIST:	*What is the (exchange) rate today?*
BANK TELLER:	*I don't know. Let me have a look.*

Another foreigner is in a Dutch bank

TOERIST:	Kan ik een reischeque wisselen?
BANKBEDIENDE:	Ja, meneer, mag ik uw paspoort zien?
TOERIST:	Nee, helaas niet. Ik heb het niet bij me.
BANKBEDIENDE:	Dan uw rijbewijs, meneer.
TOERIST:	Hier is mijn rijbewijs. (*handing it over*) Alstublieft.[4]

4 Note the way **alstublieft** is used when giving something to someone, in which case it is not equivalent to 'please' but expresses something like 'Here you are'.

BANKBEDIENDE: Dank u wel. (*pointing to the cheque*) Zou u alstublieft hier willen tekenen?

TOERIST: Ja, zeker. Waar? Hier?

BANKBEDIENDE: (*once it's signed*) Goed zo, meneer. U krijgt driehonderd vijfentachtig gulden en drieëndertig cent.

TOURIST: *Can I cash a traveller's cheque?*

BANK TELLER: *Yes, sir, may I see your passport?*

TOURIST: *No, unfortunately not. I haven't got it on me.*

BANK TELLER: *Then your driver's licence, sir.*

TOURIST: *Yes, here's my licence.*

BANK TELLER: *Thank you. Would you mind signing here?*

TOURIST: *Yes, of course. Where? Here?*

BANK TELLER: *Perfect, sir. You get 385 guilders and 33 cents.*

Language points

Dutch money

The Dutch monetary unit is **de gulden**, the guilder: **één gulden** = **100 cent**. The coins (**de munten**) are: **5 cent**, **10 cent**, **25 cent**, **één gulden**, **twee gulden vijftig**, **5 gulden**.

These coins have names (compare the use of *nickel* and *dime* in the United States). Both the amounts and the coins themselves are referred to as **een stuiver (5 cent)**, **een dubbeltje (10 cent)**, **een kwartje (25 cent)** and **een rijksdaalder (twee gulden vijftig)**.

The notes come in denominations of 10, 25, 50, 100, 250 and 1,000 guilders. Ten guilders, both the amount and the 10 guilder note, are colloquially called **een tientje**.

It is not uncommon for amounts to be referred to as follows by shopkeepers: **Het kost twee tientjes/drie kwartjes/twee dubbeltjes**.

The symbol the Dutch use for a guilder is *f*, which is an abbreviation of **florijn**, a currency unit which was previously used. Prices are written as follows: *f*10,50. This can be expressed either as **tien gulden vijftig** or **tien vijftig**. Note that a comma is used instead of a decimal point. Although one-cent coins were abolished in 1980, prices such as *f*1,98, *f*2,97 still occur. If buying one item priced in this way, the sum is rounded off to the nearest 5 cents; when buying several items, the total is rounded off.

```
■ VREEMD GELD
                (prijs in guldens)
                    Verk.   Aank.
amerik.dollar       1,630   1,750
austr.dollar        1,24    1,36
belg.frank (100)    5,28    5,58
canad.dollar        1,130   1,250
deense kroon (100)  27,00   29,50
duitse mark (100)   109,50  113,50
engelse pond        2,55    2,80
finse mark (100)    34,75   37,25
franse frank (100)  30,90   33,65
griekse dr. (100)   0,62    0,79
hongkong dlr.(100)  19,00   23,00
ierse pond          2,55    2,80
ital lire (10.000)  09,60   11,30
jap.yen (10.000)    166,00  172,00
noorse kroon (100)  24,10   26,60
oost.schill. (100)  15,67   16,17
port.escudo (100)   0,97    1,15
spaanse pes. (100)  1,19    1,35
turkse lira (100)   0,0031  0,0052
zuid.afr.rand       0,40    0,55
zweedse kr. (100)   21,30   23,80
zwits.fr. (100)     130,75  135,25
    (Advieskoersen 23/01- Bron: GWK)
```

The words **cent** and **gulden**, as well as the names of all other currencies, are not pluralised when they are used in prices, e.g. **Dat kost tien cent/gulden/dollar/pond/frank**. **Guldens** is normally only used when referring to a collection of one-guilder coins, e.g. **Kan ik tien guldens hebben, alstublieft** (handing over a ƒ10 note). **Centen** died out with the abolition of one-cent coins.

Colloquially the Dutch refer to a guilder as a **piek** (compare 'quid' or 'buck'), e.g. **Ik heb tien piek voor dat boek betaald**. 'I paid ten smackers for that book'. And similar to the use of 'grand' in American English, Dutch uses **ton** for ƒ100,000, e.g. **Die auto kost meer dan een ton** 'That car costs more than a hundred thou'.

Culture point

Dutch coins are a pleasure to use as they are a practical size. The 5 cent is copper, 10 cents, 25 cents, ƒ1 and ƒ2,50 are 'silver' and the ƒ5 coin, which in recent years replaced the ƒ5 note, is 'gold' and quite thick, to distinguish it clearly from ƒ1, which is about the same size.

Dutch banknotes are gloriously colourful, all very different from each other, and also a pleasure to use. They are supplied with a series of raised symbols in one corner to enable the blind to distinguish them, which is eminently practical as well as being an example of the admirable Dutch quality of considering the handicapped members of their society.

The Belgian monetary unit is the **frank**. The abbreviation for **frank** is **fr**. The Belgian franc consisted of 100 **centimes** and until recently the smallest coin in circulation was 50 centimes, but now it is **één frank**; nevertheless prices can thus look like this with rounding off upwards taking place: fr.10,50. The one- and fifty-franc coins are 'silver' and the five- and twenty-franc coins are 'gold'; coins of all denominations are struck in equal numbers in Dutch and French. The banknotes, which occur in denominations of 100, 500, 1,000, 2,000 and 10,000 francs, are printed in French on one side and Dutch on the other.

Dialogue 7 ▣

Two tourists are on holiday in Amsterdam

A: Ik moet geld wisselen.
B: Waarom, heb je geen guldens?
A: Nee. Wacht even, ik heb nog een briefje van honderd
    gulden, maar ik wil een ijsje kopen. Kan jij het wisselen?
B: Ik heb alleen maar twee briefjes van vijftig. Helpt dat?
A: Nee, niet veel. Ik ga naar het wisselkantoor op het station.
    Ik heb nog een biljet van 50 dollar. Dat ga ik wisselen.
B: Zoals je wilt.

A: *I'll have to change money.*
B: *Why, haven't you got any guilders?*
A: *No. Wait a moment, I've still got a hundred-guilder note, but
    I want to buy an icecream. Can you change it?*
B: *I've only got two fifty-guilder notes. Does that help?*
A: *No, not much. I'm going to the exchange bureau at the station.
    I've still got a $50 bill. I'm going to change that.*
B: *As you wish.*

Exercise 9

Write the following prices out in full: ƒ2,35; ƒ1,85; ƒ0,69; ƒ364,25;
ƒ1234; ƒ0,25; ƒ105; DM25; £80; $55.

3 Bij de groenteboer

At the greengrocer's

Dialogue 1 ⬤⬤

Pauline is at the greengrocer's

PAULINE:	Wat kosten de appels?
GROENTEBOER:	Twee vijftig per kilo.
PAULINE:	Ik wou graag één kilo appels en een halve kilo uien.
GROENTEBOER:	Zeker, mevrouw. Dat kan.
PAULINE:	Heeft u ook peren?
GROENTEBOER:	Nee, helaas niet. Anders nog iets, mevrouw?
PAULINE:	Ja. Twee bananen. Dat was het dan.
GROENTEBOER:	Dat is precies vier gulden alles bij elkaar.
PAULINE:	(*handing over the money*) Alstublieft.
GROENTEBOER:	Dank u. Tot uw dienst, mevrouw. Tot ziens.

PAULINE:	*What do the apples cost?*
GREENGROCER:	*Two fifty a kilo.*
PAULINE:	*I'd like one kilo of apples and half a kilo of onions.*
GREENGROCER:	*Certainly, madam. No problem.*
PAULINE:	*Have you also got pears?*
GREENGROCER:	*No, unfortunately I don't. Anything else, madam?*

PAULINE:	*Oh, yes. Two bananas. That's it.*
GREENGROCER:	*That's four guilders exactly all together.*
PAULINE:	*There you are.*
GREENGROCER:	*Thank you. You're welcome, madam. Bye.*

Language points

The plural of nouns

Plural nouns: He sells *apples* and *pears.*

There are two main ways of forming the plural of a Dutch noun: by adding **-s** or **-en**.

Singular		*Plural*	
een appel	an apple	**appels**	apples
de appel	the apple	**de appels**	the apples
een peer	a pear	**peren**	pears
de peer	the pear	**de peren**	the pears

The vast majority of nouns take **-en** in the plural. Note that where the **-en** ending is added, the spelling rules given on pages 7 and 8 apply:

Singular		*Plural*	
de aap	the monkey	**de apen**	the monkeys
de boom	the tree	**de bomen**	the trees
de muur	the wall	**de muren**	the walls
de duif	the dove, pigeon	**de duiven**	the doves, pigeons
de golf	the wave	**de golven**	the waves
de muis	the mouse	**de muizen**	the mice
de gans	the goose	**de ganzen**	the geese

Note that when a neuter noun is used in the plural, the definite article that accompanies it is **de**, e.g. **het huis – de huizen** 'the houses', **het wiel – de wielen** 'the wheels'.

A small number of common nouns containing a short vowel (most are neuter) lengthen their vowel in the plural, which is reflected in their spelling, e.g.

de dag – dagen	days
de weg – wegen	roads, ways
het bad – baden	baths
het dak – daken	rooves

het gat – **gaten**	holes
het glas – **glazen**	glasses
het pad – **paden**	paths
het slot – **sloten**	locks

De stad – **steden** 'cities, towns' and **het schip** – **schepen** 'ships' show a further irregularity.

The following categories of nouns take **-s**:

1 Nouns ending in unstressed **-el**, **-en**, **-em** and **-er**, e.g. **de tafel** – **tafels** 'tables', **de deken** – **dekens** 'blankets', **de bezem** – **bezems** 'brooms', **de moeder** – **moeders** 'mothers'. Note that nouns like **het wiel** 'wheel', **de schoen** 'shoe' and **het dier** 'animal' go **wielen**, **schoenen** and **dieren** as the **-el**, **-en** and **-er** in such words are stressed and are not grammatical endings.
2 Foreign nouns ending in **-a**, **-i**, **-o** or **-u**, but all of these require an apostrophe before the **-s**, e.g. **de firma** – **firma's** 'firms', **de taxi** – **taxi's** 'taxis', **de auto** – **auto's** 'cars', **het menu** – **menu's** 'menus'.
3 All diminutives with the ending **-(t)je**, e.g. **het katje** – **katjes** 'kittens', **het schoentje** – **schoentjes** 'little shoes'.

There is a handful of neuter nouns that take neither **-en** nor **-s** in the plural but **-eren**, e.g.

het blad – **de bladeren**	leaves
het ei – **de eieren**	eggs
het kalf – **de kalveren**	calves
het kind – **de kinderen**	children
het lam – **de lammeren**	lambs

There are further exceptions and additions to the above rules for forming the plural of nouns (e.g. **zoon** – **zoons** 'sons', **broer** – **broers** 'brothers', **oom** – **ooms** 'uncles' and **secretaresse** – **secretaresses** 'secretaries'), but those rules cover most nouns.

Exercise 1

Put the following nouns in the plural. Make sure you get the definite article correct too.

1 de banaan	2 de leraar	3 de vader
4 de vrouw	5 de man	6 het land
7 de school	8 de dochter	9 de zetel
10 de hoofdstad	11 de regering	12 het kind

| 13 de Duitser | 14 het oog | 15 het jaar |
| 16 de aardappel | 17 de ui | 18 de trein |

Exercise 2

Write down the Dutch translation of the following words.

1 grapes	2 bananas	3 onions
4 pears	5 potatoes	6 men
7 lambs	8 leaves	9 children
10 countries	11 Dutchmen	12 towns
13 waves	14 eggs	15 cars

Exercise 3

What is the singular of the following nouns? Also provide the appropriate form of the definite article.

1 de ogen	2 de schepen	3 de golven
4 de kalveren	5 de peren	6 de vrouwen
7 de wegen	8 de steden	9 de druiven
10 de ganzen	11 de tafels	12 de schoenen
13 de paden	14 de katten	15 de meisjes

Words and phrases for shopping

Kan ik u helpen?	Can I help you?
Waar kan ik u mee van dienst zijn?	How can I be of service?
Wat mag het zijn?	What'll it be? What do you want?
Ik wou graag ...	I would like ...
Wat kost ...?	What does ... cost?
Hoeveel kost ...?	How much does ... cost?
één/twee/drie gulden per stuk	one/two/three guilders each
één/twee/drie gulden per kilo	one/two/three guilders a kilo
één/twee/drie gulden per ons	one/two/three guilders for 100g.
Dat is te duur/erg goedkoop	That is too expensive/very cheap.

Note: All measures, like currencies, are expressed in the singular after numerals, e.g. **drie kilo, 80 gram, twee ons**. Although **ons** (100 grams) and **pond** (500 grams)[1]

1 An imperial pound as used in English-speaking countries is only 454 grams.

are no longer official measures, they are nevertheless still commonly used even if never written on price labels in shops. Thus 750 grams can be expressed as **750 gram** or **anderhalf pond**. **Pond** tends only to be used for amounts up to one kilo, except with reference to the weight of newborns, e.g. **Het kind woog zes pond bij zijn geboorte** 'The child weighed six pounds at birth'.

Dialogue 2 ▯▯

In a cheese shop

KLANT:	Goeie morgen, meneer De Rooij. Hoe gaat het?
KAASBOER:	Prima, hoor, en hoe gaat het met u, mevrouw?
KLANT:	Uitstekend, dank u.
KAASBOER:	En wat mag het zijn, mevrouw?
KLANT:	Geeft u^2 mij anderhalf kilo belegen kaas, alstublieft.
KAASBOER:	Ja zeker, mevrouw. (*puts the cheese on the scale*) Het is ietsje meer, mevrouw, mag dat?
KLANT:	Ja, hoor. Dat is niet erg.
KAASBOER:	Anders nog iets, mevrouw?
KLANT:	Nee, hoor. (*handing the money over*) Alstublieft.
KAASBOER:	(*handing the cheese to the customer*) Alstublieft, mevrouw.
KLANT:	Dank u wel, meneer. Tot ziens.
KAASBOER:	Tot uw dienst. Tot ziens, mevrouw, dáág.

CUSTOMER:	*Good morning, Mr De Rooij. How are you?*
CHEESE SALESMAN:	*Fine, and how are you faring, madam?*
CUSTOMER:	*Fine, thanks!*
CHEESE SALESMAN:	*And what would you like, madam?*
CUSTOMER:	*One and a half kilos of mature cheese, please.*
CHEESE SALESMAN:	*Of course, madam. It's just over, madam, is that alright?*
CUSTOMER:	*Yes! That doesn't matter.*
CHEESE SALESMAN:	*Anything else, madam?*
CUSTOMER:	*No! There you are.*
CHEESE SALESMAN:	*Here you are, madam.*
CUSTOMER:	*Thank you. Goodbye.*
CHEESE SALESMAN:	*Don't mention it. Goodbye, madam.*

2 See page 100 for an explanation of this form of order.

Culture point

Gouda (**Goudse kaas**) and Edam (**Edammer**), the most commonly eaten cheeses in the Netherlands, are sold according to their degree of maturity (**jonge, belegen, zeer belegen**); the older the cheese, the lower the moisture content and thus the dearer it is. They are very similar cheeses. A popular variant is **Leidse kaas**, which is the same basic cheese with cumin seed in it.

Exercise 4

Make up this dialogue between yourself and the greengrocer.

YOU:	Ask how much the bananas are.
GREENGROCER:	Says they cost three guilders a kilo.
YOU:	Say you would like four bananas. Ask if he has any grapes too.
GREENGROCER:	Says he unfortunately has no grapes.
YOU:	Ask how much the pears cost.
GREENGROCER:	Says they are four guilders fifty a kilo.
YOU:	Ask for a kilo of pears.
GREENGROCER:	Asks if you want anything else.
YOU:	Say that's it.
GREENGROCER:	Says it will be seven guilders and seventy-five cents all together.
YOU:	Say you have no change (**het kleingeld**). Ask if he can change a 100 guilders.
GREENGROCER:	Says that's no problem, madam/sir.
YOU:	Handing him the money, you say 'Here you are'.
GREENGROCER:	Handing back the change, he says 'Here you are' and bids you goodbye.

Reading text 🔘

The Netherlands has been a monarchy (**het koninkrijk**) since 1813. Most Dutch people are very sentimental about their monarchy. With the help of the following words, see how much you understand of this passage about the Dutch queen.

Vocabulary

de koningin	the queen
de man	the husband
het paleis	the palace
erg	very[3]
de afbeelding	the image
de postzegel	the stamp

The queen of the Netherlands

De koningin van Nederland heet Beatrix. Zij is getrouwd met prins Claus en hij komt uit Duitsland. Zij hebben drie zoons, kroonprins Willem Alexander, prins Johan Friso en prins Constantijn Christof. Koningin Beatrix en haar man wonen in Huis Ten Bosch, een paleis in Den Haag. Er is ook een paleis op de Dam in Amsterdam, de hoofdstad, maar daar wonen ze niet. Koningin Beatrix is erg populair. Haar afbeelding staat op veel Nederlandse postzegels en alle munten. Haar moeder, prinses Juliana, was koningin tot 1980. Prinses Juliana leeft nog en is ook erg populair. Zij is eveneens met een Duitser getrouwd, prins Bernhard. Haar moeder was koningin Wilhelmina en Juliana's vader was ook Duits.

Exercise 5

Answer the following questions in Dutch using full sentences.

1　Hoe heet Willem Alexanders grootvader?
2　Uit welk land komt zijn opa?
3　Wat is de moedertaal van zijn vader?
4　In welke stad woont het Koninklijk Gezin?
5　Wat was prinses Juliana tot 1980?
6　Wat staat op alle Nederlandse munten?

3　There are three words for 'very' in Dutch: **erg**, **heel** and **zeer**. **Zeer** sounds rather bookish and is best avoided in speech. Both **erg** and **heel** are very common, but **heel** cannot be used with a negative, e.g. **Het was erg/heel duur**, but **Het was niet erg duur** 'It was very expensive/It was not very expensive'. Thus it is simplest to stick to **erg**, which can also mean 'terrible', e.g. **De aardbeving in Japan was heel erg** 'The earthquake in Japan was really terrible'.

Dialogue 3 ▣

Pauline is talking to a colleague

PAULINE:	Ga je vaak naar de schouwburg?
COLLEGA:	Ja, ik hou van opera.
PAULINE:	Zing je zelf?
COLLEGA:	Nee, helaas niet, maar mijn vader is operazanger.
PAULINE:	Ga weg! Echt waar? Zingt hij hier in Amsterdam?
COLLEGA:	Ja, en weet je waar? In het Concertgebouw.[4]

PAULINE:	*Do you go to the theatre often?*
COLLEAGUE:	*Yes, I love opera.*
PAULINE:	*Do you sing yourself?*
COLLEAGUE:	*No, unfortunately I don't, but my father is an opera singer.*
PAULINE:	*Go on! Really? Does he perform here in Amsterdam?*
COLLEAGUE:	*Yes, and do you know where? In the Concertgebouw.*

Language points

Yes/no questions

Questions that only require 'yes' or 'no' for an answer are formed simply by swapping around (inverting) the verb and the subject.

Ga je naar de bioscoop?	Are you going to the movies?
Zing je zelf?	Do you sing yourself?
Zingt hij hier in Amsterdam?	Does he perform in Amsterdam?
Weet je waar?	Do you know where?

Here is the pattern:

F	V	N	Rest
–	Ga	je	naar de bioscoop?
–	Zing	je	zelf?
–	Zingt	hij	hier in Amsterdam?
–	Weet	je	waar?

4 This very famous concert hall is known in English by its Dutch name (**het gebouw** 'the building').

Note 1: As in English, in this type of question no other word or phrase can precede the verb.

Note 2: When **jij** is inverted with its form of the verb, the **t** is dropped, e.g.

Jij vindt het hier leuk.	You like it here.
Vind je het hier leuk?	Do you like it here?

Note 3: Common verbs containing an **ij** or **ou** followed by **d** drop both the **t** ending and the **d** of the stem,[5] e.g.

Jij rijdt te hard.	You're driving too fast.
Rij je te hard?	Are you driving too fast?
Jij houdt van mij.	You love me.
Hou jij van mij?	Do you love me?

Exercise 6

Write suitable questions for the following answers.

1 Nee, wij wonen in Utrecht.
2 Nee, ze spreekt geen Engels.
3 Nee, Amsterdam is de hoofdstad van Nederland.
4 Nee, Pauline werkt in Den Haag.
5 Nee, ik rij niet altijd zo hard.
6 Nee, ik hou niet van haar.

Dialogue 4 ▣

A conversation in the tourist bureau

KANTOORBEDIENDE:	Kan ik u helpen?
KLANT:	Ja, graag. Wij blijven twee dagen in Amsterdam. Wat is er te zien?
KANTOORBEDIENDE:	Bent u ooit in Amsterdam geweest?
KLANT:	Nee, nog nooit.
KANTOORBEDIENDE:	Bent u ook nog nooit in Nederland geweest?
KLANT:	Jawel, vier jaar geleden, maar alleen maar in Den Haag.

PAULINE:	*Can I help you?*
ASSISTANT:	*Yes, please. We are staying in Amsterdam for two days. What is there to see?*
PAULINE:	*Have you ever been to Amsterdam before?*

5 Less common verbs, like those mentioned on page 17, merely drop the **t**, which means there is no change in the way they are pronounced, e.g. **lijd je**, **vermijd je**.

ASSISTANT: *No, never.*
PAULINE: *Haven't you ever been to the Netherlands before either?*
ASSISTANT: *Yes, four years ago, but only to The Hague.*

Note: The word **jaar**, and also **uur** 'hour' and **keer** 'time', never takes a plural ending after a numeral or the expression **een paar** 'a few', e.g. **Hij is tien jaar oud** 'He is ten years old', **vijf uur** 'five hours', **een paar/drie keer** 'a few/three times'.

Culture point
The national tourist bureau, which is represented all over the Netherlands, is known by its initials, **de VVV** (pronounced **de vee vee vee**). Most people don't even know what the letters stand for so you don't need to know either. **Waar is de VVV?** or **Waar is het VVV-kantoor?** is a handy question to have up your sleeve when arriving in a Dutch city you don't know.

Language points

The use of nee, ja, and jawel when answering yes/no questions

The word used when you want to give a negative answer is **nee**, which is sometimes written **neen** but the final **n** is never pronounced:

Bent u ooit in Amsterdam geweest? Nee, nooit.

To give an affirmative answer to a question the following rules apply:

1 The affirmative answer to a positive question is **ja**:

Kan ik u helpen? Ja, graag.

2 The affirmative answer to a negative question is **jawel**:

Bent u ook nog nooit in Nederland geweest? Jawel, vier jaar geleden.

Note: In other contexts as well, **wel** has the effect of contradicting a previous negation, e.g.

Jij hebt geen fiets.	You haven't got a bike.
Ik heb wel een fiets.	I do have a bike.
Heb je geen fiets?	Haven't you got a bike?
Jawel, ik heb wel een fiets.	Yes, I do have a bike.

Exercise 7

Answer the following questions with a simple **ja**, **nee** or **jawel** as appropriate:

1 Gaat Pauline elke dag naar Den Haag?
2 Werkt Piet in Amsterdam?
3 Wonen Piet en Pauline in Amsterdam?
4 Spreekt Pauline geen Nederlands?
5 Woont Pauline in Engeland?
6 Woont Piet niet in Nederland?

Dialogue 5 🔲

Pauline wakes Marius up

PAULINE: De hoeveelste is het vandaag?
MARIUS: Het is de achtste/het is acht april.
PAULINE: En wat is dat voor een dag?
MARIUS: Ik ben jarig.
PAULINE: Hoe oud word je dan?
MARIUS: Ik ben nu zeven geworden. Ik ben nu zeven jaar oud.
PAULINE: Gefeliciteerd, hoor!
MARIUS: Dank je. Waar zijn mijn cadeautjes?

PAULINE: *What's the date today?*
MARIUS: *It is the eighth/it is the eighth of April.*
PAULINE: *What sort of day is that?*
MARIUS: *It's my birthday.*
PAULINE: *How old are you going to be?*
MARIUS: *I've now turned seven. I'm seven years old.*
PAULINE: *Happy birthday then.*
MARIUS: *Thanks. Where are my presents?*

Language points

Ordinal numerals

An ordinal numeral: It is the *eighth* today.

Apart from 'first', 'third' and 'eighth' the ordinal numerals up to 'nineteenth' are simply the cardinal numerals (the numbers you have already learned) with **-de** added to them:

eerste	tweede	derde	vierde	vijfde
zesde	zevende	achtste	negende	tiende
elfde	twaalfde	dertiende	veertiende	vijftiende *etc.*

Note the three irregularities, **eerste**, **derde** and **achtste**.

From 'twentieth' on, **-ste** is added to all numerals:

twintigste	eenentwintigste	tweeëntwintigste
drieëntwintigste	vierentwintigste	dertigste *etc.*
veertigste	vijftigste	zestigste
zeventigste	tachtigste	negentigste
honderdste	honderdeerste	honderdtiende *etc.*

The Dutch equivalents of the English abbreviations *st*, *nd*, *rd* and *th* are simply **e**, e.g. **1e, 2e, 3e, 8e, 20e, 101e**.

Days, months and festive seasons of the year

The Dutch words for the days of the week are: **maandag, dinsdag, woensdag, donderdag, vrijdag, zaterdag, zondag**.
The months are: **januari, februari, maart, april, mei, juni, juli, augustus, september, oktober, november, december**.

The festive seasons of the year are:

Nieuwjaarsdag	New Year's Day
Pasen	Easter
Pinksteren	Whitsuntide, Pentecost
Kerstmis	Christmas
Eerste Kerstdag	Christmas Day
Tweede Kerstdag	Boxing Day

Note: Unlike English, capital letters are *not* used for the names of days and months.

Exercise 8

Complete these sentences by filling in the appropriate month:

1 Kerstmis valt in _____.
2 Nieuwjaarsdag valt in _____.
3 Ik heb vakantie in _____.
4 Pinksteren valt in _____.
5 Koninginnedag is altijd in _____.
6 Ik ben in _____ jarig.
7 Pasen valt bijna altijd in _____.
8 In Nederland begint de zomer in _____.

Culture point

Special dates in the Dutch calendar are **30 april**, **Koninginnedag** 'Queen's Birthday' and **5 mei**, **Bevrijdingsdag** 'Liberation Day'. Both are public holidays.

In fact, 30 April was the birthday of the former queen, Juliana, but as Juliana abdicated on her birthday in 1980, Beatrix decided as a gesture to her mother to retain that day as the national holiday. She was after all inaugurated as queen on that day. It should be noted that Dutch monarchs are not crowned. On **Koninginnedag** the Dutch have the right to set up stalls in the street to sell whatever they like, which is particularly the case in Amsterdam. Many Dutch people have a flagpole in their garden or hanging from the balcony and they are keen to fly the Dutch flag on the occasion of all royal birthdays in particular. When the event has a royal connection, a long narrow orange-coloured pennant is hoisted with the flag, orange being symbolic of the Dutch monarchy, which belongs to the **Huis van Oranje-Nassau**.

Bevrijdingsdag relates to World War II, which has left deep scars on the Dutch national psyche. There are still residual anti-German sentiments to be found among the Dutch, even among those born long after the war. This is even reflected in how seriously the Dutch take the learning of English compared with the minimum of effort they put into learning German – in the latter case near enough is good enough, despite the fact, or perhaps because of it, that the two languages are so similar.

FEESTDAGEN IN DE KOMENDE JAREN			
	1996	**1997**	**1998**	**1999**

	1996	1997	1998	1999
Nieuwjaar	maandag	woensdag	donderdag	vrijdag
Carnaval	19 feb.	10 feb.	23 feb.	15 feb.
Pasen	7 april	30 maart	12 april	4 april
Koninginnedag	dinsdag	woensdag	donderdag	vrijdag
Bevrijdingsdag	zondag	maandag	dinsdag	woensdag
Hemelvaart	16 mei	8 mei	21 mei	13 mei
Pinksteren	26 mei	18 mei	31 mei	23 mei
Kerstmis	woensdag	donderdag	vrijdag	zaterdag

Dates

When saying a date mentioning the name of the month, it is more usual in Dutch to use the cardinal, not the ordinal numeral, e.g. **Wat is het vandaag? Het is tien februari**. But if the name of the month is omitted, the ordinal is used, e.g. **Vandaag is het de tiende**.

Exercise 9

Write out in Dutch the dates of the following events, giving the day and the month:

1 Wanneer is het Koninginnedag?
2 Wanneer ben je jarig?
3 Wanneer is het Bevrijdingsdag?
4 Op welke dag valt Eerste Kerstdag?
5 Wanneer is het Nieuwjaarsdag?

Congratulations and good wishes

(Hartelijk) gefeliciteerd	See note 1 on page 54
Prettig weekend!	Have a nice weekend!
Prettige vakantie!	Have a nice holiday!
Vrolijk Kerstfeest!	Merry Christmas!
Gelukkig Nieuwjaar!	Happy New Year!
Beterschap!	Get well soon!
Gecondoleerd	Condolences, I'm very sorry to hear that ... (used towards relatives of a deceased person)

Veel plezier!	Enjoy yourself/yourselves!
Sterkte!	Chin up! Keep at it!
Eet ze	See note 2 below
Eet smakelijk!	Bon appétit! Enjoy the meal!
Smakelijk eten!	Bon appétit! Enjoy the meal!
Slaap ze	Sleep well! See note 2 below
Welterusten	Sleep well!

Note 1: (**Hartelijk**) **gefeliciteerd** literally means 'congratulations' and is used on all occasions, from birthdays to wedding anniversaries and the passing of exams. When uttered to a birthday boy/girl, it renders 'happy birthday' or 'many happy returns', whereas when said to a newly married couple, it simply renders 'congratulations'. If the reason for the greeting needs to be made clear, which is not normally the case, however, one says (**hartelijk**) **gefeliciteerd met je verjaardag/met je examen/huwelijk.**

Note 2: **Eet ze** and **slaap ze** are very colloquial expressions and are seldom ever written. **Slaap ze** alternates with **welterusten** and has a direct English equivalent. **Eet ze** alternates with both **eet smakelijk** and **smakelijk eten** and also has a direct English equivalent, if you can regard 'bon appétit' as English – continentals feel a necessity to say something before beginning a meal, as opposed to the Anglo-Saxon custom of simply setting to.

Culture point

Birthdays are sacrosanct to the Dutch. God forbid that you should forget to ring up or pop in on a friend on their birthday. But no Dutch person would or could ever forget because hanging on the back of every toilet-door in the country is a **verjaardagskalender** (birthday calendar) with the birthday noted of every person you've ever met in your life! When visiting someone on the occasion of a birthday, you do the rounds of all relatives present, uttering the word **gefeliciteerd** as you shake their hand – apparently they too are seen as having made some contribution to the birthday boy's/girl's achievement of having survived one more year on the planet. If you have to spend your birthday at work, rather than being the fortunate recipient of goodies you are on the contrary expected to lash out and buy small cakes for all your colleagues to have with their morning coffee.

Felicitaties

Maria Dellenvoet-v.d. Berg **65 jaar** Het is niet niks en nu op naar de honderd Gefeliciteerd, JE FAMILIE	Lieve GREET hartelijk gefeliciteerd als Sarah! Ik hou van je, de rest vertel ik je zelf. Jaap.
	Hoera, JOKE LIGTENBERG wordt vandaag 50 jaar!!! Hartelijk gefeliciteerd en een oergezellige dag toegewenst door je broers en zusters
Tine VAN HARTE GEFELICITEERD.	CHIPPY, hartelijk gefeliciteerd, ik mis je! *** E.
Het leven begint bij 40! XXX en heel veel liefs, Manon, Sheila en Pim.	Hiep, hoera! MELISSA, 1 jaar. Van harte gefeliciteerd, kusjes van Opa en Oma.

Dialogue 6 ▭

A friend is visiting Piet on his birthday

VRIEND: Hoi, Piet. Je bent vandaag jarig, niet waar? Hartelijk
gefeliciteerd.
PIET: Dank je, Jaap.
VRIEND: Pauline, gefeliciteerd met de verjaardag van je man.
PAULINE: Bedankt, Jaap.
VRIEND: Hoe oud ben je nu, Piet?
PIET: Ik word vandaag 32.
VRIEND: We worden oud, hè?
PIET: Jij misschien wel, maar ik niet, hoor.
VRIEND: Wat is er met je been aan de hand?
PIET: Ik heb het gisteren gebroken.
VRIEND: Wat erg! Sterkte hoor en beterschap!

FRIEND: *Hi, Piet. It's your birthday today, isn't it? Many happy
returns!*
PIET: *Thanks, Jaap.*
FRIEND: (The equivalent greeting does not exist in English.) See
Culture point above.
PAULINE: *Thanks, Jaap.*
FRIEND: *How old are you now, Piet?*
PIET: *I turn thirty-two today.*
FRIEND: *We're getting old, aren't we?*
PIET: *You are perhaps, but not me.*

FRIEND: *What's wrong with your leg?*
PIET: *I broke it yesterday.*
FRIEND: *What a shame! Keep your chin up, and I hope you get better soon.*

Language points

How to use niet waar?

The simple expression **niet waar?** (lit. 'not true?') can be used wherever English uses the question tags *aren't they?*, *is he?*, *shouldn't we?*, *has she?*, etc. at the end of a statement. But in colloquial Dutch **hè?** is used in the same way and is in fact much more commonly heard than **niet waar?** Use of both expressions is illustrated in the above dialogue.

More words for food and drink

het eten	food	**de appel**	apple
de soep	soup	**de banaan**	banana
de groente (sing.)	vegetables	**de oploskoffie**	instant coffee
het vlees	meat	**het kruid**	spice, herb
het gehakt	minced meat	**de melk**	milk
de kip	chicken	**de kaas**	cheese
de (rook)worst	(smoked) sausage	**de roomboter**	butter
		het brood	bread, loaf of bread
de vis	fish		
de wijn	wine	**de saus**	sauce
het bier	beer	**de patat** (pl.)	chips, French fries
de pils	beer		
de sla	salad, lettuce	**de snoep**	confectionery, candy
de tomaat	tomato		
de aardappel	potato	**het gebak**	pastries, cakes (collective)
de knoflook	garlic		
het fruit	fruit		

4 Telefoneren

Telephoning

In this lesson you will learn about:

- telephone conversations
- the past tense of regular verbs (I worked/have worked)
- the past tense of irregular verbs (I saw/have seen)
- use of **zijn** and **hebben** in the perfect tense
- modal auxiliary verbs
- making and accepting apologies

Dialogues 1 and 2 🔳

Piet's brother, Hans, rings Piet up

PAULINE: Met Pauline.
HANS: Hallo, Pauline. Met Hans. Is Piet thuis?
PAULINE: Nee, hij is nog niet thuis.
HANS: Ach, het geeft niet.
PAULINE: Wil je dat-ie[1] je terugbelt?
HANS: Nee, hoor. Ik bel straks wel weer.

PAULINE: *Pauline speaking.*
HANS: *Hallo, Pauline. It's Hans here. Is Piet at home?*
PAULINE: *No, he's not home yet.*
HANS: *Oh, it doesn't matter.*
PAULINE: *Do you want him to ring you back?*
HANS: *No, I'll ring again in a little while.*

---

1 **Hij** is commonly pronounced, but never written, **ie** but only when it occurs in inverted position (e.g. **Wat heeft-ie in zijn hand?** 'What has he got in his hand?') or as in the above dialogue where a word ending in **t** precedes and makes a glide possible, i.e. this is pronounced **dattie.**

Pauline answers the phone at work

PAULINE: Van Goor en Zonen.
KLIËNT: Hallo, goeie morgen. U spreekt met Joop Scherpenzeel. Mag ik de manager even spreken?
PAULINE: Een ogenblik, meneer. – Nee, die is helaas in gesprek.
KLIËNT: Ach, wat jammer!
PAULINE: Kan ik een boodschap aan hem geven?
KLIËNT: Nee, eigenlijk niet. Geeft u mij Pauline van den Berg even!
PAULINE: Daar spreekt u mee.

PAULINE: *Van Goor and Sons.*
CLIENT: *Hallo, good morning. It's Joop Scherpenzeel speaking. May I speak to the manager?*
PAULINE: *Just a moment, sir. – No, unfortunately he's on the phone (= is engaged).*
CLIENT: *Oh, what a shame!*
PAULINE: *Can I give him a message?*
CLIENT: *No, not really. Can I speak to Pauline van den Berg?*
PAULINE: *Yes of course, it's Pauline speaking.*

Language points

Telephone conversations

The person answering the phone may (1) give his/her first name, surname or both names preceded by **met**, or (2) give the name of the office, shop, etc.

Note 1: It is not usual to give the phone number when answering the phone. When phone numbers are otherwise given, the figures are read out in pairs, either as 34 56 78 **vierendertig zesenvijftig achtenzeventig** or as **drie vier – vijf zes – zeven acht**. With seven-digit numbers either the first or the last number can be read on its own and the rest coupled as illustrated.

Note 2: **Mag ik** (name) **even spreken?** is a rather formal way of asking to speak to someone, i.e. omitting **met** and using **spreken**, whereas **Mag ik ... even?** is somewhat less formal.

Note 3: **Even** (lit. 'just') is commonly used as a softener in putting requests and demands; it has the force of 'if you don't mind', e.g. **Mag ik Pauline even spreken?** 'Can I speak to Pauline?', **Ga even zitten!** 'Sit down!' **Wacht even!** 'Wait a moment!' **Eens** (pronounced **'s**) has a similar function and is often used in combination with **even**, e.g. **Wacht eens even!**

Note 4: As the use of **mag** and **kan** in the above dialogue illustrates, they frequently alternate in usage just as *may* and *can* do in English.

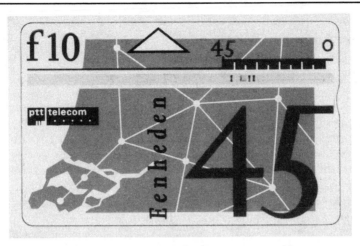

Useful words and phrases for a telephone conversation:

Hallo! Ik ben het – Jaap.	Hello! It's me – Jaap.
Ben jij het, Hilde?	Is that you, Hilde?
Je/u spreekt met ...	... speaking.
Met wie spreek ik?	Who am I speaking to?
Is ... thuis?	Is ... at home?
Wilt u even wachten!	Would you please hold on!
Wacht even!	Hold on!
(Een) ogenblik/ogenblikje.	Just a moment.
U bent verkeerd verbonden.	You have the wrong number.
de telefoonkaart	telephone card

Exercise 1

Write out the following telephone conversation taking the role of the person who has been rung.

YOU: Say it's Paul speaking.

CALLER: Asks if Joop is at home.

YOU: Say that he is at home. Ask who you are speaking to.

CALLER: Gives his name (André de Schutter) and asks if he can speak to Joop. (Use a less formal form as this is not a business.)

YOU: Tell the caller to hang on. (Use a polite form as you don't know the caller.)

JOOP: He says who's speaking.

CALLER: Does likewise.

JOOP: Says he does not know the person and tells the chap he has the wrong number.

Language points

The two groups of verbs

Dutch verbs can be divided into two groups, regular and irregular. Although the distinction between the two groups is not obvious in the present tense, which we have already covered, it is important to be aware that there is a difference in the way these two groups of verbs form their past tenses – compare *loved/have loved* and *worked/have worked*, which are regular verbs in English, with *saw/have seen* and *did/have done*, which are irregular verbs. The concept is basically the same in the two languages.

Dialogue 3 🔲

Pauline tells Piet about a recent phone-call

PAULINE: Ik heb vandaag van Hilde gehoord. Ze belde. We hebben een uur lang gepraat.
PIET: Wat zei ze?
PAULINE: Ze heeft de hele week gekookt. Haar man is zaterdag jarig.
PIET: Ik heb haar man nooit ontmoet.
PAULINE: Ik ook niet.

PAULINE: *I heard from Hilde today. She rang. We talked for an hour.*
PIET: *What did she say?*
PAULINE: *She has been cooking all week. It's her husband's birthday on Saturday.*
PIET: *I've never met her husband.*
PAULINE: *I haven't either.*

Language points

The perfect tense of regular verbs

Perfect tense: I *have worked* very hard.

The perfect tense in both Dutch and English consists of a form of the verb **hebben** 'to have' followed by the past participle.

The past participle of regular verbs in English ends in *-ed*, whereas in Dutch one takes the stem of the verb (see page 16, where verbal stems were discussed) and adds **ge-** to the front of it and **-d** or **-t** to the end:

Infinitive	*Stem*	*Past participle*
horen (hear)	**hoor**	**gehoord** (heard)
bellen (ring)	**bel**	**gebeld** (rung)
praten (talk)	**praat**	**gepraat** (talked)
zeggen (say)	**zeg**	**gezegd** (said)
koken (work)	**kook**	**gekookt** (cooked)

Whether you add **-d** or **-t** to the end depends on the last sound of the stem – compare English *worked*, where the *d* is pronounced as a *t* and *loved*, where the *d* is pronounced as a *d*, and you can see that a similar distinction exists in English but you don't write it. The Dutch use a mnemonic to help them remember whether to write **-d** or **-t**, because a final **d** is pronounced **t** and thus you can't hear the difference: remember the made-up word **'t kofschip**; if a stem ends in any of the consonants in this word, it adds **-t**, otherwise **-d**. Thus **werken** and **koken** above take a **-t** and **bellen**, **horen** and **zeggen** a **-d**.

You need to be careful with verbs that have a **v** or **z** in the infinitive but a stem that ends in **f** or **s** because the original **v** and **z** determine if the **'t kofschip** rule is to be applied, despite appearances:

Infinitive	*Stem*	*Past participle*
reizen (travel)	**reis**	**gereisd** (travelled)
leven (live)	**leef**	**geleefd** (lived)

The **ge-** prefix is not stressed; the stress falls on the next syllable, e.g. **ge'hoord**, **ge'werkt**, **ge'leefd**. Verbs that start with unstressed **be-**, **ge-**, **her-**, **ont-** and **ver-** don't add **ge-**; an example of this is **ontmoet** in the above dialogue.

Exercise 2

Derive the past participles of the following verbs applying the **'t kofschip** rule and enter them into the crossword.

Horizontaal	*Verticaal*
2 vertalen	1 wonen
5 roken	3 doden
6 leven	4 antwoorden
8 tellen	5 zeggen
9 trouwen	6 doven
10 bedanken	7 zetten
11 blaffen	8 dansen
12 beloven	

Language points

Use of the perfect tense and position of the past participle

In dialogue 3 all the verbs are in the perfect tense whereas only two of the English verbs, 'She has been cooking' and 'I've never met', are in the perfect. This illustrates a fundamental difference between Dutch and English: in Dutch the perfect tense is much more commonly used than the imperfect tense. 'I heard', 'she rang', 'she talked', 'What did she say?' are all examples of English using the imperfect (we deal with this tense in Dutch later) where Dutch prefers the perfect. Get used to using this tense whenever you use a verb in the past: 'she cooked', 'she did cook', 'she has cooked' and 'she has been cooking' are all most usually rendered by **zij heeft gekookt**.

Note that the past participle is always placed at the end of the clause in Dutch, however long the clause is; the finite verb stands in second position and the past participle dependent on it forms a sort of final bracket to the statement:

Ik heb gebeld.	I rang/have rung.
Ik heb hem gebeld.	I rang/have rung him.
Ik heb hem gisteren gebeld.	I rang him yesterday.
Ik heb hem gisteren thuis gebeld.	I rang him at home yesterday.

Note: The above sentences illustrate the difference in English between the perfect and the imperfect. The use of *yesterday* in the last two sentences makes it impossible to say *have rung*, whereas context may demand it in the first two examples. This distinction is unknown in Dutch and the perfect can be used throughout.

Exercise 3

Give the stem and the past participle of the following verbs:

1 ontmoeten (*meet*)
2 wekken (*wake*)
3 herhalen (*repeat*)
4 blaffen (*bark*)
5 verven (*paint*)
6 blozen (*blush*)
7 praten (*talk*)
8 huren (*rent*)

Exercise 4

Translate the following into Dutch:

1 I worked today.
2 He has worked all week.
3 They have been working all day.
4 I met him last night.
5 Piet has translated a book.
6 She rang this morning.
7 He said nothing.
8 Have you been working?
9 She painted the wall.
10 We have rented a house.

Dialogue 4 ▣

Pauline tells Piet about a girlfriend's good luck

PAULINE: Ik heb Hilde vandaag gezien.
PIET: Hoe gaat het met haar?

PAULINE: Prima! Ze heeft net een nieuwe auto gekregen.[2]
PIET: Gekregen? Echt waar? Hoe dan?
PAULINE: Haar tante heeft hem gewonnen en ze heeft hem aan Hilde gegeven.
PIET: Wat leuk! Wat heeft ze geboft, zeg!

PAULINE: *I saw Hilde today.*
PIET: *How's she doing?*
PAULINE: *Great! She just got a new car!*
PIET: *She was given one? Really? How come?*
PAULINE: *Her aunt won it and she gave it to Hilde.*
PIET: *How wonderful! Gee, she was lucky.*

Language points

The perfect tense of irregular verbs

There are not nearly as many irregular as there are regular verbs. Assume every new verb you meet is regular unless told it is irregular. Generally speaking, it is not obvious from the infinitive of a verb whether it is regular or irregular in the past tense. Irregular past tense forms are given in parentheses after the infinitive in the word list at the back of the book; where there are no parentheses, a verb can be assumed to be regular, e.g.

horen   to hear
vinden (vond/vonden, gevonden)   to find

The past participle of an irregular verb adds **ge-** to the front and **-en** to the end of the stem, with or without a change in the vowel of the stem, e.g. **geven – gegeven**, **krijgen – gekregen**, **winnen – gewonnen**, **zien – gezien**.

If a verb is irregular, there are several ways in which it can be irregular; there are a few rules for identifying patterns, but these are only a rough guide anyway and will be dealt with later. There are just a few irregular verbs whose past participle has both a change of vowel and ends in a **-t** like a regular verb, e.g. **brengen**

---

2 Unlike *to get* in English, **krijgen** always has the connotation of having been given something for nothing, thus Piet's reaction **Gekregen?**, which means 'What, she was given a car?' For this reason if asking someone 'Where did you get that coat?' 'get' must be rendered by **kopen**, not **krijgen**, e.g. **Waar heb je die jas gekocht?**

– **gebracht** 'to bring', **denken – gedacht** 'thought', **kopen – gekocht** 'to buy'.

Exercise 5

Look up the past participles of the following verbs in the list of irregular verbs on pages 249–54 or under the respective verb in the glossary and enter them into the crossword.

Horizontaal	*Verticaal*
1 doen	1 winnen
4 geven	2 kopen
5 vinden	3 snijden
6 zoeken	5 kijken
8 zijn	6 slaan
9 denken	7 hebben
10 komen	

Exercise 6

Translate the following into Dutch. The verb in each case is irregular. You can get the correct form either from the list of irregular verbs on pages 249–54 or from the Dutch–English word list where it is given in parentheses after the infinitive:

1 She gave the book to me.
2 He's won a trip to Greece.
3 I saw Hilde in town.
4 Piet drank too much beer.
5 We've found it.

Exercise 7

Your partner has just come home from work and you tell him/her what you have been doing all day. Write out sentences like the one below using the word pairs given. Some of the verbs are irregular and some are regular.

Example: de afwas/doen: Ik heb de afwas gedaan.

1 boodschappen/doen
2 brood/bakken
3 de auto/wassen
4 overhemden/strijken
5 mijn moeder/bellen
6 aardappels/schillen

Dialogue 5

Pauline is asking Piet about a friend she hasn't seen for a while

PAULINE: Waar is Wim? Ik heb hem erg lang niet gezien.
PIET: Hij is naar Maastricht verhuisd.
PAULINE: Waarom heeft-ie dat gedaan?
PIET: Hij is 65 geworden en werkt niet meer. Hij is namelijk in Maastricht geboren.
PAULINE: Is-ie nog getrouwd?
PIET: Nee, hij is getrouwd geweest maar is nu gescheiden.
PAULINE: Leeft zijn moeder nog?
PIET: Nee, die is vorig jaar overleden.

PAULINE: *Where's Wim? I haven't seen him for a long time.*
PIET: *He's moved to Maastricht.*
PAULINE: *Why did he do that?*
PIET: *He turned sixty-five and doesn't work any more. He was born in Maastricht, you see.*
PAULINE: *Is he still married?*
PIET: *No, he was married but is now divorced.*
PAULINE: *Is his mother still alive?*
PIET: *No, she passed away last year.*

Language points

The perfect tense with zijn

So far we have seen that the perfect tense is formed by a form of the verb **hebben** followed by the past participle, as in English:

Ik heb gewerkt.	I have worked/been working.
Hij heeft het gedaan.	He's done it.

A small group of common verbs, most but not all of them irregular, don't use **hebben** to form this tense, but **zijn**:

Ze zijn naar de stad gegaan.	They've gone/went to town.
Hij is gisteren aangekomen.	He has arrived/arrived yesterday.
Haar man is gestorven.	Her husband has died/died.
Wat is je man veranderd!	How your husband has changed!
Mijn vrouw is ziek geweest.	My wife has been/was ill.

Verbs that take **zijn** in this way belong to one of three categories:

1 They indicate a motion, such as **gaan** and **aankomen** above.
2 They indicate a change of state, such as **sterven** and **veranderen** above.
3 There are just a few that don't seem to fit logically into either of the above categories, e.g. **blijven**, **vergeten**, **zijn**.

Verbs that take **zijn** in the perfect are indicated in the Dutch–English word list as follows: **sterven (stierf/stierven, is gestorven)**, **verhuizen (is verhuisd)**. Irregular verbs are also marked as taking **zijn** in the list of irregular verbs on page 249.

Exercise 8

Complete the following statements and questions using either **hebben** or **zijn** where appropriate.

1 De computer _____ verdwenen. (infinitive **verdwijnen** 'to disappear')
2 _____ Marius het genomen? (**nemen** 'to take')
3 _____ Pauline al thuisgekomen? (**thuiskomen** 'to come home')
4 Zij _____ naar Amsterdam gereden. (**rijden** 'to drive')
5 Piet _____ naar huis gegaan. (**gaan** 'to go')
6 Ze _____ koffie gedronken. (**drinken** 'to drink')
7 _____ Lien al verhuisd? (**verhuizen** 'to shift')

8 _____ je Hilde gebeld? (**bellen** 'to ring')
9 Ze _____ ja gezegd. (**zeggen** 'to say')
10 We _____ de hele dag thuis gebleven. (**blijven** 'to stay')

Verbs that can take either zijn or hebben in the perfect

A small group of verbs (mostly irregular but there are a few regular ones among them) can take either **zijn** or **hebben** depending on whether they are expressing motion from one point to another or not (i.e. the destination must be mentioned):

Hij is naar huis gelopen.	He walked home.
Hij heeft de hele dag gelopen.	He's been walking all day.
Ik ben alleen naar Rusland gereisd.	I travelled to Russia on my own.
Ik heb in Rusland veel gereisd.	I've travelled a lot in Russia.

These verbs are indicated as follows in the Dutch–English word list:

lopen (liep, is/heeft gelopen)
reizen (is/heeft gereisd)

Exercise 9

Complete the following statements and questions using either **hebben** or **zijn** where appropriate.

1 Ik ____ naar huis gereden.
2 Ik ____ nooit een Mercedes gereden.
3 ____ je ooit in de Noordzee gezwommen?
4 Ik ____ een keer van Frankrijk naar Engeland gezwommen.
5 We ____ gisteren naar Den Helder gefietst.
6 ____ jij nooit gefietst?

Modal auxiliary verbs

There is a group of verbs, collectively called modal auxiliary verbs, which have totally irregular forms, even in the present tense. In English *can*, *may* and *must* are examples of such verbs. Some Dutch modal verbs have already been used in the dialogues, and you have had no trouble understanding them, but attention now needs to be drawn to them. Here they are with their irregular present tense:

kunnen 'to be able/can'	**moeten** 'to have to/must'
ik kan 'I am able to/I can'	ik moet 'I have to/I must'
jij kan/kunt	jij moet
u kunt	u moet
hij kan	hij moet
wij kunnen	wij moeten
jullie kunnen	jullie moeten
zij kunnen	zij moeten
mogen 'to be allowed to/may'	**willen** 'to want to'
ik mag 'I am allowed to/I may'	ik wil 'I want to'
jij mag	jij wil/wilt
u mag	u wilt
hij mag	hij wil
wij mogen	wij willen
jullie mogen	jullie willen
zij mogen	zij willen

We have already seen how past participles are put at the end of the clause as only one verb, the finite verb, can stay at the front of the clause in second position. Modal verbs all have in common that they are usually followed by another verb, always an infinitive,[3] and that second verb must stand at the end of the clause:

Ik wil een nieuwe auto kopen.	I want to buy a new car.
Mag ik even met Piet spreken?	May I speak to Piet?
Zij moet naar de dokter gaan.	She has to go to the doctor.
Kan ik u helpen?	Can I help you?

The following is a schematic view of what one does with non-finite verbs, both past participles and infinitives. The latter stand in position V2:

F	V	N	OTHER	V2
Wim	is		naar Maastricht	verhuisd.
	Is	hij	nog	getrouwd?
We	zijn		gisteren thuis	gebleven.

3 The reason modal verbs are called auxiliary verbs is because they support infinitives.

Exercise 10

What are your options or possibilities in the following situations?
Use **kunnen** plus the words in parentheses to form your answers.

Example: You are fed up with your dog. (buy/a cat)
Ik kan een kat kopen.

1 You can't pay your bills. (forget/them)
2 You don't like the country you live in (move/to Belgium)
3 You ring somebody up but get no answer. (ring/again)
4 You don't want people to know you are in. (switch off/the light)
5 You don't like to say no to an invitation. (say/yes)
6 You have broken down on the motorway. (stop/a car)
7 You have been in town for hours and are tired. (go/home)
8 The electricity has gone off. (light/a candle)

Exercise 11

Complete the sentence **Je kan met een** ___ ___ by choosing a noun
from the first box and an appropriate verb from the second to put
in the two gaps in the sentence.

Example: Je kan met een mes snijden.

| potlood kwast schaar naald lepel schop pen |

| graven knippen naaien verven schrijven roeren tekenen |

Dialogues 6 and 7 [CD]

Pauline is annoyed there is no more milk

PAULINE: Waar is de melk?
MARIUS: Ik heb hem opgedronken.
PAULINE: Nu hebben we geen melk voor het ontbijt.
MARIUS: Sorry. Daar heb ik niet aan gedacht.

PAULINE: *Where's the milk?*
MARIUS: *I drank it.*
PAULINE: *Now we haven't got any milk for breakfast.*

MARIUS: *I'm sorry. I didn't think of that.*

Piet arrives home late from school

PIET: Het spijt me dat ik zo laat thuiskom.
PAULINE: Het geeft niet. Waar was je?
PIET: We hebben een vergadering gehad.
PAULINE: Nu kunnen we eindelijk eten. Ik heb honger.
PIET: Hebben jullie op mij gewacht? Sorry, hoor!
PAULINE: Het maakt niet uit. We eten alleen maar brood.
PIET: Wat? Alleen maar brood? Ik heb vandaag niet warm gegeten.
PAULINE: (*angrily*) Ik had geen tijd om te koken. Ik heb ook de hele dag gewerkt en ben pas laat thuisgekomen.[4]
PIET: Neem me niet kwalijk, maar ik heb razende honger. (*his stomach rumbles*) Pardon!

PIET: *I'm sorry I've got home so late.*
PAULINE: *It doesn't matter. Where've you been?* (= What kept you?)
PIET: *We had a meeting.*
PAULINE: *We can finally eat now. I'm hungry.*
PIET: *Did you all wait for me? I am sorry.*
PAULINE: *It doesn't matter. We are only having a bread meal.*
PIET: *What? Only bread?* (i.e. not a cooked meal) *I haven't had a cooked meal today.*
PAULINE: *I didn't have time to cook. I've worked all day too and didn't get home till late.*
PIET: *Forgive me, but I'm starving. Pardon!*

Language points

Making and accepting apologies

Saying sorry:

Sorry.	Sorry.
Het spijt me (dat ...).	I'm sorry (that ...).
Neem me niet kwalijk/Neemt u me niet kwalijk.	I'm sorry/Forgive me/Don't take offence.

---

4 **Thuis** normally renders 'at home'; 'home', i.e. motion towards, is expressed by **naar huis**; only in the expression **thuiskomen** 'to come home' is **thuis** used where you might otherwise expect **naar huis**.

Pardon.   Excuse me.

The word **sorry** has a wider application in Dutch than in English. When pushing your way through a crowd, for instance, you could say **sorry** where in English it would be more appropriate to say *excuse me*. If you trod on someone's toe you could say **Sorry hoor! Neem me niet kwalijk** or **Pardon. Het spijt me** is commonly used when you go on to give the reason for your apology but this can also be expressed by **sorry dat ...**

Accepting an apology:

Het geeft niet.   It doesn't matter.
Het maakt niet uit.   It doesn't matter.

Exercise 12

Pauline and Charlotte, her daughter, are in the kitchen. Pauline opens the cupboard door. Write the dialogue.

PAULINE: Asks Charlotte if she has seen the biscuits.
CHARLOTTE: Says yes and says she has eaten two biscuits and Marius has eaten two biscuits too.
PAULINE: Complains that they now have no biscuits for this evening.
CHARLOTTE: Apologises that she ate the biscuits.

Exercise 13

Pauline and the children have sat down at the table for lunch. Piet comes in from the garden. Write the dialogue.

PIET: Asks if they have been waiting for him.
PAULINE: Says yes and asks what kept him.
PIET: Says he's been washing the car.
PAULINE: Asks if he's hungry.
PIET: Says yes, that he is starving and apologises for being so late.
PAULINE: Brushes the problem aside and tells him that Jaap rang.
PIET: Asks how Jaap is.
PAULINE: Says he's getting along fine.

> **Culture point**
> The Dutch wouldn't dream of having more than one hot meal a day. It is not uncommon to be asked when arriving at a Dutch house with the intention of staying the night **Heb je al warm gegeten?**, the implication being that if you have, the evening meal will be a bread meal not unlike a Dutch breakfast. If you are to be honoured with a hot meal (**een warme maaltijd**), there is little likelihood that potatoes in one or other form, but usually simply boiled, will not be on the menu. The meat is most likely to be fried and the frying medium plus meat juices will be avidly collected to form **de sju**, which will be poured onto the potatoes after you have crushed them with your fork and formed a hollow (**een kuiltje**) to hold the **sju** – never cut them with a knife! This custom is reminiscent of mixing cement.

Reading text

Vocabulary

lieveling, **schat**, **lieverd**   darling, honey, etc.
helemaal niet   not at all

A late phone call

Het is avond. Meneer De Bruyn belt zijn vrouw. Zij neemt de telefoon op.
'Hallo, lieveling. Ik kom vanavond heel laat thuis. Ik heb een heel belangrijke vergadering', zegt hij.
'Dat geeft helemaal niet, schat', antwoordt zij.
'Wat zeg je?', vraagt hij.
'Het maakt helemaal niet uit, lieverd', zegt zij.
'Sorry, hoor, maar ik ben verkeerd verbonden, geloof ik', zegt hij.
(His wife would never be so understanding)

Language points

How to say that you have not heard or understood someone

Wat zeg je?	
Wat zegt u?	I beg your pardon? Sorry?
Wat?	What? Eh?
Ik heb/kan u niet verstaan.	I can't hear/understand you.
Wat betekent dat?	What does that mean?
Zeg dat nog eens, alstublieft!	Please say that again!

Note: Although **Wat zegt u?** also of course translates 'What did you say?', it does not sound as abrupt as in English and is in fact as polite as 'I beg your pardon?' or 'Sorry?' **Wat?** is colloquial and only appropriate where people know each other well, as in English.

5 Bij Piet en Pauline

At Piet's and Pauline's

In this lesson you will learn about:

- personal pronouns as objects (me, him, etc.)
- possessives (my, your, his, etc.)
- demonstratives (this/these, that/those)
- independent possessives (mine, yours, his, etc.)
- indicating possession (apostrophe s)
- adjectives

Dialogue 1 🎧

Pauline is looking for Piet and Charlotte

PAULINE: Marius, ik zoek je vader. Heb je hem gezien? En ik heb ook Charlotte nodig. Heb je haar gezien?

MARIUS: Nee, ik heb ze geen van beiden gezien. Is Charlotte niet buiten in de tuin?

PAULINE: Ik heb haar ongeveer een uur geleden in de tuin gezien, maar ze (die) is er niet meer. Is ze soms bij de buren?

MARIUS: Ja, waarschijnlijk. Ze is altijd bij hen als we haar nodig hebben.

PAULINE: Marius, kom me hier even helpen, alsjeblieft.

MARIUS: Nee, ik kan je nu niet helpen. Ik ben bezig.

PAULINE: Jou help ik ook nooit meer.

PAULINE: *Marius, I'm looking for your father. Have you seen him? And I need Charlotte too. Have you seen her?*

MARIUS: *No, I haven't seen either of them. Isn't Charlotte outside in the garden?*

PAULINE: *I saw her in the garden about an hour ago but she isn't there any more. Is she perhaps at the neighbours'?*

MARIUS: *Yes, probably. She is always at their place when we need her.*
PAULINE: *Marius, please come and help me here.*
MARIUS: *No, I can't help you now. I'm busy.*
PAULINE: *I won't ever help you again either.*

Language points

Personal pronouns as objects

A personal object pronoun: I saw *her* in the garden.

Singular		Plural	
mij/me	me	**ons**	us
jou/je	you	**jullie/je**	you
u	you	**u**	you
hem	him	**ze/hen/hun**	them
haar	her		
het	it		

We have been seeing object pronouns in use all along but they have not previously been dealt with formally. The concept is the same as in English except that *you* is both a subject and object pronoun in English, whereas in Dutch as a subject you use **jij** and as an object **jou**, but the unemphatic form of both is **je**. 'Me' also has an unemphatic form, **me**.

Note 1: All third-person pronouns, both singular and plural and subject and object forms, are often replaced in colloquial Dutch by **die**, as illustrated by the alternative form in parentheses in dialogue 1. Except in questions, **die** commonly stands in front position as it is usually emphasised. Context always makes it clear what **die** is referring to:

Die is in de tuin.	She/he (subject) is in the garden.
Die heb ik niet gezien.	I haven't seen him/her/them (object).
Die wonen naast ons.	They (subject) live next-door to us.

Of course **die** cannot stand in first position in questions, e.g.

| **Waar is Jaap? Heb je die gezien?** | Where is Jaap? Have you seen him? |
| **Dat is Jaap. Ken je die?** | That's Jaap. do you know him? |

Note 2: There are complications with rendering 'them' in Dutch. **Ze** is always correct if no emphasis is required, e.g.

| **Ik ken ze.** | I know them. |

| **Ik heb ze het geld gegeven.** | I gave them the money. |
| **Ik heb het geld aan ze gegeven.** | I gave the money to them. |

Ze can refer to both things and people but **hen** and **hun** are only used with reference to people and are both emphatic forms; **hen** is a direct object (and is used after prepositions) and **hun** an indirect object (i.e. = 'to them'), e.g.

Ik heb hun het geld gegeven.	I gave them the money.
Ik heb het geld aan hen gegeven.	I gave the money to them.
Ik heb hen in de stad gezien.	I saw them in town.

In practice the Dutch do not observe the distinction between **hen** and **hun**, other than in writing, and always use **hun** where emphasis is required and otherwise **ze**.

Exercise 1

Give the right form of the object pronoun.

1 Hij heeft (*her*) in de stad gezien.
2 Heb je (*him*) gezien?
3 Ik heb (*them*) bij de buren gezien.
4 Hij woont bij (*us*). (**bij** + object pronoun = 'at the house of')
5 Ik heb het aan (*them*) gegeven.
6 Zij kennen (*me*) niet. Ken jij (them)?
7 Ik zoek (*you*).
8 Ik heb (*them*, i.e. things, not people) gevonden.

Replacing a noun by the pronoun 'it'

When you were presented with the subject pronouns on page 11, you were not told the full story. The paradigm given there indicates that **hij** means 'he' and **het** means 'it'. But if an 'it' refers to a previously mentioned common gender noun, you must use **hij** not **het**, e.g.

Hoe vind je mijn nieuwe keuken?	How do you like my new kitchen?
Hij was erg duur.	It was very expensive. (*de* **keuken**)
Waar is mijn potlood?	Where's my pencil?
Het is rood.	It is red. (*het* **potlood**)

The same applies to the object pronouns. On page 76 **hem** is given as meaning 'him' and **het** as 'it', but in fact **hem** also translates 'it' when reference is being made to a common gender noun, e.g.

Ik vind hem prachtig.　　　I think it's fabulous.
(i.e. je nieuwe keuken)

Exercise 2

Give the right form of the subject or object pronoun.

1 Wat een auto! Waar heb je (*it*) gekocht?
2 Mijn oom heeft een marmot. (*It)* heet Rob. Wil je (*it*) zien?
3 Ik heb een konijn. (*It*) heet Lies. Wil je (*it*) aaien?

Dialogue 2 ▧

Piet has lost his savings book

PIET: Heb je mijn spaarboekje gezien?
PAULINE: Nee, maar dat van mij zit in mijn handtas.
PIET: Ik zoek niet dat van jou, maar dat van mij.
PAULINE: Heb je in je zakken gekeken?
PIET: Ja, en ook in jouw handtas.
PAULINE: Ik kan deze week de rekeningen betalen. Hoeveel heb ik op mijn rekening?

PIET: *Have you seen my savings book?*
PAULINE: *No, but mine is in my handbag.*
PIET: *I'm not looking for yours, but for mine.*
PAULINE: *Have you looked in your pockets?*
PIET: *Yes, and in your handbag as well.*
PAULINE: *I can pay the bills this week. How much have I got in my account?*

Language points

Possessives

A possessive: This is *my* savings book.

Singular	Plural		
mijn	mine	**ons** *or* **onze**	our
jouw/je	your	**jullie/je**	your
uw	your	**uw**	your
zijn	his	**hun**	their
haar	her		
zijn	its		

The concept of possessive adjectives indicating what belongs to whom is as in English. Only **jouw** and **jullie** have unemphatic forms that are written, e.g.

Ik ken je moeder niet. I don't know your (pronounced 'ya') mother.

Jouw **moeder ken ik niet.** I don't know **your** mother.

Mijn and **zijn** are pronounced, but seldom ever written, **m'n** and **z'n** if unstressed.

Ons takes an **-e** ending, with the **s** changing to **z**, before **de** words and plurals, e.g. **ons huis** 'our house', but **onze vader** 'our father' and **onze boeken** 'our books'. This concept is dealt with later in the lesson.

Exercise 3

Fill in the correct form of the possessive.

1 Ken je (*his*) vader?
2 Nee, maar ik ken (*her*) moeder.
3 (*Our*) ouders en (*their*) ouders kennen elkaar.
4 Heb je (*your*) huiswerk gedaan?
5 Heeft u (*your*) auto gewassen?

Dialogue 3 ▄▄

Marius and Charlotte are arguing about their possessions

MARIUS: Dat is mijn pen, Charlotte.
CHARLOTTE: Nee, dat is jouw pen en dit is mijn pen.
MARIUS: Deze pen heb ik voor mijn verjaardag gekregen.
CHARLOTTE: Die pen heb je gekregen, niet deze. Deze heb ik voor mijn verjaardag van Tante Lien gekregen.

MARIUS:	Onzin, zij heeft je dat spaarpotje gegeven.
CHARLOTTE:	Ja, dat klopt. Ik heb dit spaarpotje èn[1] deze pen gekregen.

MARIUS:	*That's my pen, Charlotte.*
CHARLOTTE:	*No, that is your pen and this is my pen.*
MARIUS:	*I got this pen for my birthday.*
CHARLOTTE:	*You got that pen, not this one. I got this one from Aunt Lien for my birthday.*
MARIUS:	*Nonsense, she gave you that money-box.*
CHARLOTTE:	*Yes, that's right. I got this money-box AND this pen.*

Language points

Demonstratives

Demonstratives: This/that book is mine.

Singular		Plural	
die/dat	that	**die**	those
deze/dit	this	**deze**	these

Die expresses 'that' before a singular common gender noun and **dat** before a singular neuter noun, but **die** is used before all plural nouns to express 'those' (compare **de** and **het**, where **het** is also replaced by **de** before a neuter noun in the plural), e.g.

die tafel	that table	**die tafels**	those tables
dat huis	that house	**die huizen**	those houses

Following a similar pattern, **deze** expresses 'this' before a singular common gender noun and **dit** before a singular neuter noun, but **deze** is used before all plural nouns to express 'these', e.g.

deze tafel	this table	**deze tafels**	these tables
dit huis	this house	**deze huizen**	these houses

Note 1: In sentences like 'This is my car' or 'That is his uncle', **dit** and **dat** are used despite the fact that there is ultimately reference to a common gender noun, because at the point of utterance that noun has not been mentioned. But compare **Ik heb**

---

1 The Dutch designate stress in writing in this way rather than underlining or bolding. In fact this word **èn** with its accent can render 'both . . . and'.

twee fietsen gekocht: deze is voor Marius, en die is voor Charlotte 'I have bought two bikes: this one is for Marius and that one for Charlotte'. Here **deze** and **die** stand for 'this one' and 'that one', i.e. where the gender of the noun being referred to is known. Because at the point of utterance in the following sentences the noun being referred to has not been mentioned, it is possible for **dit** and **dat** to render even 'these' and 'those' with reference to plural nouns occurring after the verb, e.g.

Dit zijn mijn kinderen.   These are my children.
Dat zijn oude kopjes.   Those are old cups.

And in a similar way **het** can render 'they', e.g.

Van wie zijn die kinderen? Het zijn mijn kinderen.
Whose children are those? They are my children.

Note 2: In dialogue 3 you will see how **deze pen** and **die pen** often stand at the beginning of the sentence, for emphasis, something which we do not do in English. We merely stress the 'this/these' or 'that/those'. The fronting of any expression one wishes to draw attention to, which of course causes inversion of subject and verb, is typical of Dutch.

Note 3: Remember that back on page 76 it was pointed out that **die** often replaces third-person pronouns, in which case it renders 'he/him', 'she/her', 'it' and 'they/them'.

Exercise 4

Fill in the correct form of the demonstrative.

1 Ken je (*that*) man?
2 (*That one*) ken ik niet, maar (*this one*) wel.
3 (*That*) is mijn broer.
4 (*This*) is mijn zus.
5 (*These*) zijn zijn boeken.
6 Ik wil (*these*) stoelen verven.
7 Ken je (*those*) mensen. (*They*) zijn mijn buren.
8 (*That*) boom is te groot voor (*this*) tuin maar (*that one*) is niet te groot.

Exercise 5

Put the appropriate word for 'this/these' and 'that/those' in front of the following nouns, e.g. **vloer – deze/die vloer.**

koelkast lamp appels
fornuis bed bedden
vogel honden ooms

Independent possessives

Independent possessives: This is *mine. Yours* is red.

Singular			Plural		
(die/dat) **van mij**	mine		(die/dat) **van ons**	ours	
(die/dat) **van jou**	yours		(die/dat) **van jullie**	yours	
(die/dat) **van u**	yours		(die/dat) **van u**	yours	
(die/dat) **van hem**	his		(die/dat) **van hen**	theirs	
(die/dat) **van haar**	hers				

When uttering a statement like 'This is mine' or 'Is that yours?', where the possessive stands after the verb 'to be', you simply say **Dit/deze is van mij**, **Is dat/die van jou?**, where the choice of **dit** or **deze** (or **dat** or **die**) depends on whether the noun has been previously mentioned and thus whether you know the gender of it. But 'mine', 'yours', etc. as the subject or object of a sentence are rendered by **die/dat van mij** where the choice of **die** or **dat** is determined by the gender of the noun being referred to, which in this case is always known at the point of utterance, e.g.

Hier staat mijn auto.	Here's my car.
Ik kan die van jou niet zien.	I can't see yours.
Waar staat je auto?	Where's your car (parked)?
Die van mij staat om de hoek.	Mine is (parked) around the corner.

Exercise 6

Fill in the correct form of the independent possessive.

1 Ik woon in een groot huis. Hoe groot is (*yours*)?
2 Mijn kinderen heten Marius en Charlotte. Hoe heten (*yours*)?
3 Ken je (*mine*) niet?
4 Ik heb een mooie handtas gekocht maar (*hers*) was duurder.
5 Die hond is (*theirs*) maar (*ours*) is veel leuker, vind je niet?

> ## Culture point
>
> A typical Dutch abode is a quite narrow terrace house (**het rijtjeshuis**) – the Dutch like uniformity in their residential streetscapes. Immediately inside the front door is a staircase (**de trap**) leading upstairs to the bedrooms (**de slaapkamer**) and bathroom (**de badkamer**) as well as an attic (**de zolder**), often reached by a small collapsible step-ladder (**de zolderladder/-trap**) that pulls down out of the ceiling on the landing (**de overloop**). The roof space above the attic, used for storage, is called **de vliering**. Under the staircase at the end of the passage inside the front door is the (usually tiny) toilet (**de wc**), never with a window to the outside (bare bottoms and draughts don't mix) but with a long flue extending up to the roof. Next to the toilet, at the end of the passage, is the kitchen (**de keuken**) with a door leading out to the handkerchief-sized garden. To the left or right of the front door, on the opposite wall to the staircase, is the lounge (**de woonkamer**), which runs the full depth of the house from the front garden (**de voortuin**) – if there is one, but in the inner city they usually front directly onto the footpath – to the back garden (**de achtertuin**). It either has no curtains at all, or if it does, they are seldom drawn. (What have we got to hide? And anyway, I bet your TV is not as big as ours!) The window sills accommodate veritable jungles of potted plants. The windows themselves are spotless – now a monthly, but formerly a weekly, chore performed with great gusto and pride – and the public footpath outside the front door is also scrubbed on at least a weekly basis, which is usually necessary to remove the ubiquitous dog droppings (**de hondepoep**) for which Dutch cities are notorious.

Reading text 📼

Vocabulary

gescheiden	divorced
boven	upstairs
overleven	to survive
opruimen	to tidy up
de puinhoop	the mess
net zoals	just like

Pauline talks about her home and her family

Mijn ouders zijn gescheiden. Mijn vader heeft een flat in Londen en mijn moeder woont in een oud Victoriaans huisje in Oxford. Het huis van mijn schoonouders hier in Amsterdam-Noord is ook erg oud. Het is een typisch Hollands huis. Het is niet groot en heeft hele[2] kleine kamers, maar ik vind het leuk. Het heeft een prachtige tuin want mijn schoonvader heeft groene vingers.

Mijn gezin bestaat uit vier mensen en ons huis is nieuw en erg modern. De kamers van de kinderen zijn boven, ver weg van de woonkamer gelukkig. Piet en ik kunnen het dus overleven als de vrienden van de kinderen op visite komen. Marius en Charlotte ruimen hun kamers zelf op en Charlottes kamer is altijd erg netjes maar Marius z'n kamer is altijd een puinhoop en hij wordt boos als ik wat zeg.

Onze tuin is vol fruitbomen. Piet is net zoals zijn vader. Hij werkt ook erg graag in de tuin en ik kook graag. Wij helpen elkaar met boodschappen doen en schoonmaken.

Language points

Indicating possession (apostrophe s)

Indicating possession with apostrophe s: The *man's* name.

Piets vrouw heet Pauline.	Piet's wife is called Pauline.
Marius' fiets is stuk.	Marius' bike is broken.
De tuin van zijn vader is prachtig.	His father's garden is fabulous.[3]

Generally speaking, the Dutch only use a possessive s after a first name and do not require an apostrophe unless an s has been left off, thus **Marius' fiets**. In all other cases it is usual to express possession with **van**, e.g. **de auto van meneer Smid**. This is also possible, although perhaps less usual, with first names, e.g. **de fiets van Marius**.

---

2 Strictly speaking, **heel** 'very' is an adverb and should not take an ending but this word commonly does get an ending in spoken (but not written) Dutch when the adjective that follows has an ending. The rules for adjectival endings are given later in this lesson.

3 It should be added that the form **zijn vaders tuin** is possible but *****mijn mans tuin** 'my husband's garden' is not. Thus learning at this stage that all such possessives are rephrased using **van** (e.g. **de tuin van mijn man**) will avoid any errors being made.

In spoken Dutch unemphatic forms of **zijn** (**z'n**) 'his', **haar** (**d'r**) 'her' but **hun** for 'their' are placed between the possessor (but only when it is a person) and the thing possessed, e.g.

Marius z'n fiets is stuk.	Marius' bike is broken.
Die man z'n auto was duur.	That man's car was expensive.
Charlotte d'r pop is stuk.	Charlotte's doll is broken.
De kinderen hun fietsen zijn stuk.	The children's bikes are broken.

Exercise 7

Express the following in Dutch:

1 Pauline's parents-in-law (3 ways)
2 Piet's children (3 ways)
3 the neighbour's dog (2 ways)
4 the neighbours' cat (2 ways)
5 Lien and Jaap's parents (3 ways)
6 the country's capital (only 1 way possible)
7 the cat's face (only 1 way possible)

Culture point

The Dutch are very family orientated. Family birthdays and anniversaries are red-letter days in their calendar. They even have two words for family, **het gezin** and **de familie**. The former relates to the nuclear family and the latter to the extended family. In the above passage Pauline starts telling us about her **familie** and ends up giving a few details about how her **gezin** lives. There are of course Dutch words to express all the family relationships, but curiously enough the words **de neef** and **de nicht** express two relationships: the former means both nephew and male cousin and the latter both niece and female cousin.

Exercise 8

Imagine you are Piet in his old age and complete this family tree from Piet's point of view, placing the following relationships on the appropriate branches of the tree, i.e. each number on the tree corresponds to one of the following relationships.

moeder	vader	zoon	dochter
nicht	neef	oom	tante
schoonmoeder	schoonvader	zwager	schoonzuster
schoondochter	schoonzoon	kleindochter	kleinzoon
grootvader	grootmoeder	overgrootmoeder	overgrootvader
betovergrootvader		betovergrootmoeder	
achterkleinzoon		achterkleindochter	

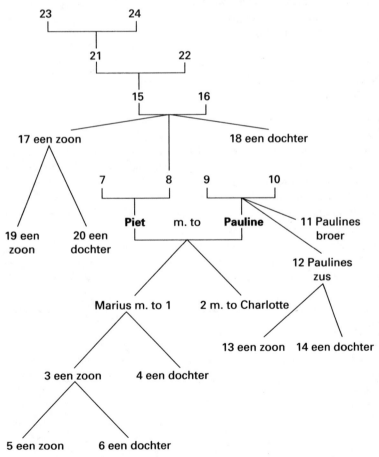

Dialogue 4 ▢▢

Piet and Pauline have an altercation

PIET: Pauline, geef me de schaar, alsjeblieft!
PAULINE: Welke schaar? De grote of de kleine?
PIET: Het kleine schaartje. Ik wil een leuk artikel uit dit tijd-schrift knippen.
PAULINE: Ben je gek? Uit dat splinternieuwe tijdschrift? Ik heb het nog niet gelezen.

PIET: *Pauline, please hand me the scissors!*
PAULINE: *Which scissors? The big ones or the little ones?*
PIET: *The little scissors. I want to cut a good article out of this magazine.*
PAULINE: *Are you crazy? Out of that brand new magazine? I haven't read it yet.*

Language points

Adjectives

Adjectives: The house is *large*. The *large* house.

When adjectives are used predicatively, i.e. not before a noun but after a verb, they are indeclinable, e.g.

Het huis is groot. Het is ook erg oud.
The house is large. It is also very old.

But when an adjective is used attributively, i.e. before a noun, it takes an **-e** ending in certain circumstances, e.g. **het oude huis**. This is called inflecting the adjective. The rules for inflecting are not at first glance simple and are difficult to apply because they rely on the speaker often intuitively knowing whether the following noun is common gender or neuter. Adjectives standing in front of common gender nouns, both singular and plural, inflect. Adjectives standing in front of neuter singular nouns that are indefinite (i.e. the noun is preceded by **een, geen, welk** 'which' and **ieder/elk** 'each/every') do not inflect. But adjectives standing in front of neuter singular nouns that are definite (i.e. the noun is preceded by **de/het, die/dat, deze/dit, mijn/jouw/zijn,** etc.) or plural, do inflect:

een ronde tafel 'a round table'	**een klein huis** 'a small house'
welke (ronde) tafel	**welk (klein) huis**
de ronde tafel	**het kleine huis**
deze/die ronde tafel	**dit/dat kleine huis**
mijn ronde tafel	**mijn kleine huis**
de ronde tafels	**de kleine huizen**
ronde tafels	**kleine huizen**
welke ronde tafels	**welke kleine huizen**

Note 1: The same spelling changes apply to adjectives when adding the **-e** ending as applied when we pluralised nouns and derived the verbal stems from their infinitives:

kaal	**kale**	bald	**dik**	**dikke**	fat
breed	**brede**	wide	**wit**	**witte**	white
groot	**grote**	big, large	**doof**	**dove**	deaf
duur	**dure**	expensive	**vies**	**vieze**	dirty

Note 2: The adjectives **goed**, **rood** and **oud**, when inflected, are pronounced **goeie**, **rooie** and **ouwe** although they are usually written **goede**, **rode** and **oude**, e.g. **goeie morgen, een rooie auto, een ouwe man**.

Note 3: The possessive **ons** (see page 79) also inflects like an adjective, e.g. **ons huis** but **onze tuin, onze kinderen**.

Exercise 9

Decide whether the adjectives in parentheses in the sentences below require an **-e** ending.

1 (Groot) bomen zijn soms gevaarlijk.
2 Ik heb (rood èn groen) appels gekocht.
3 Wat een (breed) weg!
4 Ik heb geen (Nederlands) geld.
5 (Welk) boeken heb je me geleend?
6 Het (dik) over Shakespeare en dat (dun) over de oorlog.
7 Was het een (goedkoop) of een (duur) fiets?
8 Ik heb geen (wit) overhemd en ook geen (wit) broek.
9 Hij komt (elk) dag/(elk) jaar.
10 Ze heeft de (vies) vloer geveegd.

Dialogue 5 ▐▄▐

Pauline is finishing a chat in the street with her friend Lien

PAULINE: Zeg, ik moet naar huis, hoor. Ik moet het eten klaarmaken.

Lien:	Goed, hoor. En ik moet ook naar de supermarkt. Doe de groeten aan Piet.
Pauline:	Doe ik. Wanneer zien we mekaar weer, Lien?
Lien:	Wil je morgen bij mij op de koffie komen?
Pauline:	Ja zeker. Gezellig. Tot dan. Dáág!

Pauline:	*I say, I really have to get home. I have to cook dinner.*
Lien:	*OK. And I have to go to the supermarket. Give my regards to Piet.*
Pauline:	*I shall. When are we going to see each other again, Lien?*
Lien:	*Do you want to come to my place for morning tea tomorrow?*
Pauline:	*Of course. How nice. Till then. Bye!*

Note 1: When the infinitive that is dependent on **moet** is **gaan**, it is often left unsaid as the implication is obvious.

Note 2: **Doe de groeten aan Piet**: relaying regards to the rest of the family is an important part of Dutch etiquette.

Note 3: **Elkaar** 'each other' is often pronounced **mekaar** in spoken Dutch.

Note 4: 'Nice' is expressed in many ways depending on what is being referred to. 'Nice weather' is **mooi weer**, 'nice food' is **lekker eten** and people are **aardig**, whereas here the reference is to the prospect of the companionship of the forthcoming event. But the most useful and exceedingly commonly used word is **leuk**, e.g. **wat een leuke film/man/avond** 'what a nice film/man/evening'. **Wat leuk!** is a common reaction to something one approves of or rejoices in, e.g. **Lien: Mijn dochter gaat trouwen. Pauline: Wat leuk!** 'Lien: My daughter is getting married. Pauline: How wonderful!'

6 Fietsen

Cycling

In this lesson you will learn about:

- interrogatives (what, where, when, how, etc. questions)
- first names and family names
- expressing future events
- the position of expressions of time, manner and place
- the position of objects in a sentence

Reading text 🔳

Vocabulary

bijna	almost, nearly
bezitten	to own, possess
smal	narrow
het verkeer	the traffic
het fietsenrek	the bicycle stand
de fietsenstalling	the bicycle garage
af en toe	now and then
voorop/achterop	on the front/back
zelfs	even
helemaal geen	no/none/not any at all
de heuvel	the hill

Cycling

Bijna elke Nederlander bezit een fiets. De straten van de meeste Nederlandse steden zijn erg smal en er is veel te veel verkeer. Het is niet leuk in een Nederlandse stad te rijden. Je kunt veel beter met de tram of op de fiets. Je vindt fietsenrekken overal waar je je fiets kunt laten staan en op het station kun je hem in de fietsenstalling laten. Je ziet af en toe een moeder op een fiets met één kind voorop en één kind achterop. De hond gaat soms ook mee op de fiets. Zelfs oude mensen fietsen graag. Nederland is een vlak land zonder bergen en weinig heuvels – het is dus ook praktisch om alles op de fiets te doen.

Dialogue 1

Pauline and Piet are sitting in the lounge

PAULINE: Wat heb je in je hand, Piet?
PIET: Het is een pop.
PAULINE: Waar heb je hem gevonden?
PIET: In de tuin achter een boom.
PAULINE: Wat is het voor een pop?
PIET: Een rubberen pop, maar waarom vraag je dat? Van wie is de pop dan?
PAULINE: Van Martine, Charlottes vriendinnetje. Ze heeft zo'n pop verloren.
PIET: Wanneer?
PAULINE: Vorige week.

PAULINE: *What have you got in your hand, Piet?*
PIET: *It's a doll.*
PAULINE: *Where did you find it?*
PIET: *In the garden behind a tree.*
PAULINE: *What sort of a doll is it?*
PIET: *A rubber doll, but why do you ask? Whose doll is it then?*
PAULINE: *It's Martine's, Charlotte's friend. She lost a doll like that.*
PIET: *When?*
PAULINE: *Last week.*

Language points

Interrogatives

Questions can be formed from the following words, which are called interrogatives:

wanneer	when
Wanneer komt hij?	When is he coming?
hoe	how
Hoe weet je dat?	How do you know that?
hoeveel	how much/many
Hoeveel heeft het gekost?	How much did it cost?
Hoeveel kinderen heeft hij?	How many children does he have?
waarom	why
Waarom woon je hier?	Why do you live here?
wat	what
Wat heb je in je hand?	What have you got in your hand?
wat voor een ...	what sort of a ...
Wat voor een auto heb je?	What sort of a car have you got?
or, **Wat heb je voor een auto?**	
wie	who
Wie heb je gezien?	Who did you see?
van wie	whose
Van wie is deze trui?	Whose pullover is this?
waar	where
Waar woont u?	Where do you live?
waar ... vandaan	where ... from
Waar komt u vandaan?	Where do you come from?
waar ... naartoe	where ... (to)
Waar ga je naartoe?	Where are you going (to)?
welk(e)[1]	which
Welke oom bedoel je?	Which uncle do you mean?
Welk huis heb je gekocht?	Which house did you buy?

Note: In combination with **gaan** (as well as other verbs of motion like **rijden** 'to drive'), 'where' is always translated with **waarnaartoe**; the 'to' is often superfluous in English, but never in Dutch; **naartoe**, which expresses 'to' in combination with **waar**, can either be joined to **waar** or stand separated from it at the end of the question, separation being much more common in spoken Dutch, e.g. **Waar ga je tijdens de vakantie naartoe? Waarnaartoe ga je tijdens de vakantie?** 'Where are you going (to) during the holidays?'

---

1 **Welk** is an adjective and takes an **-e** ending according to the rules given on page 87.

Exercise 1

Fill in the correct interrogative.

1 Met (*whom*) werkt je vader?
2 (*Whose*) is deze kat?
3 (*Where from*) komen de buren?
4 (*How much*) heb je voor je nieuwe jurk betaald, Pauline?
5 (*Who*) woont naast jullie?
6 (*Where*) ga je vanavond?
7 (*Which dress*) ga je dragen?
8 In (*what sort of a*) huis wonen jouw ouders?

Reading text ▣

Piet's parents and their neighbours

Paulines schoonouders zijn Jaap en Jo van den Berg. Pauline vindt meneer Van den Berg erg aardig maar ze heeft een hekel aan mevrouw Van den Berg. De Van den Bergs wonen naast meneer en mevrouw De Rooij. Ruud de Rooij werkt op hetzelfde kantoor als Pauline in Den Haag en Ria de Rooij is huisvrouw.

Language points

Dutch names

A Dutch first name (**de voornaam**) is more often than not abbreviated. Jaap is a shortened form of Jacob, Jo of Jacoba, Ruud of Rudolf (also abbreviated to Dolf) and Ria of Maria, for example. The Dutch can have three or four first names and the name they are called by (**de roepnaam**) is not necessarily derived from the first of these. You may have the name Cornelius Wilhelmus Theodorus van Staden and be known as Wim or Theo. Consequently in Dutch telephone books a surname (**de familienaam, achternaam**) is listed alphabetically but once you have found the Van Stadens, for example, they are then arranged alphabetically according to the street name, not the initial, because you cannot possibly know that Wim van Staden's first name is in fact Cornelius (abbreviated form Kees). Note the use in the reading text above of capital and small letters with surnames in **de**, **van**

and **van de/den**. When such a surname is preceded by the first
name or the initial, these words are written with small letters (e.g.
G. van de Molen, B. de Beer), but when the surname stands alone
or is preceded by **meneer** or **mevrouw**, the first word of the surname
is capitalised (e.g. Van Staden, meneer Van den Berghe).

Culture point

When meeting someone for the first time, it is customary to utter
your name as you put out your hand to shake theirs. Inevitably you
both say your names (both first name and surname) simultaneously,
with the result that neither hears the other's name distinctly, but
that's what the ritual demands.

It is common but not a necessary practice for married women –
and this was the case long before women's liberation – to hyphenate
their maiden name to their married surname in writing. Although
mevrouw Smit will be addressed as such, when writing her name
on the back of an envelope or on a cheque, for example, she is quite
likely to write her name as follows **A. Smit-Molenaar**.

Dialogue 2 🔘

Piet and Pauline are discussing what they are going to do

PIET: Wat doen we vanavond? Zullen we naar de bioscoop
gaan?
PAULINE: Nee, ik ga televisie kijken. Morgen moeten we vroeg
op.
PIET: Ach ja, dat klopt. Ik rij morgenochtend naar Groningen.
PAULINE: Dan breng ik de kinderen naar school.
PIET: Goed, en ik haal ze later op.

PIET: *What'll we do tonight? Shall we go to the movies?*
PAULINE: *No, I'm going to watch TV. We('ll) have to get up early
tomorrow.*
PIET: *Oh yes, that's right. I'll be driving to Groningen
tomorrow morning.*
PAULINE: *I'll take the kids to school then.*
PIET: *Okay, and I'll pick them up later.*

Language points

The future tense

There are three ways of expressing future events in Dutch, just as there are in English:

1 by using the present tense, e.g.

We kopen een nieuw huis.   We're buying a new house.

2 by using the verb **gaan** 'to go', e.g.

We gaan een nieuw huis kopen.   We're going to buy a new house.

3 by using the verb **zullen** 'will', e.g.

We zullen een nieuw huis kopen.   We'll buy a new house.

Generally speaking, although the three ways of forming the future tense are the same in the two languages, they differ from each other in the frequency of use of the various forms; English uses the form with 'will' more often than Dutch. Where English uses the present tense to express the future, so does Dutch; where English uses 'to go' to express the future, so does Dutch; but where English uses 'will' (particularly in combination with an adverb of time like *tomorrow*, *next week*, etc.), Dutch normally uses the present, e.g.

Ik koop volgend jaar een nieuwe auto.   I'm buying a new car next year.

Ik ga het aan mijn zuster geven.   I'm going to give it to my sister.

Ik doe het morgen.   I'll do it tomorrow.

The future with **zullen** may be used if there is no adverb of time, e.g. **Ik zal het doen, alleen niet vandaag** 'I will do it, just not today'. Note that **zullen** has irregular forms like modal verbs do (see pages 68–9):

ik zal	wij zullen
jij zal/zult	jullie zullen
u zult	u zult
hij/zij/het zal	zij zullen

'Would' is expressed by the past tense of **zullen, zou/zouden**, e.g.

Dat zou leuk zijn. That would be nice.
We zouden naar de bioscoop We could go to the movies.
kunnen gaan.

The useful phrase 'I would like ... ' is expressed by **ik zou ...
willen**, e.g.

Ik zou graag een nieuwe fiets willen (hebben).
I would like a new bike.

Ik zou graag naar de bioscoop willen (gaan).
I would like to go to the movies.

Zullen we ... translates 'shall we ... ' when suggesting a plan of
action to someone, e.g. **Zullen we vanavond thuis blijven?** 'Shall
we stay home tonight?' The almost synonymous expression 'Let's
... !' is rendered by **laten we ...** , e.g. **Laten we vanavond thuis
blijven!** 'Let's stay home tonight!'

Exercise 2

Translate the following sentences using a form of the future. In
some cases more than one of the above future forms is possible.

1 I'm going to visit Aunt Lies tomorrow.
2 I'll do the shopping tomorrow.
3 Where will she be living? (two forms possible)
4 Marius will have to go to bed now.
5 I'll do it for you.
6 They'll be coming next week.

Exercise 3

Suggest to your friend that the two of you do these things:

Example: go for a walk
         Zullen we gaan wandelen?

1 watch television
2 drive to Germany
3 drink coffee
4 buy an icecream
5 visit Granny

Exercise 4

Now make the same suggestions to your friend using the **Laten we ...** form:

Example: go for a walk
            Laten we gaan wandelen!

The position of expressions of time, manner and place

As you have probably already observed, Dutch word order is often quite different from English word order. An important rule of Dutch word order is the TMP rule, i.e. that expressions of time (T), manner (M) and place (P) occur in that order, e.g.

T   M   P

Pauline gaat   <u>elke dag</u>   <u>met de trein</u>   <u>naar Den Haag</u>.

Often there are only two such adverbial expressions but the same order applies, e.g.

T   P

Piet rijdt   <u>morgen</u>   <u>naar Groningen</u>.

M   P

Marius gaat   <u>op de fiets</u>   <u>naar school</u>.

T   M

Charlotte is   <u>op het ogenblik</u>   <u>alleen</u>.

It is very common in Dutch to put expressions of time at the front of the sentence. This causes inversion of subject and verb, because the finite verb must always be in second position, as you know, and in so doing time automatically precedes manner and place, e.g.

Morgen rijdt Piet naar Groningen.
Op het ogenblik is Charlotte alleen.

Exercise 5

Rewrite the following sentences starting them with the expression of time, making the necessary adjustments to the word order.

1 We kunnen op het ogenblik niet komen.
2 Je moet me morgen komen helpen.

3 Marius is vandaag op school.
4 De kinderen spelen elke middag in het park.
5 Hij heeft vijftien jaar geleden in Utrecht gewoond.

The position of objects in a sentence

When a sentence not only contains adverbial expressions of time, manner and place, but also an object, certain word order rules apply. If the direct object is a noun, time precedes that object, but not if it is a pronoun, e.g.

Hij heeft gisteren zijn auto verkocht. He sold his car yesterday.
Hij heeft hem gisteren verkocht.   He sold it yesterday.

But in both these cases it is of course also possible to start with time:

Gisteren heeft hij zijn auto/hem verkocht.

Exercise 6

Rewrite the following sentences replacing the noun in italics by a pronoun. Remember that 'it' may be **het** or **hem**, depending on the gender of the noun being replaced (see page 77), and that you will need to change the word order.

1 Charlotte heeft vanochtend *haar pop* aan haar vriendin gegeven.
2 Piet heeft gisteren *Lien* in de stad gezien.
3 Hij gaat nu *de krant* lezen.
4 Ze hebben vorige week *hun huis* verkocht.
5 Ze zit op het ogenblik *haar huiswerk* te doen.
6 De kinderen hebben dit jaar *fietsen* gekregen.

7 Pannenkoeken

Pancakes

In this lesson you will learn about:

- giving orders (i.e. the imperative)
- separable verbs
- polite requests
- writing letters and addressing envelopes
- use of **te** and **om te**

Dialogue 1 🔲

Pauline comes into the living room where Charlotte is watching television

CHARLOTTE:	Maak niet zo veel herrie!
PAULINE:	Wat zeg je?
CHARLOTTE:	Hou je mond. Dit is spannend.
PAULINE:	Praat niet zo tegen je moeder. Kom, sta op, ga naar bed.

CHARLOTTE:	*Don't make so much noise!*
PAULINE:	*I beg your pardon?*
CHARLOTTE:	*Shut up! This is exciting.*
PAULINE:	*Don't talk like that to your mother. Come on, get up, go to bed.*

Language points

The imperative

Imperative: Shut the door!

The imperative is used for giving orders and has the same form as the stem of the verb, e.g. **kom** 'come', **maak** 'make', **praat** 'talk'. The imperative of the five monosyllabic verbs (see page 17) is: **doen** – **doe**, **gaan** – **ga**, **slaan** – **sla**, **staan** – **sta**, **zien** – **zie**.

The imperative of **zijn** 'to be' is **wees**, e.g. **Wees niet zo wreed!** 'Don't be so cruel!'

Verbs like **houden** and **rijden**, where a **d** occurs after the diphthongs **ou** and **ij**, drop this **d** as they do in the first person of the present tense (see page 48), e.g. **Hou je mond!** 'Shut up!', **Rij langzamer!** 'Drive more slowly!'

Although the stem is used as the imperative for **jij**, **u** and **jullie**, there is an alternative **u** form which is particularly polite, e.g. **Gaat u zitten** (otherwise **Ga zitten**) 'Sit down', **Komt u binnen** (otherwise **Kom binnen**) 'Come in'.

Reading text 1 🔲

The Dutch regard pancakes as a traditional Dutch dish. Their pancakes are different from elsewhere in the world in that they are made as large as the frying pan they are prepared in and are topped with all manner of things. Whatever the topping (even cheese or smoky bacon), a thick, extremely sweet syrup (**de stroop**) is poured over them. They are eaten as a meal in themselves and one is quite sufficient!

Vocabulary

een snufje	a pinch of
glad	soft
het beslag	the batter
hiervan	of this
het schijfje	the slice
het deeg	the dough

Appelpannenkoeken

Ingrediënten:

250 gram zelfrijzend bakmeel
1 ei
een halve liter melk
een snufje zout
60 gram boter
één appel

Klop het ei mooi los. Maak van het meel, het ei, de melk en een snufje zout een mooi glad beslag. Bak hiervan in de hete boter in de koekenpan op een niet te groot vuur pannenkoeken. Leg tijdens het bakken dunne schijfjes appel in het deeg. Keer de pannenkoeken wanneer de bovenzijde droog is.

Exercise 1

Find the imperatives in the recipe above and write them down together with their infinitive and their meanings.

Exercise 2

Pretend you have followed the above recipe and now relate what you did in the past tense; in other words, write out the recipe in the perfect tense, e.g. **Ik heb het ei mooi los geklopt**.

Dialogue 2 🔲

Piet has a bone to pick with Pauline[1]

PIET: Doe het licht in de keuken uit!
PAULINE: Ik heb het al uitgedaan.
PIET: Jij doet het nooit uit. Je laat het altijd aan.
PAULINE: Ik zal het voortaan altijd uitdoen, o.k.?

PIET: *Turn the light off in the kitchen!*
PAULINE: *I've already turned it off.*
PIET: *You never turn it off. You always leave it on.*
PAULINE: *I'll always turn it off in future, OK?*

---

1 Dutch uses a similar colourful idiom: **Piet heeft een appeltje met Pauline te schillen** literally 'Piet has an apple to peel with Pauline'.

Language points

Separable verbs

The infinitives of verbs like 'to turn on' and 'to turn off' that contain a preposition are written as one word in Dutch, i.e. **aandoen**, **uitdoen**. Such verbs which contain a stressed prepositional prefix are called separable verbs because in certain tenses the preposition separates from the verb and is placed at the end of the sentence. In the present tense and imperative this is the case, e.g.

opbellen 'to ring up'
Ik bel elke dag mijn moeder op. I ring my mother up every day.
Bel je moeder onmiddellijk op! Ring your mother up immediately!

The past participle is formed by placing the **ge-** prefix between the preposition and the verb, e.g.

Ik heb vanmorgen mijn moeder opgebeld.
I rang my mother this morning.

Separable verbs can be regular, like **opbellen** above, or irregular, but the principle is the same for both, e.g.

weggaan 'to leave, go away'
We gaan morgen heel vroeg weg.
We're leaving very early tomorrow.
Ga weg. Go away.
We zijn met Kerstmis niet weggegaan.
We didn't go away at Christmas time.

Note: The new verb that results from affixing a prepositional prefix to an existing verb often has a figurative meaning: for example, although **uitgeven** can mean 'to give out', it also and more usually means 'to spend (money)' or even 'to publish'. Similarly **voorstellen** (lit. 'to put forward') usually means 'to suggest' or 'to introduce (someone)'.

Exercise 3

Form imperative sentences from the following couplets.

Example: dichtdoen/de deur
        Doe de deur dicht!

1 opstaan/onmiddellijk
2 uitnodigen/je broer

3 opeten/de appel
4 aannemen/het geld
5 binnenkomen/alsjeblieft
6 opendoen/het raam
7 uitgeven/het geld

Exercise 4

Form the past participle of the verbs in exercise 3.

Example: dichtdoen
              dichtgedaan

Exercise 5

Put the following sentences into the past tense.

Example: Ik doe de deur dicht.
              Ik heb de deur dichtgedaan.

1 Hij staat onmiddellijk op.
2 Ik nodig je broer uit.
3 Marius eet een appel op.
4 Pauline neemt het geld niet aan.
5 Hij komt niet binnen.
6 Zij doet het raam open.
7 Zij geeft het geld uit.

How to make a request sound polite

Merely adding **alsjeblieft** or **alstublieft** to a command is frequently not sufficient to make it sound polite. There are various ways of softening it: compare English 'Come here' with 'Come here a moment'. The adverb **even** 'just', which was discussed on page 58, is one common simple method:

Wacht even! Wait a moment! Just wait a jiffy!

A variant of this is **eventjes**:

Sta eventjes op!   Get up for a moment!

The underlying meaning of **even/eventjes** is not just 'a moment' but also 'would you mind?' But this can be expressed even more emphatically by using **willen** or **zou ... willen**, usually used in combination with **even** or **eventjes**:

Wil je het raam even dichtdoen?
Would you mind shutting the window?

Zou je de deur even willen opendoen?
Would you mind opening the door?

In the **u** form the same requests would be expressed as follows:

Wilt u het raam even dichtdoen?
Zou u de deur even willen opendoen?[2]

All these requests can be concluded with **alsjeblieft/alstublieft** but it is not necessary as they already sound very polite.

Exercise 6

Translate the following sentences giving the simple imperative and the two polite forms with **willen** and **zou willen**.

Example: helpen/me
Help me (even(tjes))!
Wil je me even(tjes) helpen?
Zou je me even(tjes) willen helpen?

1 opstaan
2 opbellen/me morgen
3 aansteken/de kaars
4 binnenkomen
5 voorlezen/die brief
6 wegdoen/die rommel

Reading text 2 ▮▮

Vocabulary

het feest(je)	the party
meebrengen	to bring along
beloven	to promise
tot kijk	a colloquial variant of **tot ziens**

---

2 Even higher style is the form **zoudt u ...**

A letter from Piet to his brother Joop in Belgium

```
                              .        Keizersgracht  132
                                       3520  RT  Amsterdam
                                       NEDERLAND
                                       22  juli  1996
Beste  Joop,

Mijn  schoonmoeder  komt  op  bezoek  en  we  willen
een  klein  feestje  voor  haar  houden,  want  ze  wordt
dit  jaar  65.  Ze  is  op  zaterdag  17  augustus  jarig.
Zouden  jullie  voor  dat  feest  naar  Nederland  willen
komen?  We  zouden  het  erg  leuk  vinden.  Kom  op
vrijdag  en  blijf  het  weekend  bij  ons.  Breng  de
kinderen  ook  mee!  Het  belooft  erg  gezellig  te
worden.  Tot  kijk.

Hartelijke  groeten,

*Piet*

P.S.  Groeten  aan  allemaal  van  Pauline.
```

Language points

Informal letters

It is optional whether the address of the sender is written in the top right-hand corner, but it is always written on the back of the envelope, often preceded by the abbreviation **afz.** (= **afzender** 'sender'). Dutch postal codes all consist of four numbers followed by a space and two capital letters placed before the name of the town; this code is specific to the city block the abode is located in. The date, which can also be written 22/7/96 (7/22/96, as in the United States, is unknown), does not have any abbreviation after the 22 corresponding to 'nd' as cardinal numerals are used in such dates (see page 53).

The greeting **lieve** is only used between relatives, lovers and very close friends but not from one man to another. Where there is no intimate or really close relationship, as well as between two men who are friends or related, **beste** is used, e.g. **Beste Piet/Pauline, Beste meneer en mevrouw Scherpenzeel** (i.e. the neighbours). **(Zeer) geachte** is used in non-personal letters.

(**Met**) **hartelijke groeten**, a variation of which is (**met**) **vriendelijke groeten**, is a standard way to finish off a letter; **met vriendelijke groet** also occurs. **Veel liefs** 'lots of love' can be used instead, as can simply **Je** 'Yours' followed by your first name.

Addressing an envelope

The titles used are **De heer, Mevrouw** or **Mejuffrouw** followed by the initial and surname. **Mejuffrouw** is somewhat on the wane these days unless it is a young girl. Political correctness now demands that young women be addressed as **mevrouw**. Note that although the above is written on the envelope (i.e. with capital letters), a letter to someone you address as Mr or Mrs requires the following forms: **Beste** or **Geachte heer/ mevrouw/mejuffrouw Scherpenzeel** (i.e. with small letters). The abbreviations used on an envelope are **Dhr., Mevr., Mej.** or **Mw.** for 'Ms.'

Note: The form **meneer** is chiefly used when addressing a man directly. It renders both 'sir', when used alone, and 'Mr' when followed by a surname. The word **mevrouw** is used in both cases (i.e. 'madam' and 'Mrs'), whereas **juffrouw** 'miss' (not **mejuffrouw**, which is only used in letters) is the form used to a young female shop assistant, for example; it too can be followed by the surname.

The street number always follows the name of the street and the words for 'street', 'road', 'lane', etc. are always written together with the name as one word, e.g. **Zadelstraat** 'Saddle Street', **Hoofdweg** 'Main Road', **Zilversteeg** 'Silver Lane'. Note that when using street names in speech, they are always accompanied by the definite article, e.g. **Ik woon in de Zadelstraat.**

Exercise 7

Translate the following letter into Dutch. Pretend you are a man writing to another male friend:

Dear Alistair,

We are now in Amsterdam. We are staying here for two days. Two days is not very long but we have to be in London on (**op**) Wednesday. We would like to visit the National Museum (**het Rijksmuseum**) but we don't have enough time. We can't do everything unfortunately. And we don't have much money left (**over**) either (**ook**).

What are you going to do in the summer? Shall we go to Athens together (**samen**)? Let's save our money for that trip!

I have to go to the post-office. Give my regards to your parents.

Kind regards,

Johan

Dialogue 3

Piet and Pauline are waiting for Joop and his wife to arrive

PIET: Wat zit je te doen?
PAULINE: Ik probeer het station te bellen maar ik heb het verkeerde nummer gedraaid.
PIET: Joop en Karin hopen met de trein van negen uur uit Brussel te komen, niet waar?
PAULINE: Ja, maar ik wil weten wanneer die trein hier aankomt.
PIET: Er is geen tijd te verliezen, denk ik. Het is al elf uur.

PIET: *What are you doing?*
PAULINE: *I'm trying to ring the station but I dialled the wrong number.*
PIET: *Joop and Karin are hoping to come on the nine o'clock train from Brussels, aren't they?*
PAULINE: *Yes, but I want to know when it arrives here.*
PIET: *There's no time to lose, I think. It's already eleven o'clock.*

Language points

Use of te before an infinitive

Although you have learnt infinitives as follows, i.e. **wachten** 'to wait', **komen** 'to come', where the 'to' is not translated, there are instances in Dutch where this English 'to' is rendered by **te**. As a general rule it can be said that an infinitive at the end of a Dutch clause is preceded by **te** except when the finite verb in the clause is a modal verb. There is one example of this in dialogue 3, **ik wil weten**; compare **Hij kan niet komen, Zij moet morgen teruggaan, Ze zullen je helpen**. In all other cases where a finite verb is followed by an infinitive later in the clause, that infinitive is preceded by **te**, e.g. **Ik probeer het station te bellen**. Further examples:

Dat is moeilijk te doen.	That is difficult to do.
Hij wenst naar Marokko te gaan.	He wishes to go to Morocco.
Het kind begint te huilen.	The child starts crying/to cry.

Dialogue 4 ▣

Joop and his wife have arrived from Belgium

JOOP: Piet! Wat leuk om jullie weer te zien! Kijk eens wat we voor jullie uit België meegebracht hebben.

PIET: Heerlijke Belgische chocola! Wat lekker! Hartstikke[3] bedankt, zeg!

JOOP: Waar zijn Marius en Charlotte?

PIET: Ze zijn naar hun opa gegaan om zijn nieuwe tanden te zien.

JOOP: Gekke kinderen!

PIET: Een goede reis gehad?

JOOP: Ja, maar we waren te laat opgestaan om met de trein van negen uur te komen.

PIET: We hebben het niet erg gevonden om een half uur op het station te wachten. Er was veel te zien.

---

3 This is a common way of intensifying adjectives and adverbs. It is considered very colloquial.

Joop: *Piet! How nice to see you again! Look what we've brought you from Belgium.*

Piet: *Wonderful Belgian chocolate! How delicious! Gee, thanks a lot!*

Joop: *Where are Marius and Charlotte?*

Piet: *They've gone to their granddad's to see his new teeth.*

Joop: *Crazy kids!*

Piet: *Had a good trip?*

Joop: *Yes, but we got up too late to catch the nine o'clock train.*

Piet: *We didn't mind waiting at the station for half an hour. There was lots to see.*

Language points

Use of om te

Whenever a *to* standing before an infinitive in an English sentence means 'in order to', **om te** is required in Dutch, not just **te**, e.g. **We gaan nu naar huis om televisie te kijken** 'We're going home now (in order) to watch TV'. But the Dutch now use **om te** in many instances where it does not mean 'in order to' and where in fact a simple **te** would be sufficient – purists frown at this but it is now the norm. In dialogue 4 there is only one example of **om te** meaning 'in order to', e.g. **Ze zijn naar hun opa gegaan om zijn nieuwe tanden te zien.** Here 'to see his new teeth' means 'in order to see his new teeth' (i.e. purpose). In all the other **om te** clauses in the above dialogue **te** could have been used.

In dialogue 3 **om te** could also have been used instead of just **te** in the following cases:

Ik probeer om het station te bellen.
Joop en Karin hopen om met de trein van negen uur uit Brussel te komen.
Er is geen tijd om te verliezen.

Only in **Wat zit je te doen?** is **om te** not possible because this is a standard expression, which will be dealt with later.

Note: When the infinitive that is dependent on **(om) te** is a separable verb, the **te** is inserted between the prefix and the verb and the three are written as separate words, e.g. **Hij zal proberen (om) vroeg aan te komen** 'He'll try to arrive early'.

Exercise 8

Complete the following sentences using **om te**.

1 Hij belt je op *to invite you to a party.*
2 Pauline heeft geprobeerd *to help Marius.*
3 We waren te moe *to get up so early.*
4 Hij wenst *to stay in Germany longer.*
5 Het is niet gemakkelijk *to find Lunteren on the map.*
6 Ik vind het moeilijk *to speak French.*
7 Ze had heel veel *to do.*
8 Het is niet mogelijk voor haar *to come home.*

Culture point
The Dutch words **vriend** and **kennis**, although literally meaning 'friend' and 'acquaintance' respectively, are used differently from their English equivalents. The Dutch consider that they have relatively few **vrienden** but a host of **kennissen**. A **vriend** must be a close friend, whereas anyone you otherwise know is a **kennis**. For instance, where in English we might say 'A friend of mine also lives in Moscow', where the emphasis is on the fact that you also know someone who lives there, rather than on the closeness or otherwise of your relationship to that person, the most natural thing to say in Dutch would be **Een kennis van mij woont ook in Moskou**. **Vriend/vriendin** also render 'boyfriend/girlfriend', where the use of **mijn**, **zijn**, etc. makes the meaning clear, e.g.

Mijn vriendin is op het ogenblik in Warschau.
My girlfriend is in Warsaw at the moment.

Een vriendin/kennis van mij is op het ogenblik in Warschau.
A female friend of mine/friend is in Warsaw at the moment.

8 Piets ouders zijn op visite

Piet's parents are visiting

In this lesson you will learn about:

- Dutch table manners
- diminutives
- colours
- expressions of time (periods of the day)

Dialogue 1 ▣

Piet's parents are having lunch with Piet and Pauline

PIET:	Eet smakelijk! (*all others respond with either* **eet smakelijk** *or* **smakelijk eten**)
OMA:	Mag ik een snee brood, alsjeblieft Piet?
PIET:	Pardon, pa! (*as he stretches in front of dad*) Alsjeblieft, ma.
OMA:	Geef me alsjeblieft ook de kaas. (*tastes it*) Hmm, die smaakt verrukkelijk.
PIET:	Heb je zin in nog een pilsje, pa?
OPA:	Dank je. Ik heb nog wat.
PIET:	Ik drink nog een glaasje. Proost!

PIET:	*Bon appétit!* (= enjoy the meal)
GRANDMA:	*Can I have a slice of bread please, Piet?*
PIET:	*Excuse me, dad! There you are, mum.*
GRANDMA:	*Please pass me the cheese too! Hmm, it tastes wonderful.*
PIET:	*Do you feel like another beer, dad?*
GRANDPA:	*No thanks. I still have some.*
PIET:	*I'm having another glass. Cheers!*

Lunch is drawing to a close

PAULINE: Er is geen brood meer. Ik haal nog wat.
OPA: Laat maar! We hebben allemaal genoeg gegeten.
PAULINE: Weet je het zeker? Heeft het gesmaakt?
OPA: Het was heerlijk, dank je.
PAULINE: Graag gedaan. Ik ga nu afwassen.
OPA: Goed, ik droog af.

PAULINE: *There's no more bread. I'll fetch some more.*
GRANDPA: *Don't bother! We've all had enough to eat.*
PAULINE: *Are you sure? Did you like it?*
GRANDPA: *It was delicious, thank you.*
PAULINE: *My pleasure. I'm going to do the washing-up now.*
GRANDPA: *Okay, I'll dry the dishes.*

Language points

Table manners

Once seated, prior to starting the meal and after grace in those
families where it is still said, everyone at the table utters one of
the following three greetings:

Eet smakelijk!	Bon appétit! (see page 54)
Smakelijk eten!	
Eet ze! (very colloquial)	
Geef me alsjeblieft de/het …	Please pass the …
Mag ik de/het/een … (hebben)	Please pass the/a …
Heb je zin/trek in … ?	Do you feel like … ?
Het smaakt heerlijk/verrukkelijk.	It tastes delicious.
Smaakt het?	How's it taste? How do you like it?
Pardon.	Excuse me. (see page 72)
Proost!	Cheers! (also said when someone sneezes)
Op je/uw gezondheid!	To your very good health!
Ik heb genoeg gehad/gegeten.	I'm full.

Note 1: You will have noticed by now how common it is for the Dutch to utter exclamations consisting of **wat** plus an adjective, e.g. **Wat leuk!** 'How nice/wonderful!', **Wat
prachtig!** 'How beautiful!', **Wat vreselijk!** 'How terrible!' **Wat heerlijk/verrukkelijk!**
are also appropriate exclamations of appreciation of what is being devoured.

Note 2: 'Another' can be ambiguous in English but is never so in Dutch. In the first dialogue Piet asks his father **Heb je zin in nog een pilsje?** and later says **Ik drink nog een glaasje. Nog een** means literally 'an additional' whereas **een ander(e)** means 'a different', e.g.

Ik heb nu nog een auto.
'I now have another car' (i.e. two).
Ik heb nu een andere auto.
'I now have another car' (i.e. a different one).

More often than not 'another' in English corresponds to the former.

Note 3: Note that when Piet asks his father if he would like another beer, he answers in the negative with **Dank je** (see page 111).

The expression **trek hebben in** 'to feel like' is used only in reference to food, but **zin hebben in** refers to both food and anything else you feel like (doing), e.g.

Ik heb trek/zin in een appel.
I feel like an apple.
Ik heb zin om naar de bioscoop te gaan.
I feel like going to the movies.

Exercise 1

Translate the following dialogue.

PIET: Enjoy the meal!
PAULINE: Enjoy the meal! Please pass the ham, Piet.
PIET: Certainly. Here you are.
PAULINE: Thanks. May I have another glass of wine?
PIET: You've still got some.
PAULINE: Oh yes. Cheers! Please pass the butter!
PIET: But you haven't got any bread yet.
PAULINE: Oh yes. How stupid of me! May I have the bread?
(*a little later*)
PIET: It was delicious but I'm full.
PAULINE: Me too. Let's do the washing up (**de afwas doen**).

Note: In expressions like 'a cup of coffee', 'a glass of wine', 'a box of matches', 'a pound of mince', the 'of' is not translated, e.g.

een kopje koffie   **een glas wijn**
een doosje lucifers   **een pond gehakt**

Culture point
Although native Dutch cuisine tends to be simple and frequently stodgy, a 'Dutch' speciality is Indonesian food (**Indisch eten**). Every Dutch town has numerous Indonesian restaurants (**het Chinees-Indisch restaurant**, commonly abbreviated to **Chin.-Ind.**). The food is usually a combination of Chinese and Indonesian, the result of the influential role the Chinese played in the commercial life of the Dutch

East Indies (**Nederlands-Indië**). It is good value for money. **We gaan vanavond chinezen** is the way they express that they are going out for a Chinese–Indonesian meal tonight. Take-away is not common in Holland but is not unknown (**het meeneemcentrum** 'take-away Chinese restaurant'). The ultimate in Indies cuisine is a Dutch invention, **de rijsttafel** (verb **rijsttafelen**). A rijsttafel (**de rijst** = 'rice') consists of a basis of limitless steamed rice to which are added very small portions of a host of different exotic dishes which flavour the rice.

Het café is the Dutch equivalent of a pub (also called **de kroeg**), where it is often also possible to get a cheap meal and it is just as common to go into a **café** for a cup of coffee as it is for a beer. Dutch cafés pride themselves on being **gezellig, gezelligheid** being their great drawcard. But be warned! The Dutch are a nation of heavy smokers, roll-your-owns (**het sjekkie**) and cigars (**de sigaar**) being very commonplace. The rights of non-smokers are scarcely recognised. If you are a non-smoker, look out for the signs **Niet roken** or **Verboden te roken** to assert your rights. It'll be a rare privilege.

A traditional Dutch café, which is darkish, with Persian rugs on the tables (**het persje**) and oom-pah-pah music playing is called **een bruin café** or **een bruine kroeg**; this is the domain of the Dutch working class (**de arbeidende klasse**).

Reading text 🔲

Eating out in the Netherlands

Het is altijd nogal duur geweest om in Nederland uit eten te gaan maar Chinees-Indisch eten is meestal vrij goedkoop. Je vindt een Chin.-Ind. restaurant in bijna elk dorp in Nederland maar je kunt ook vaak een hapje eten in een café. Dat is gewoonlijk niet duur, maar het is doorgaans erg eenvoudig eten – patat, een kroketje, of een uitsmijter of zo. Je kunt er ook een pils, een kopje koffie of een borrel drinken in een zeer gezellige sfeer. In een bruin café in Amsterdam of Rotterdam zul je ook dikwijls het dialect van die steden horen want arbeiders gaan ernaartoe voor een borrel of een biertje na het werk. Zulke cafés zijn erg gezellig en de gemiddelde Nederlander vindt gezelligheid erg belangrijk.

Exercise 2

Answer the questions on page 116 by studying the details given on the menu of this **eetcafé** (a 'pub' or bar that serves meals).

EETCAFÉ
de Poort

DAGSCHOTELS VOOR 24/01 TOT 30/01

✱ ✱ ✱ ✱ ✱ ✱ ✱ ✱ ✱ ✱ ✱ ✱ ✱ ✱ ✱ ✱ ✱ ✱

DINSDAG
1/2 GEBRADEN KIP MET
CHILLISAUS & FRANSE FRITES

WOENSDAG
ZALMMOOT MET ROOMSAUS
& RIJST

DONDERDAG
SHASLICKPENNEN
MET FRITES

VRIJDAG
KIPFILET
GEVULD MET ASPERGES

ZATERDAG
RUNDERSTOOFSCHOTEL
MET AARDAPPELPUREE

ZONDAG
ITALIAANSE VARKENSSCHIJF
MET KRIELTJES

MAANDAG
ZIGEUNERSCHNITZEL MET
VRUCHTEN & KRIELTJES

✱ ✱ ✱ ✱ ✱ ✱ ✱ ✱ ✱ ✱ ✱ ✱ ✱ ✱ ✱ ✱ ✱ ✱

elke zondag vanaf 11.00 uur
ENGLISH BREAKFAST F 12,50
ROEREI, BACON, TOAST, GEB.SPEK,
GEBRADEN WORST, CHAMPIGNONS

✱ ✱ ✱ ✱ ✱ ✱ ✱ ✱ ✱ ✱ ✱ ✱ ✱ ✱ ✱ ✱ ✱ ✱

Alle schotels worden geserveerd met
aardappelgarnituur, groente en salade,
tenzij anders staat vermeld.

De schotels kosten

f14,50

De keuken is geopend van
17.00 uur tot 21.00 uur.

TOLSTEEGBARRIÈRE 2 – UTRECHT – 314572

1 Hoe heet het café?
2 In welke stad staat dit café?
3 Ik hou van kip. Welke dag of dagen zou je mij aanraden om bij
   De Poort te gaan eten?
4 Ik lust geen vis. Wanneer moet ik dus niet naar De Poort gaan?
5 Hoeveel goedkoper is een Engels ontbijt dan een gewone
   dagschotel?
6 De dagschotel op vrijdag bij De Poort is kipfilet gevuld met
   asperges. Wat krijg je nog meer op je bord?
7 Hoeveel verschillende soorten aardappels kun je bij je eten
   krijgen?
8 Wanneer kun je bij De Poort eten?

Dialogue 2 ▣

Piet has bought Charlotte a dolly

PIET: Lotje, ik heb een mooi popje voor je gekocht.
CHARLOTTE: Laat eens zien, papa.
PIET: Kom 's hier liefje! Geef me een kusje! (*she kisses
him*) Dank je, schatje. Hier is je popje.

PIET: *Lotte, I've bought a lovely dolly for you.*
CHARLOTTE: *Let me see, dad.*
PIET: *Come here, sweetie. Give me kiss. Thank you,
darling. Here's your dolly.*

Language points

Diminutives

Diminutives: dog – *doggy,* doll – *dolly*

You have probably already noticed how many Dutch nouns end in
-je and that the ending is often optional. Earlier in this lesson you
saw both **pils** and **pilsje** being used. This ending is called the
diminutive ending. Its primary function is to make something small.
Whereas words like *doggy* and *bickie* (from *biscuit*) are highly
colloquial in English and more commonly found in children's
language, the equivalent formation in Dutch is not at all childish,
although it is often (but not by any means always) colloquial.

Although very few nouns can take such an ending in English, virtually every Dutch noun can take this ending. The effect may be to make the noun small (e.g. **katje** 'kitten'), but it can also express gezelligheid (**een leuk avondje** 'a nice night') or affection (e.g. **wat een lief huisje** 'what a sweet house') or contempt (**een burgermannetje** 'a petit-bourgeois'). The diminutive ending is one of the most unique and charming aspects of Dutch, the force of which is seldom translatable into English.

The ending is not always merely **-je**, but may be **-tje**, **-etje**, **-pje** or **-kje**. The choice of ending depends on the phonetics of the base noun. Here are the rules:

1 The basic form is the addition of **-je** to any noun:

aap – aapje 'monkey'   **huis – huisje** 'house'
boek – boekje 'book'   **oog – oogje** 'eye'
hond – hondje 'dog'   **pet – petje** 'cap'

2 Nouns containing a long vowel or diphthong, either at the end of the word or followed by **l**, **n** or **r**, take **-tje**:

ei – eitje 'egg'   **stoel – stoeltje** 'chair'
ui – uitje 'onion'   **schoen – schoentje** 'shoe'
vrouw – vrouwtje 'woman,   **deur – deurtje** 'door'
wife'

Nouns ending in **-el**, **-en** and **-er** also take **-tje**:

tafel – tafeltje 'table'   **kamer – kamertje** 'room'
deken – dekentje 'blanket'

Nouns ending in **a**, **o** or **u** (nearly all foreign) double the vowel before adding **-tje**:

oma – omaatje 'granny'   **paraplu – parapluutje** 'umbrella'
auto – autootje 'car'   Note: **café – cafeetje** 'café, pub'

3 Nouns containing a short vowel and ending in **l**, **m**, **n**, **ng** or **r** take **-etje**:

bel – belletje 'bell'   **ding – dingetje** 'thing'
kam – kammetje 'comb'   **ster – sterretje** 'star'
pan – pannetje 'pot, pan'

A few nouns containing a short vowel and ending in **b**, **g** or **p** also add **-etje**, but most belong in group 1:

rib – ribbetje 'rib'   **kip – kippetje** 'chicken'
vlag – vlaggetje 'flag'

4 Nouns ending in **m** take **-pje**:

boom – boompje 'tree'   **bezem – bezempje** 'broom'

5 Nouns ending in **-ing** are complicated. If they consist of one syllable the ending is **-etje**, e.g.

ring – ringetje 'ring'   **ding – dingetje** 'thing'

Those ending in **-eling** and **-ening** also take **-etje**:

wandeling – wandelingetje   tekening – tekeningetje 'drawing' 'walk'

But all other nouns ending in unstressed **-ing** take **-je** and change the **g** to **k**, e.g.

koning – koninkje 'king'   **regering – regerinkje** 'government'

6 Several of those nouns that have a short vowel in the singular but a long vowel in the plural (see page 41) also have a long vowel in the diminutive form:

gat – gaatje 'hole'   **pad – paadje** 'path'
glas – glaasje 'glass'   **schip – scheepje** 'ship'

Note: All diminutives are neuter, whether the base noun is neuter or not: **de brug – het bruggetje** 'bridge', **het fornuis – het fornuisje** 'stove'. The plural of diminutives is always formed in **s**: **de bruggen – de bruggetjes, de fornuizen – de fornuisjes**.

Exercise 3

Form the diminutive of the following nouns changing the definite article where necessary: **de vader, de broer, de kast, het huis, het dak, de stoel, de deur, de lepel, de sigaret, het blad, het bed, de kussen, de rekening.**

Exercise 4

Give the diminutive of the following nouns. Note that they are all plural: **de schoenen, twee lampen, drie appels, deze peren, die twee boeken, die mannen, de kranen, de honden, de sterren, de bellen.**

Colours 〔OO〕

The principal colours are:

blauw	blue	**purper/paars**	purple
bruin	brown	**rood**	red
geel	yellow	**rose**	pink
grijs	grey	**wit**	white
groen	green	**zwart**	black
oranje	orange		

The in-between colours are created by putting the names of the two colours together:

blauwgroen   blueish-green   **geelbruin**   yellowish-brown

'Light' and 'dark' are expressed by **licht-** and **donker-** being prefixed to the name of the colour:

lichtgroen   light green   **donkerblauw**   dark blue

Exercise 5

What am I talking about? Give the Dutch word and say whether it is **de** or **het**.

1   Het is rood en vegetariërs eten het niet.
2   Het is geel en het smelt in de zon.
3   Ze zijn bijna wit en je huilt als je ze schilt.
4   Het is zwart en ik kan niet slapen, als ik het gedronken heb.
5   Het is lichtbruin en je drinkt het koud.
6   Het is wit en je strooit het op je eten.

Expressions of time – periods of the day 🔲

Learn the following adverbs of time:

vanochtend	this morning
vanmorgen	this morning
vanmiddag	this afternoon
vanavond	this evening, tonight
vannacht	tonight/last night (see explanation below)
morgen	tomorrow
morgenochtend	tomorrow morning
morgenmiddag	tomorrow afternoon
morgenavond	tomorrow evening/night
overmorgen	the day after tomorrow
overmorgenochtend, **-middag, -avond**	the morning of the day after tomorrow etc.*
gisteren	yesterday
gisterochtend	yesterday morning
gistermiddag	yesterday afternoon
gisteravond	last night

eergisteren   the day before yesterday
eergisterochtend,   the morning of the day before yesterday
  -middag, -avond   etc.*

Note: * In such cases we tend to say Wednesday morning/afternoon/evening or whatever the day might be.

Vannacht can refer back to the night just past or forward to the one coming up, but in both cases it means that period after midnight. When referring to that period of 'last night' or 'tonight' prior to going to bed, the words **gisteravond** and **vanavond** respectively are used.

Exercise 6

Fill in the appropriate expression of time.

1 Hij komt pas (*the day after tomorrow*).
2 Wat doe je (*tonight*)?
3 Wat heb je (*last night*) gedaan?
4 Ik heb hem (*this morning*) in de stad gezien.
5 Mijn vader komt (*Wednesday evening – it is now Monday*) terug.

Exercise 7

Answer the following questions giving the day and the date assuming **Vandaag het is donderdag 4 april**.

maandag	dinsdag	woensdag	donderdag
1	2	3	4

vrijdag	zaterdag	zondag
5	6	7

1 Wat is het morgen?
2 Wat is het overmorgen?
3 Wat was het gisteren?
4 Wat was het eergisteren?
5 Wat was het afgelopen maandag? (**afgelopen** 'last')
6 Wat is het aanstaande zondag? (**aanstaande** 'next')

9 Na het ontbijt

After breakfast

In this lesson you will learn about:

- coordinate and subordinate clauses
- interrogatives in indirect questions
- the simple past tense
- more expressions of time (in the morning, next week, etc.)

Dialogue 1 ▣

At Piet and Pauline's just after breakfast

PIET: Wat ga je doen als we ontbeten hebben?
PAULINE: Nadat ik de bedden heb opgemaakt, ga ik de stad in. Als je wilt, kun je mee(gaan).[1]
PIET: Ik kan niet omdat ik vanochtend de auto wil wassen. Wanneer kom je thuis?
PAULINE: Ik weet nog niet wanneer ik thuiskom. Je weet dat de bus erg onbetrouwbaar is.

PIET: *What are you going to do when we've had breakfast?*
PAULINE: *After I've made the beds, I'm going to town. If you like, you can come too.*
PIET: *I can't because I want to wash the car this morning. When are you coming home?*
PAULINE: *I don't know yet when I'm coming home. You know that the bus is very unreliable.*

---

1 **Gaan** is optional here as it is implied.

Language points

Coordinate and subordinate clauses

A coordinate clause: He works in Utrecht *and she works in The Hague.*
A subordinate clause: He said *that he worked in Amsterdam.*

You have been making longer sentences joining two clauses together by means of **en** 'and', **maar** 'but', **of** 'or' and **want** 'because' for some time already without any problem. Normally when you join two clauses in Dutch – each with its own subject and finite verb – you need to apply a change of word order. Only when the joining word (i.e. the conjunction) is one of the above four words, is no change in word order necessary, e.g.

Pauline blijft in Den Haag want er is een treinstaking.
Ze heeft een auto maar ze gaat veel liever op de fiets.

These four joining words, which cause no change in word order, are called coordinating conjunctions.

All other conjunctions, which do cause a change in word order, are called subordinating conjunctions.[2] The finite verb in the subordinate clause is sent to the end of that clause when the clause is introduced by one of the following conjunctions:

dat	that	**alsof**	as if
voordat	before	**zoals**	as
nadat	after	**terwijl**	while
omdat	because	**hoewel**	although
zodat	so that	**sinds**	since
als	when, if	**zodra**	as soon as
toen	when (past tense)	**of**	whether

There are in fact quite a few more of these conjunctions, but the above are the most common. Observe the effect they have on the finite verb that follows them:

Weet je dat hij op het ogenblik in Duitsland is? (from **Hij is op het ogenblik in Duitsland**)
Do you know (that) he is in Germany at the moment?

---

2 As there is no difference in word order in English whether you are using a coordinating or a subordinating conjunction, the distinction is usually somewhat artificial in English, but is certainly not so in Dutch.

Zij maakt het bed op terwijl hij de afwas doet. (from **Hij doet de afwas**)
She is making the bed while he does the washing-up.

Kom thuis zodra de film afgelopen is. (from **De film is afgelopen**)
Come home as soon as the film is over.

Note: The first example above illustrates that the conjunction 'that' can be omitted in English but can never be omitted in Dutch, e.g. **Ik geloof dat hij het gedaan heeft** 'I think (that) he did it'.

Observe what happens when the finite verb in the subordinate clause is a separable verb – the verb and the prefix join up again:

Ik weet niet of hij morgen terugkomt. (from **Hij komt morgen terug**)
I don't know if he is coming back tomorrow.

As in English, it is often possible to start with the subordinate clause, in which case the finite verb in that clause still stands at the end of that clause, but the subject and verb in the main clause must be inverted to retain the finite verb in that clause in overall second position in the sentence as a whole – the Dutch regard the subordinate clause at the beginning as one idea:

       Idea 1   Idea 2
Als jij mij met de afwas helpt, zal ik jou met je huiswerk helpen.
If you help me with the washing-up, I'll help you with your home-work.

      Idea 1   Idea 2
Omdat hij ziek is, blijft hij vandaag thuis.
Because he is ill, he's staying at home today.[3]

The above sentences are stylistic variations of the following in which **zal** and **blijft** respectively are still the second idea:

    Ik zal jou met je huiswerk helpen als jij mij met de afwas helpt.
    Hij blijft vandaag thuis omdat hij ziek is.

Because this inversion puts the finite verbs in the two clauses side by side, it is customary to use a comma between the clauses but not necessarily when the subordinate clause follows the main clause.

---

3 You will have noticed that both **want**, which is a coordinating conjunction, and **omdat**, which is a subordinating conjunction, translate 'because' but the former can never be used when the sentence starts with 'because'; compare English *for* in the sense of 'because', e.g. *He's staying home for he is feeling ill.*

Note what happens when you turn a clause that has a past participle or an infinitive at the end of it into a subordinate clause:

Ik heb vanochtend brood gekocht.
Weet je dat ik vanochtend brood heb gekocht/gekocht heb?
Ik moet vanmiddag brood kopen.
Ik weet dat ik vanmiddag brood moet kopen.

When the finite verb that is being sent to the end of the clause by the conjunction is a form of **hebben** or **zijn** (i.e. when a sentence is in the past tense), you can choose whether it precedes or follows the past participle. But when the finite verb is a modal verb, it stands before the infinitive (after the infinitive is possible, but not very common).

There are a few tricks to watch out for when using the above conjunctions. What follows may seem a bit confusing, but you'll soon get the hang of it.

You may have noticed that **of** is used both as a coordinating conjunction meaning 'or' with no change in word order, and as a subordinating conjunction meaning 'whether' with a change in word order. Context and word order always make it clear what the meaning is:

Kom je vandaag of kom je morgen?
Are you coming today or are you coming tomorrow?
Ik weet niet of ik morgen of overmorgen kom.
I don't know whether/if I'm coming tomorrow or the day after tomorrow.

As just illustrated, when 'if' means 'whether' it is rendered by **of**, but an 'if' that does not mean 'whether' is **als**:

Als het morgen regent, blijf ik thuis.
If it rains tomorrow, I'll stay home.

There are several tricks associated with translating 'when' in Dutch. As you saw on page 92, 'when' introducing a question is **wanneer**, e.g. **Wanneer komt hij?** 'When is he coming?' But when 'when' occurs in a statement, i.e. when it is a subordinating conjunction, it is rendered by **als**, e.g. **Ik doe de brief op de bus als ik terugkom** 'I'll post the letter when I get back' (here logic tells you **als** does not mean 'if').

When 'when' refers to one single incident in the past, it is rendered by **toen**, usually followed by the simple past tense, which we will be looking at later in this lesson:

Ik heb heel goed gegeten toen ik in België was.
I ate really well when I was in Belgium.

But when the action took place on repeated occasions in the past, i.e. when 'when' means 'whenever', **wanneer** is used:

Ik heb altijd heel goed gegeten wanneer ik in België was.
I always ate really well when(ever) I was in Belgium.

But the subordinating conjunction **als** can also mean 'if' (but not 'if' which means 'whether', because that is **of**). It is often ambiguous whether **als** means 'if' or 'when' but it makes little difference to the overall meaning:

Geef het hem als je hem ziet 'Give it to him if/when you see him'.

Exercise 1

Put **Hij heeft gezegd dat** 'He said that' in front of the following sentences, thereby turning them into subordinate clauses, and make the necessary changes to the order of the verbs.

1 Pauline werkt in Den Haag.
2 Pauline is in Engeland geboren.
3 Piet wil vroeg thuiskomen.
4 De kinderen moeten opstaan.
5 Paulines moeder heeft haar opgebeld.

Exercise 2

What is the appropriate word for 'when' in the following sentences? You have a choice of **als**, **wanneer** or **toen**:

1 ____ ga je naar Engeland?
2 ____ hij thuis komt, ga ik boodschappen doen.
3 Marius heeft de schaar teruggegeven ____ hij klaar was.
4 ____ Piet zijn buurman op straat tegenkwam, heeft hij hem altijd gegroet.

Exercise 3

Rewrite the following sentences putting the subordinate clause first and making the necessary changes to word order.

1 Hij was al thuis toen ik thuiskwam.

2 Piet heeft het gedaan hoewel Pauline hem toch gewaarschuwd had.
3 Pauline kookt terwijl de kinderen televisie kijken.
4 We willen morgen niet gaan als het gaat regenen.

Culture point

A Dutch breakfast consists of bread, usually pre-sliced at the bakery, with a vast array of **beleg** (goodies for putting on bread); Dutch cheese, an assortment of very thinly sliced cold meats (**vleeswaren**), which are sold in quantities of 100 grams, unofficially still referred to by the old-fashioned term of **ons**. In fact the Dutch will put almost anything on bread – they even consume a crisp, spicy biscuit (**de speculaas**) and gingercake (**de ontbijtkoek**) on bread. The idea of a cooked breakfast (other than a boiled egg) like the traditional British breakfast is anathema to the Dutch. Porridge (**de pap**) may be eaten at breakfast time and cereals, although not traditional, are no longer uncommon.

Interrogatives in indirect questions

An interrogative in a direct question: When is she coming?
An interrogative in an indirect question: I don't know *when* she's coming.

Interrogatives (question words) like **wanneer, hoe, wie**, etc. in direct questions were dealt with on page 92. There you saw that inversion of subject and verb occurs, just as in English. When replying to a direct question, it is common to repeat the interrogative, as in the example above; this construction is called an indirect question. In indirect questions in Dutch, the interrogatives act like subordinating conjunctions by sending the finite verb in their clause to the end of the clause:

Ik weet niet wanneer zij komt.
I don't know when she's coming.

Hij heeft mij gevraagd waar zij op het ogenblik woont.
He asked me where she is living at the moment.

Hij heeft niet gezegd hoeveel het gekost heeft.
He didn't say how much it cost.

Exercise 4

What are the direct questions to which the following are the answers?

1 Ik weet niet waar Piet nu werkt.
2 Ik geloof dat Marius het kopje gebroken heeft.
3 Ik weet niet hoeveel ze verdient.
4 Ik weet niet wat ze gezegd heeft.

The simple past tense

The simple past tense: He *worked* in Amsterdam.

This tense, which is also called the imperfect tense, is formed by adding **-te** or **-de** to the stem of the verb in the singular and **-ten** or **-den** in the plural; the choice of **-te/-ten** or **-de/-den** is determined by the **'t kofschip** rule given on page 61. Here are two typical verbs with these endings:

koken 'to cook'	**horen** 'to hear'
ik kookte 'I cooked' *etc.*	ik hoorde 'I heard' *etc.*
jij kookte	jij hoorde
hij kookte	hij hoorde
wij kookten	wij hoorden
jullie kookten	jullie hoorden
zij kookten	zij hoorden

Note that just as **ik kook** in the present tense translates 'I cook', 'I am cooking' and 'I do cook', so **ik kookte** can mean 'I cooked', 'I was cooking', 'I did cook' as well as 'I used to cook'. Note what happens with verbs like **praten** 'to talk' and **verbranden** 'to burn' that already end in **t** and **d**:

ik praatte	ik verbrandde
wij praatten	wij verbrandden

Wij praten 'we are talking' and **wij praatten** 'we were talking' and **wij verbranden** 'we are burning' and **wij verbrandden** 'we were burning' are pronounced the same but are distinguished from each other in writing. In fact, because the **n** in the ending **-en** tends to be dropped, as we have seen, **praten**, **praatte** and **praatten** and **verbranden**, **verbrandde** and **verbrandden** are all pronounced alike.

The above endings only apply to regular verbs. Irregular verbs form their imperfect tense in a variety of ways, e.g.

brengen – bracht/brachten	to bring – brought
denken – dacht/dachten	to think – thought
geven – gaf/gaven	to give – gave
komen – kwam/kwamen	to come – came
kopen – kocht/kochten	to buy – bought
krijgen – kreeg/kregen	to get – got
vinden – vond/vonden	to find – found
winnen – won/wonnen	to win – won
zien – zag/zagen	to see – saw

Example:

ik gaf 'I gave' *etc.*	wij gaven
jij gaf	jullie gaven
hij gaf	zij gaven

Now you have covered all the major tenses of the verb. When you look up a verb in the vocabulary at the back of the book, if it is irregular, the parts of the verb are given in parentheses after the infinitive, e.g.

kopen (kocht/kochten, gekocht) to buy
gaan (ging/gingen, is gegaan) to go

On pages 249–54 there is an alphabetical list of all the main irregular verbs in Dutch, which you can use for quick reference.

Back on page 62, where you were introduced to the perfect tense, you were told to get used to using that tense whenever you use a verb in the past and that 'she cooked', 'she did cook', 'she has cooked' and 'she has been cooking' are all most usually rendered by **zij heeft gekookt**. Now you have learnt the imperfect and have been told that **zij kookte** can also mean 'she cooked', 'she was cooking', 'she did cook'. In English the time perspective determines whether you say 'she cooked' or 'she has cooked', e.g.

She cooked a lovely meal last night.
She has cooked a lovely meal.

You cannot say *She has cooked a lovely meal last night.* This distinction is unknown in Dutch and the Dutch tend to use the perfect tense rather than the imperfect tense for isolated events that took place in the past,[4] especially in speech. You will see the imperfect

---

4 Knowing where the two tenses are not interchangeable and thus where an imperfect is required is a little tricky. Repeated actions in the past and descriptions (neither of them isolated events in the past) are expressed in the imperfect, e.g.

more often in written texts than you will hear it in conversation. In short, **Ik heb hem gisteravond in de stad gezien** and **Ik zag hem gisteravond in de stad** are synonymous but the former is the more usual in conversational Dutch. For this reason you were introduced to the perfect tense first.

Remember this: a perfect in English is always a perfect in Dutch[5] (i.e. 'I have not seen it' **Ik heb het niet gezien**), whereas an imperfect in English can be either an imperfect or a perfect in Dutch, but is more usually the latter (i.e. 'She bought it last year' **Ze kocht het vorig jaar/Ze heeft het vorig jaar gekocht**).

Exercise 5

Put the following sentences into the simple past or imperfect tense.

1 Hij komt elke dag erg laat thuis.
2 Pauline werkt in Den Haag.
3 Marius gaat maandag niet naar school.
4 Charlotte krijgt een tientje voor haar verjaardag van haar opa.
5 De kinderen spelen gezellig met elkaar in de tuin.
6 Die hond bijt iedereen.
7 Mijn zus praat te veel.
8 Mijn ouders werken te hard.

Exercise 6

The following story is in the present tense. Put it into the simple past.

Wim heeft een prachtige auto en hij koopt elke drie jaar een nieuwe. Zijn auto's zijn altijd rood. Hij houdt van auto's en hij rijdt graag hard. Hij parkeert zijn auto achter zijn huis. Hij wast hem elke week en geeft hem één keer in de maand een servicebeurt. Zijn vrouw vindt het lastig dat hij altijd met zijn auto bezig is. Om de drie jaar krijgt zij een nieuwe fiets van Wim. Wim verwent zijn vrouw niet.

Vroeger kwam ik altijd te laat 'I always used to come late', **De zon scheen** 'The sun was shining'. And as mentioned previously in this lesson, the verb in a **toen** clause is always in the imperfect.
5 See page 187 for one exception to this rule.

Dialogue 2 ▨

Piet and Pauline are discussing their plans for the coming week

PAULINE: Wat doe je op zondagochtend, Piet?
PIET: Ik doe wat ik altijd 's zondags doe – ik was de auto.
PAULINE: Dat heb je afgelopen zondag niet gedaan.
PIET: Misschien niet, maar aanstaande zondag doe ik het wel.
PAULINE: En wat doen we vanavond?
PIET: Wat we altijd 's avonds doen, natuurlijk. Televisie kijken.
PAULINE: Moet dat elke avond? Kunnen we niet één avondje gaan wandelen?

PAULINE: *What are you doing on Sunday morning, Piet?*
PIET: *I'll be doing what I always do on Sundays – I'll be washing the car.*
PAULINE: *You didn't do that last Sunday.*
PIET: *Perhaps not, but I will be next Sunday.*
PAULINE: *And what are we going to do this evening?*
PIET: *What we always do in the evening, of course. Watch TV.*
PAULINE: *Do we have to do that every evening? Can't we go out for a walk at least one evening?*

Language points

More expressions of time ▨

volgende week/maand	next week/month
volgend jaar	next year
vorige/verleden week/maand	last week/year
vorig/verleden jaar	last year
(op) maandag/dinsdag *etc.*	on Monday/Tuesday, etc.
's zondags, 's maandags, 's woensdags	on Sundays etc.
dinsdags, donderdags, vrijdags, zaterdags	on Tuesdays etc.
vorige/afgelopen zaterdag *etc.*	last Saturday etc.
aanstaande zaterdag *etc.*	next Saturday etc.
in het weekend	at the weekend

Note: 'Next' with **week**, **maand** and **jaar** is **volgend**, but with days of the week it is **aanstaande**. For 'last' **verleden** is only used with **week**, **maand** and **jaar**, but **vorig** can be used with those words as well as with the days of the week. Note the following expressions too: **volgende week zondag** 'Sunday after next', **verleden week zondag** 'Sunday before last'.

's ochtends/'s morgens	in the morning(s)
's middags	in the afternoon(s)
's avonds	in the evening(s)
's nachts	at night
op een avond/dag/middag	one evening/day/afternoon

Note: The **'s** in the above expressions of time is a remnant of the genitive case, which has now died out in Dutch and is only found in fixed expressions. It is an abbreviation of **des** (lit. 'of the'). Note that it is used with only three days of the week. If a sentence starts with an expression with **'s**, the first letter of the following noun is capitalised, e.g.

's Nachts is het hier doodstil.	It is as quiet as can be here at night time.

Seasons

The four seasons are:

de zomer	summer	
de herfst	autumn	(also known as **het najaar**)
de lente	spring	(also known as **het voorjaar**)
de winter	winter	

The definite article must always be used with the seasons, e.g.

Het regent hier in de zomer niet vaak.
It doesn't rain much here in summer.

You can say either **in de zomer/winter/lente/herfst** or in the case of summer and winter, you can also say **'s zomers** and **'s winters**, e.g. **Het regent hier 's zomers niet vaak.**

The expressions **van de zomer/winter/lente/herfst** render either 'this summer/winter', etc. or 'last summer/winter', etc. The tense of the verb always makes the meaning clear, e.g.

Waar gaan jullie van de zomer naartoe?
Where are you going this summer?

Waar ben je van de winter geweest?
Where were you last winter?

Exercise 7

Translate the following:

1 What do you do on Thursdays?

2 Where do you work on Wednesdays?
3 What are you doing next Friday?
4 Where were you last Monday?
5 Where are you going at the weekend?
6 The grass grows so quickly in spring.
7 I'm going to Italy this summer.

Exercise 8

Someone wants to make an appointment with you. This is your schedule. You are hard to catch. Tell him where you will be if he came when he suggests:

Example: Monday   in Utrecht
        **Het spijt me, meneer/mevrouw, maar maandag ben ik
          in Utrecht.**

1 Tuesday   at the university
2 Thursday   in Groningen, in the north of the country
3 Friday   abroad
4 on the weekend   in England
5 next week   in Paris
6 next month   back in the Netherlands

10 Pauline is haar horloge kwijt

Pauline can't find her watch

In this lesson you will learn about:

- past tense of modal verbs and double infinitives
- telling the time
- reflexive verbs
- use of **mezelf** etc. with reflexive verbs
- getting dressed and clothing
- the comparative and superlative of adjectives and adverbs
- how to say 'to like'

Dialogue 1 🎞

Pauline has mislaid her watch

PIET: Heb je je horloge kunnen vinden, Pauline?
PAULINE: Nee, helaas niet. Misschien heb ik het vanochtend bij het zwembad laten liggen.
PIET: Ben je al gaan kijken?
PAULINE: Nee, ik heb vanmorgen niet terug willen gaan[1] want ik had zo veel om te doen.
PIET: Heb je gebeld om te vragen of ze je horloge gevonden hebben?
PAULINE: Nee, ik heb niet durven bellen want ik vind de directeur van het zwembad niet aardig. Wij hebben een keer ruzie gehad.
PIET: Wat belachelijk! Dan bel ik.

PIET: *Have you been able to find your watch, Pauline?*

---

1 The separation of **terug** from **willen** is explained on p. 213.

PAULINE: *No, unfortunately I haven't. Perhaps I left it at the swim-*
          ming pool this morning.
PIET: *Have you been to look?*
PAULINE: *No, I didn't want to go back this morning because I had*
          so much to do.
PIET: *Have you rung to ask if they've found your watch?*
PAULINE: *No, I didn't dare ring because I don't like the manager*
          of the swimming pool. We once had an argument.
PIET: *How ridiculous. I'll ring then.*

Language points

Past tense of modal verbs and double infinitives

The imperfect of modal auxiliary verbs, which were introduced on page 68, is as follows:

kunnen – kon/konden 'could' *or* 'was/were able'
moeten – moest/moesten 'had to'
mogen – mocht/mochten 'was/were allowed to'
willen – wou, wilde/wilden 'wanted to'[2]

Although the perfect tense is more usual than the imperfect in spoken Dutch, the imperfect of these modal verbs is commonly used, as is that of **hebben** and **zijn**:

hebben – had/hadden   zijn – was/waren

But when the above modals are used in the perfect, a grammatical complication arises which you must be acquainted with. These verbs do have a past participle (i.e. **gekund**, **gemoeten**, **gemogen**, **gewild**) but it is not commonly heard. Let's take a sentence in the present tense where the finite verb is a modal verb, and put it into the two past tenses:

present   **Ik kan mijn horloge niet vinden.**
imperfect   **Ik kon mijn horloge niet vinden.**
perfect   **Ik heb mijn horloge niet kunnen vinden.**

The final example translates as 'I haven't been able to find my watch'. Literally translated, this would be *Ik heb mijn horloge niet gekund vinden*, but this is incorrect for the following reason:

---

2 The two singular forms **wou** and **wilde** are completely interchangeable.

in a sentence where a modal verb stands in the perfect tense and is followed by an infinitive (which is nearly always the case as modal verbs are auxiliary verbs, i.e. they support another verb, which is always an infinitive) you must not use the past participle of the modal verb, but its infinitive. This leads to two infinitives at the end of the clause where the first is the past participle of the modal 'in disguise' and the second is a true infinitive. This is known as the double-infinitive rule. It is only on rare occasions, when for stylistic reasons the second infinitive is omitted, that the past participle of the modal is used, e.g.

Heb je het kunnen doen?	Were you able to do it?
Nee, ik heb het niet kunnen doen.	No, I haven't been able to do it.

or

Nee, **ik heb het niet gekund.**	No, I haven't been able to.[3]

This double-infinitive construction is very common in Dutch: first, because of the tendency to relate past events in the perfect tense; second, because of the frequency of modal verbs; and third, because it is not limited to the perfect tense of modals, but is also used with a few other common auxiliary verbs. Take note of the following, for example:

present	**Ik ga kijken.**	I'm going to have a look.
perfect	**Ik ben gaan kijken.**	I went and looked.
present	**Zij komt helpen.**	She's coming to help.
perfect	**Zij is komen helpen.**	She came and helped.
present	**Hij blijft zitten.**	He remains seated.
perfect	**Hij is blijven zitten.**	He remained seated.
present	**Hij hoort/ziet haar weggaan.**	He hears/sees her leave.
perfect	**Hij heeft haar horen/ zien weggaan.**	He heard/saw her leave.

In the first three cases the auxiliary verbs that are actually in the perfect – although what you see is their infinitive, not their past participle – are verbs of motion and thus the finite verb is **zijn**, but this makes no difference to the application of the double-infinitive rule. This is one of the most difficult aspects of Dutch grammar which you will have to learn to master.

---

3 When this form is used, an object **het** is required.

Exercise 1

Put the following sentences into the two past tenses, i.e. first the imperfect and then the perfect. The perfect will require double-infinitive constructions.

1 Pauline moet met de trein naar Den Haag (gaan).
2 De kinderen kunnen vandaag niet buiten spelen.
3 Ze mogen ook niet boven spelen.
4 Piet wil niet naar school (gaan).
5 Ik ga mijn tante bezoeken.
6 Hij komt ons elk jaar met Kerstmis bezoeken.
7 Ik zie hem in de tuin werken.
8 Zij hoort mij altijd binnenkomen.

Telling the time ▮▮

The Dutch use the twelve-hour clock rather than the twenty-four hour one except for bus and train timetables etc.

Hoe laat is het?   What time is it?

Het is tien uur.

Het is vijf over tien.

Het is kwart over tien.

Het is veertien voor half elf.

Het is tien voor half elf.

Het is vijf voor half elf.

Het is half elf.

Het is vijf over half elf.

Het is tien over half elf.

Het is kwart voor elf.

Het is vijf voor elf.

Note 1: From a quarter past the hour the Dutch refer to the hour to come, not the one just past.

Note 2: Railway timetables and the like use the twenty-four-hour clock. Such times are spoken as follows: 13.45 **dertien uur vijfenveertig**, 20.15 **twintig uur vijftien**, 21.20 **éénentwintig uur twintig**.

The expressions **'s ochtends/'s morgens**, **'s middags**, **'s avonds** and **'s nachts** (see also page 131) render 'a.m.' and 'p.m.', i.e. two or three in the morning is **twee/drie uur 's nachts** whereas seven or eight in the morning is **zeven/acht uur 's ochtends**. From about 6.00 p.m. **'s avonds** replaces **'s middags**. The written abbreviations, if the twenty-four-hour clock is not used, are **vm** and **nm** (for **voormiddags** and **namiddags**).

Exercise 2

Answer the following questions by referring to the television programme on p. 139. Write out all times in the answers in words using the twelve-, not the twenty-four-hour clock plus the expressions **'s ochtends**, **'s middags** or **'s avonds**, **'s nachts**. The acronyms given in parentheses after each programme indicate which **omroep** is responsible (see Culture point).

1 Hoeveel keer per dag kun je het NOS-Journaal op Nederland 1 zien? En hoe laat?
2 De EO (de Evangelische Omroep) zendt uit op welk net?
3 Ik heb een lottokaartje gekocht. Wanneer en naar welk net moet ik kijken om uit te vinden of ik iets gewonnen heb?
4 Naar welk programma moet ik kijken als ik iets over Cuba wil leren? Hoe laat is de uitzending en op welk net?
5 's Avonds heb ik geen tijd om naar het journaal te kijken. Ik ben alleen maar geïnteresseerd in de hoofdpunten uit het nieuws en het weerbericht. Hoe laat moet ik kijken en naar welk net?
6 Mijn oom is doof en kan alleen maar Nederland 1 op zijn televisie ontvangen. Wanneer moet hij naar het nieuws kijken?
7 De speelfilm op Nederland 1 is een programma van welke omroep en hoe laat begint hij?

Culture point
The Dutch have a unique broadcasting system. They do not believe in privately owned, commercially run radio and television stations, although some commercial television is now reaching them via satellite. Your radio and television licence is called **het kijk- en luistergeld**. In addition to paying this you subscribe to **de televisiegids**

ZATERDAG TV 14 JANUARI

NEDERLAND 1

15.26 Nws voor slechthorenden (NOS)
15.34 Bugs Bunny, superstar (KRO)
VS 1975. Tekenfilmcompilatie van Larry
Jackson. Compilatie van Bugs Bunny-teken-
films uit de periode 1940-1948, afgewisseld
met korte interviews met de verschillende te-
kenaars van deze stripfiguur. *Zie Etalage.*
17.02 Kijk, de bijbel (KRO/RKK/IKON)
Afl: *De twaalfjarige Jezus. Herh.*
17.07 Studio op stelten (KRO)
Noddy Afl: *Noddy en de aardmannetjes.*
Nijntje Afl: *Assepoester. Herh.*
Medisch Centrum Muis Nederlandse pop-
penserie. Afl: *Slaapwandelen.*
17.32 De confetticlub (AVRO)
1) Captain Cockpit. 2) Klimrekkwizz.
18.25 Boggle (KRO)
**18.53 De legende van de
Bokkerijders** (KRO) ⊕
13-delige Nederlands/Belgische dramaserie.
Afl 13 (slot): *Ontsnapt aan de galg.* Met oa
Lennert Hillege en Eugène Bervoets.
19.21 Waku waku (KRO) ⊕
Dierenquiz olv Rob Fruithof.
20.00 NOS-JOURNAAL ⊚ ⊕
20.24 NOS-Weeroverzicht ⊕
20.30 Wie van de drie (AVRO)
Raadspel. Presentatie: Rob van Hulst.
20.59 Internal affairs ⊚ (AVRO)
VS 1990. Politiethriller van Mike Figgis. Met
oa Richard Gere, Andy Garcia, Nancy Travis
en Laurie Metcalf. Nieuwkomer bij de afde-
ling Internal Affairs van de politie doet onder-
zoek naar corruptie binnen het politie-appa-
raat en stuit op een agent die connecties
heeft in de onderwereld.
22.56 Karel (AVRO)
Talkshow olv Karel van de Graaf.
23.41 Still of the night (AVRO)
VS 1982. Thriller van Robert Benton. Met oa
Meryl Streep, Roy Scheider en Jessica Tan-
dy. Patiënt van een psychiater valt dood
neer op straat. De politie verdenkt de minna-
res van het slachtoffer, die op 18-jarige leef-
tijd ook betrokken was bij de dood van haar
vader. De psychiater wordt echter verliefd op
de vrouw en gaat er met haar vandoor.
1.08-1.13 NOS-JOURNAAL ⊚

NEDERLAND 2

16.31 Als je durft (EO)
Afl 2: *Schepping of evolutie?*
16.58 Danger bay (EO)
Canadese jeugdserie. Afl: *Stormachtig.*
17.23 Deze is voor jou (EO)
Documentaire serie. Afl 3: *Trouwen.* Mira en
Marc, studenten in resp. Utrecht en Amsterdam, gaan niet samenwonen, maar trouwen.
Uit (christelijke) overtuiging.
17.49 Clip (EO)
17.58 2 Vandaag (EO/TROS/VOO) ⊕
  18.00 NOS-JOURNAAL ⊚
  18.15 Actualiteiten (NOS/EO/TROS/VOO)
  18.40 Sportjournaal (NOS)
  18.48 Lottotrekking (NOS)
  **18.51 De hoofdpunten uit het nieuws en
  weerbericht** (NOS)
18.59 Op weg naar Avonlea (EO)
Canadese serie. Afl: *De vrijwillige brand-
weer.* Met oa Jackie Burrough.
19.49 Overal en nergens (EO)
Vandaag: *Het drama van Guantanamo Bay.*
Reportage over Cubaanse bootvluchtelingen
in het interneringskamp op de Amerikaanse
marinebasis Guantanamo Bay, Cuba. Sa-
menstelling/regie: Jan van den Bosch.
20.18 Dr. Quinn, medicine woman (EO)
Amerikaanse serie. Afl 2: *De epidemie.*
21.06 AMC-tv (EO)
26-delige documentaire serie over het Aca-
demisch Medisch Centrum in Amsterdam.
Aandacht voor de behandelpraktijk en de
wetenschappelijke aspecten van het 'medisch bedrijf'. Afl 1. Een patiënt die lijdt aan
de ziekte van Parkinson ondergaat geavan-
ceerde neurochirurgische ingreep.
21.40 Tijdsein (EO)
22.13 De verandering (EO)
Feike ter Velde praat met ex-Jehova-getuige
Juno Sanchez.
22.39 Nederland zingt (EO)
23.05 Omega (EO)
6-delige serie over 'de bovennatuurlijke wer-
kelijkheid'. Afl 3: *Goddelijke genezing.*
23.54 Lied (EO)
23.59 NOS-JOURNAAL (NOS)
0.04-0.09 Nws voor slechthorenden (NOS)

(radio and television programme magazine) of one of the ten or so broadcasting associations (**een omroep**) which most closely corresponds to your philosophy of life. Many have a religious, and thus also a political, bent (some political parties have a religious affiliation). Or alternatively you nominate the **omroep** whose taste in radio and television programmes is in accordance with your own. **Omroepen** are known by acronyms, e.g. **de AVRO, de EO, de KRO, de NCRV, de TROS, de VPRO** and **de VARA** – most people are no longer aware of what these letters stand for. Each **omroep** is allotted a share of the **kijk- en luistergeld** and transmission time in accordance with the proportion of the population that subscribes to its magazine. This is considered one of the democratic pillars of Dutch society. On the down side of things, it does tend to lead to cheap programming as the various **omroepen** either don't have enough money to acquire or make expensive programmes, or are more interested in informing the people of their point of view than in entertaining them.

All broadcasting is national: radio is based in Hilversum and television in Bussum, both towns to the north of Utrecht. The names of Hilversum and Bussum are synonymous with radio and television respectively.

Dialogue 2 🔲

Piet has just arrived at school and meets a colleague

COLLEGA:	Morgen, Piet. Jij hebt je niet geschoren, zeg!
PIET:	Nee, dat klopt. Ik heb me verslapen en ik had geen tijd om me te scheren.
COLLEGA:	Ik heb me ook moeten haasten maar ik heb me wel kunnen scheren.
PIET:	Hoe laat ben jij dan opgestaan?
COLLEGA:	Ik kan het me niet meer herinneren – het was bij ons een gekkenhuis vanochtend.

COLLEAGUE:	*Morning, Piet. I say, you haven't shaved.*
PIET:	*No, that's right. I overslept and I didn't have any time to shave.*
COLLEAGUE:	*I had to hurry too but I was able to shave.*
PIET:	*What time did you get up then?*
COLLEAGUE:	*I can't remember any more – it was a madhouse at our place this morning.*

Language points

Reflexive verbs

A reflexive verb: I *scratched myself.*

The concept of reflexive verbs is a difficult one to grasp. They exist in English too but there are many more of them in Dutch and they contain several pitfalls for the learner.

Take a verb like **krabben** 'to scratch'. If you scratch someone or something, there is no problem, e.g.

Ik krab mijn rug.	I'm scratching my back.
Ik heb de hond z'n rug gekrabd.	I scratched the dog's back.

But the verb 'to scratch oneself' you learn in the form **zich krabben** and you conjugate it as follows:

ik krab me	I scratch myself
jij krabt je	you scratch yourself
u krabt u/zich	you scratch yourself
hij krabt zich	he scratches himself
zij krabt zich	she scratches herself
het krabt zich	it scratches itself
wij krabben ons	we scratch ourselves
jullie krabben je	you scratch yourselves
zij krabben zich	they scratch themselves

The **me**, **je**, **zich**, etc. are called reflexive pronouns and are used where the doer of the verb does the action of the verb to him- or herself, i.e. the action reflects back on the subject of the verb.

Note that **u** is used together with either **u** or **zich**, but it is safer to stick to **zich**, which is certainly more common when inversion takes place, e.g.

Heeft u zich niet geschoren?   Haven't you shaved?

A verb like **scheren** in dialogue 2 is similar to **krabben**, but unlike English, if you are not shaving someone else, you have to say in Dutch that you are shaving yourself, i.e. whereas we can say 'I didn't shave today', the Dutch must express this as **Ik heb me vandaag niet geschoren** utilising the reflexive pronoun **me**. Similarly, 'He hasn't washed for more than a week' is **Hij heeft zich al langer dan een week niet gewassen**.

To this point the concept, although a little different from English, is not hard to grasp. There are, however, many reflexive verbs in Dutch whose reflexivity simply has to be accepted as part of the idiom of the language. For example, the verb 'to remember' is **zich herinneren**, e.g.

Ik kan me zijn naam niet herinneren.
I can't remember his name.

Similarly, 'to oversleep' is **zich verslapen** and 'to hurry' is **zich haasten**, e.g.

Piet heeft zich vanochtend verslapen.
Piet overslept this morning.

Piet moest zich haasten.   Piet had to hurry.

The reflexive pronoun always stands after the finite verb whether that verb is the reflexive verb itself (e.g. **Hij versliep zich**) or an auxiliary verb as in the previous two examples.

Verbs like **zich herinneren**, **zich verslapen** and **zich haasten** are always reflexive and are given in the vocabulary at the back of the book as follows:

herinneren (zich)   'to remember'

If you have a Dutch–English dictionary, it is sure to use a symbol (most usually 'vr.') to indicate whether a verb is reflexive or not.

Verbs like **scheren** and **wassen** are not true reflexive verbs because their actions can be performed by the subject on someone or something else, but when they are performed on the subject, such verbs are said to be used reflexively.

Exercise 3

Translate the following sentences, which all contain a reflexive verb in Dutch, using the reflexive verbs given in parentheses. Use the perfect tense where the verbs are in the past.

1 The children are getting bored. (**zich vervelen**)
2 Marius behaved very badly. (**zich gedragen**)
3 The children must behave themselves. (**zich gedragen**)
4 You are mistaken. (**zich vergissen**) (use **u**)
5 I am ashamed. (**zich schamen**)
6 The children couldn't behave themselves. (**zich gedragen**)
7 Do you remember where he lives? (**zich herinneren**)
8 We are looking forward to the trip. (**zich verheugen op**)

9 He introduced himself. (**zich voorstellen**)

Use of mezelf etc. with reflexive verbs

The reflexive pronouns given above also occur with the addition of **-zelf**, e.g. **mezelf, jezelf, zichzelf, onszelf**, etc. Despite the similarity with English 'myself', 'yourself', etc. Dutch only uses these forms where a certain emphasis is required, i.e. where one needs to stress that the action is being performed on the doer of the verb, e.g.

Piet scheerde zijn vader, want die was ziek, en toen scheerde hij zichzelf.
Piet shaved his father, for he was sick, and then he shaved himself.

Pauline heeft geen tijd gehad om zichzelf te wassen want ze heeft de kinderen moeten wassen.
Pauline hasn't had time to wash because she had to wash the kids.

Note how 'myself' etc. is expressed when it is not part of a reflexive verb:

Ik heb het zelf moeten doen.   I had to do it myself.
Hij verft het huis zelf.   He's painting the house himself.

Getting dressed and clothing

Getting dressed, undressed and changed are expressed by the following three reflexive verbs: **zich aankleden, zich uitkleden, zich omkleden**, e.g.

Pauline kleedt eerst Charlotte aan en dan kleedt ze zichzelf aan.
Pauline first dresses Charlotte and then she dresses herself.

Marius heeft zich uitgekleed.   Marius (has) got undressed.
Piet kleedt/kleedde zich om.   Piet gets/got changed.

These verbs must not be confused with **aantrekken** 'to put on' and **uittrekken** 'to take off', which are not reflexive verbs, e.g.

Hij trekt zijn nieuwe schoenen aan.   He's putting on his new shoes.
Zij heeft haar jurk uitgetrokken.   She took off her dress.

Although 'she changed' is expressed by **zich omkleden**, 'She changed her dress' is **Ze heeft een andere jurk aangetrokken**.

Handy expressions associated with clothing:

aanpassen	to try on
passen	to fit
Welke maat heeft u/heb jij?	What size are you?
Ik heb/draag maat 36.	I take a size 36.
Deze broek is te strak.	These pants are too tight.[3]
Hij zit goed.	They fit nicely.
Hij staat u/je goed.	They suit you.
Hij staat u/je niet goed.	They don't suit you.

Exercise 4

Look up the Dutch words for the following items of apparel (or parts of them) and fill them in vertically from left to right. If you get them all right, the name of a Dutch city will appear across the middle. Of which province is it the capital city?

scarf collar pullover coat shoelace belt
glove hat tie fly bra

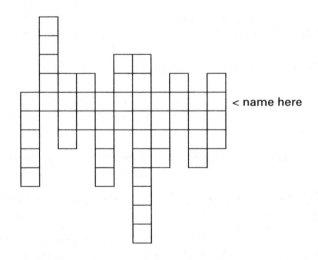

< name here

---

3 Note that 'pants' are expressed by a singular in Dutch. There are several nouns which are plural in English but singular in Dutch: **de groente** 'vegetables', **de bril** 'glasses', **de tang** 'tongs', **de schaar** 'scissors', **de vakantie** 'holidays' and even **Nederland** 'the Netherlands'.

Reading text 🔲

Here's a passage about a part of the Netherlands where local pride runs very high. It includes some useful expressions you need to know.

Vocabulary

gebruikelijk	common
trots op	proud of
net zoals	just like
bijvoorbeeld (bv.)	for example (e.g.)
in het Nederlands	in Dutch
d.w.z. (< **dat wil zeggen**)	i.e. (that is to say)

Friesland

Friesland ligt in het noorden van Nederland. De inwoners van die provincie noemen zich Friezen – een mannelijke inwoner heet een Fries en een vrouwelijke een Friezin. Er zijn omtrent 500 000 Friezen[4] in Nederland en De Vries (een oude spelling) is een van de gebruikelijkste familienamen. Friezen spreken allemaal Nederlands maar daarnaast nog een andere taal, het Fries, waar ze erg trots op zijn. Net zoals het Nederlands, kent het Fries ook dialecten – op de Friese eilanden spreekt men bijvoorbeeld anders dan op het vasteland. Het Fries van de steden (het Stadsfries) is anders dan dat van het platteland. Men ziet in Friesland tegenwoordig veel tweetalige borden, d.w.z. borden in het Nederlands en in het Fries.

Exercise 5

Give full-sentence answers to the following questions.

1 Waar spreekt men Fries?
2 Hoe noemen zich de inwoners van de provincie Friesland?[5]
3 Hoeveel Friezen zijn er in Nederland?
4 In welke talen zijn veel borden in Friesland?

---

4 An exact figure is difficult to come by but in 1990 the population of Friesland numbered 599,070, most of whom are Frisian-speaking.
5 Note that Dutch uses **hoe** here where English uses *what*. Compare **Hoe heet hij?** 'What is his name?' and **Hoe is uw naam?** 'What is your name?'

Dialogue 3 🔲

Piet and Pauline are planning their summer holidays

PIET: Waar zullen we van de zomer met vakantie naartoe gaan?
PAULINE: Kunnen we niet weer naar Italië zoals vorig jaar?
PIET: Ik denk het niet. We kunnen het ons niet veroorloven.[6] We zijn helaas blut.
PAULINE: Zullen we dan naar Friesland gaan? Dat kan niet te duur zijn.
PIET: Wat een goed idee! Dat is beslist betaalbaar.
PAULINE: We kunnen ergens aan zee kamperen en elke dag gaan zwemmen.
PIET: Dat hangt natuurlijk van het weer af maar het lijkt me heerlijk. Dat doen we dan. Ik verheug me al op de vakantie.

PIET: *Where will we go for our holidays this summer?*
PAULINE: *Can't we go to Italy again like last year?*
PIET: *I don't think so. We can't afford it. We're broke unfortunately.*
PAULINE: *Shall we go to Friesland then? That can't be too expensive.*
PIET: *What a good idea. That is definitely affordable.*
PAULINE: *We can camp somewhere near the sea and go swimming every day.*
PIET: *That depends on the weather of course but it sounds great to me. That's what we'll do then. I'm already looking forward to the holidays.*

Language points

The comparative and superlative of adjectives and adverbs

The comparative of an adjective: This house is *larger.* The *larger* house.

---

6 It was stated on page 142 that the reflexive pronoun always comes immediately after the finite verb. The only exception to this is when the sentence contains a **het** as an object. Compare **Ik kan het me niet herinneren** and **Ik kan me zijn adres niet herinneren**.

The comparative of an adverb: He speaks *more clearly.*
The superlative of an adjective: The *largest* house.
The superlative of an adverb: He speaks (*the*) *clearest.*

Generally speaking, English distinguishes between adjectives and adverbs, e.g. *He is slow* (adjective) and *He speaks slowly* (adverb, i.e. describing not him, but how he speaks). This distinction is not made in Dutch:

Hij is langzaam.   Hij spreekt langzaam.

Forming the comparative and superlative of the adjective is similar in both languages:

groot 'large'	**groter** 'larger'	**grootst** 'largest'
langzaam 'slow'	**langzamer** 'slower'	**langzaamst** 'slowest'
dik 'fat'	**dikker** 'fatter'	**dikst** 'fattest'
doof 'deaf'	**dover** 'deafer'	**doofst** 'deafest'
vies 'dirty'	**viezer** 'dirtier'	**viest** 'dirtiest'

As **dik**, **doof** and **vies** illustrate, the spelling changes we have been seeing from the beginning are applied when the **-er** ending is added to the root form.

Note what happens to those that end in **-r**:

duur 'expensive'	**duurder** 'more expensive'	**duurst** 'most expensive'
lekker 'delicious'	**lekkerder** 'more delicious'	**lekkerst** 'most delicious'

The previous examples illustrate a basic difference between English and Dutch. In English there is a point (usually more than two syllables) where it is no longer possible simply to add *-er* and *-st* to the adjective and where we resort to *more* and *most* to express the comparative and superlative. This is not the case in Dutch, where those endings are applied whatever the length of the adjective, e.g.

interessant 'interesting'	**interessanter**	**interessantst**
belangrijk 'important'	**belangrijker**	**belangrijkst**

When these comparative and superlative forms with their **-er** and **-st** endings stand in front of a noun, they are subject to the usual rules governing the inflection of adjectives, i.e. they too take an **-e** ending according to the rules on page 87, e.g.

een grotere auto	a larger car
een duurdere vakantie	a more expensive vacation

een rijkere man	a richer man
de grootste auto	the largest car
de duurste vakantie	the most expensive vacation
de rijkste man	the richest man

Note: The following English comparative requires a superlative in Dutch:

Hij is de kleinste van de twee.	He is the smaller of the two.
De kleinste jongen.	The smaller boy.

Handy expressions associated with comparatives:

groter/kleiner/langer dan	bigger/smaller/taller than
niet zo groot/klein/lang als	not as big/small/tall as
net zo groot/klein/lang als	just as big/small/tall as
even groot/klein/lang als	just as big/small/tall as

Ik ben net zo lang als mijn vader maar goddank niet zo dik als hij.
I am just as tall as my father but not, thank God, as fat as he.

Mijn moeder is nog langer dan mijn vader, gek genoeg, en ze is helaas nog dikker dan hij.
My mother is even taller than my father, funnily enough, and she is unfortunately even fatter than he.[7]

The comparative of the adverb is easy because in Dutch it does not differ from that of the adjective, e.g.

Ik rij langzamer dan jij.	I drive more slowly than you.
Jij rijdt harder dan ik.	You drive faster than me.

The superlative of the adverb is formed by adding **-st(e)** to the root form and putting **het** before it, e.g. **het langzaamst(e)** '(the) slowest', **het hardst(e)** '(the) fastest'. 'The best singer' and 'Who is the best?' (i.e. the superlative of the adjective) are simply **de beste zanger** and **Wie is de beste?**, but 'Who sang (the) best' (i.e. the superlative of the adverb) is **Wie heeft het best(e) gezongen?** The final **-e** here is always optional. You can usually ascertain whether you are dealing with the superlative of the adverb rather than that of the adjective by asking yourself if 'the' can be omitted – if so, you are dealing with the superlative of the adverb, e.g.

---

7 Note that the following extremely common 'error' in English must not be applied to Dutch:

Zij is mooier dan ik.	'She's prettier than me (= I).'
Jij bent mooier dan zij.	'You're prettier than her (= she).'

Ik reed het hardst   I was driving (the) fastest.
Wanneer zijn deze bloemen het mooist?
When are these flowers (the) prettiest?

Exercise 6

Contradict these statements as illustrated in the examples:

Example: De Mont Blanc is net zo hoog als de Everest.
              Nee, de Everest is hoger dan de Mont Blanc.
              Nee, de Mont Blanc is niet zo hoog als de Everest.

1 Nederland is net zo warm als Italië.
2 België heeft net zo veel inwoners als Duitsland.
3 Dieren zijn even intelligent als mensen.
4 De Noordzee is groter dan de Atlantische Oceaan.
5 Een Amerikaanse dollar is meer waard dan een Engels pond.

Exercise 7

Translate the following sentences.

1 These bananas are riper than those.
2 These are the most delicious apples.
3 When are potatoes (the) dearest?
4 These pears are just as dear as those.
5 The boys are just as well behaved (**braaf**) as the girls.
6 He spoke even louder (**hard**) but not as loudly as she.
7 This is the most interesting building in the city.
8 He was more successful (**succesvol**) than me.
9 My uncle is the poorer of the two.

How to say 'to like'

There are several ways of expressing liking in Dutch depending on what it is you like. One very handy way is to use **vinden** with an appropriate adjective, e.g.

Ik vind hem erg aardig.   I really like him. (people)
Ik vind dit niet lekker.   I don't like this. (food)
Ik heb de film erg leuk   I liked the film a lot. (anything)
   gevonden.

Smaken (lit. 'to taste', see page 112) can also express 'to like' with reference to food, but the person doing the liking is in the object form, e.g.

Het vlees smaakt mij niet.	I don't like the meat.
Heeft het jou gesmaakt?	Did you like it?

Houden van, which is actually the verb 'to love', can also express 'to like', but only with reference to food and things, not people, e.g.

Ik hou van haar.	I love her.
Hou je van ananas?	Do you like pineapple?
Hij houdt helemaal niet van Amsterdam.	He doesn't like A. at all.[8]

Bevallen (lit. 'to please'), where the person doing the liking is in the object form as with **smaken**, is another common way of expressing liking, but it is not used for food, e.g.

Hij bevalt me niet.	I don't like him.
Het is haar goed bevallen in Zweden.	She liked Sweden a lot.

Note that **bevallen** takes **zijn** in the perfect.

When you like to do something, as opposed to liking a person or thing, you express this with **graag** (lit. 'gladly)' plus the appropriate verb, e.g.

's Avonds kijken we graag televisie.	We like watching TV in the evenings.
Ik leer heel graag Nederlands.	I like learning Dutch.
Hij woont graag in Den Haag.	He likes living in The Hague.

Graag eten is another way of saying 'to like food', e.g.

Ik eet graag erwtensoep.	I like pea soup.

Because **graag** is an adverb, it has a comparative and a superlative form, **liever** and **het liefst**. These words are used in combination with verbs to express 'to prefer doing something' and 'to like doing something most of all' respectively, e.g.

---

8 Another common idiom meaning 'to dislike' is **een hekel hebben aan**, e.g. **Hij heeft een hekel aan Amsterdam/zijn zwager** 'He doesn't like Amsterdam/his brother-in-law'.

Ik lees graag maar ik brei liever.
I like reading/to read but I prefer knitting/to knit.

Ik leer het liefst vreemde talen.
I like learning foreign languages most of all.

Clothing

de kleren	clothes
het overhemd	shirt
de broek	trousers, pants
de riem	belt
de zak	pocket
het pak	suit
de trui	jumper, pullover
de jurk	dress
de rok	skirt
de shoen	shoe
de sok	sock
de (strop)das	tie
de muts	cap
het T-shirt	T-shirt
de spijkerbroek	jeans
het colbert	jacket, suit coat
het katoen	cotton
de wol	wool
de laars (pl. laarzen)	boot
de (nylon)kous	stocking
de zakdoek	handkerchief
de sjaal	scarf
de handschoen	glove
de hoed	hat
de handtas	handbag
de portefeuille	wallet

11 Een retourtje Maastricht, alstublieft

A return ticket to Maastricht, please

> **In this lesson you will learn about:**
>
> - expressions for travelling by train
> - transitive and intransitive verbs
> - relative pronouns
> - swearwords and exclamations
> - meanings of the verb **laten**
> - some variations of word order

Dialogue 1 ▣

Pauline is buying a train ticket to Maastricht

PAULINE: Een retourtje Maastricht, alstublieft, maar ik wil pas morgen terugkomen.

LOKETBEDIENDE: Een dagretour kost ƒ60, mevrouw. U kunt het beste morgen een enkele reis kopen om terug te komen. Een enkele reis kost ƒ35.

PAULINE: Goed, hoor. Geeft u me dan een enkele reis Maastricht. Hoe laat gaat de Intercity?

LOKETBEDIENDE: Op het hele en op het halve uur.

PAULINE: Prima, dan kan ik al over tien minuten vertrekken.

LOKETBEDIENDE: Helaas niet, want de trein van half negen heeft een kwartier vertraging.

PAULINE: Jeetje, en ik heb haast. Moet ik ergens overstappen?

LOKETBEDIENDE: Nee, hoor. De Intercity rijdt rechtstreeks naar Maastricht en stopt alleen maar in Eindhoven.

Hij vertrekt van spoor tien en komt om elf uur in Maastricht aan.

PAULINE: *A return to Maastricht, please, but I don't want to come back till tomorrow.*

TICKET CLERK: *A day return costs f60, madam. Otherwise you simply buy a one-way ticket tomorrow to return. A one-way ticket costs f35.*

PAULINE: *Fine, then give me a one-way to Maastricht. What time does the Intercity depart?*

TICKET CLERK: *On the hour and at half past the hour.*

PAULINE: *Great, then I can leave in ten minutes' time.*

TICKET CLERK: *Unfortunately not as the half past eight train is running a quarter of an hour late.*

PAULINE: *Oh Lord, I'm in a hurry. Do I have to change trains anywhere?*

TICKET CLERK: *No, the Intercity goes directly to Maastricht and only stops in Eindhoven. It leaves from platform ten and arrives in Maastricht at eleven o'clock.*

Language points

Words and phrases for travelling by train in the Netherlands

het kaartje	the ticket
de retour/het retourtje	the return (ticket)
vertrekken	to depart, leave
aankomen	to arrive
het spoor	the line, platform[1]
het perron	the platform
op tijd	on time
vertraagd	delayed
het spoorboekje	railway timetable book
tien minuten vertraging	ten minutes' delay, ten minutes late
de zitplaats	seat (only in a train, bus or theatre)
reserveren	to book
overstappen	to change (trains, buses, trams)
instappen	to get in
uitstappen	to get out
de (niet-)roker-coupé	the (non-)smoking compartment

```
┌─────────────────────┐   Nederlandse Spoorwegen | ⧖
│                     │
│                     │
└─────────────────────┘
    Geldig op/van      Geldig tot en met              Klasse
    04.04.94                                            2
    Dagretour
H   UTRECHT CS                        331      4866  T
    NIJMEGEN
    Via
    Afgiftepunt      Reductie      Nummer         Prijs
    897.33            40%          867072         19  75
    Bijz.
         MA T/M VR NIET GELDIG VAN 0U TOT 9U
                                            PL 873531
```

Notes on word usage: 'to go by train/bus/tram/car' is expressed by **met de trein/bus/tram/auto gaan**. 'To go by bicycle' is both **met** and **op de fiets gaan**.

The three verbs **overstappen**, **instappen** and **uitstappen** all take **zijn** in the perfect, e.g. **Ik ben in Eindhoven overgestapt** 'I changed in Eindhoven'. **Overstappen** expresses to change trains, buses, etc. – the mode of transport is not mentioned but is implied by the context.

Although you learn **instappen** and **uitstappen** as separable verbs, when the mode of transport is mentioned, they behave as if you are dealing with **stappen in/uit**, e.g. **Ik ben ingestapt** 'I got in', **Ik ben in de trein gestapt** 'I got into the train'.

Culture point

When it comes to public transport (**het openbaar vervoer**) the Dutch system can't be beaten. It's reliable and fast. A delay of five minutes in the arrival or departure of a train in the Netherlands is enough to give the Dutch travelling public heart failure. It simply must not be allowed to occur and very seldom does. **De NS (de Nederlandse Spoorwegen** 'Dutch Railways') pride themselves on their efficiency. If the train from Rome or Paris is late, the fault is unlikely to lie at their end of the track!

The bus depot for onward travel is always at or near the station. Both **stadsbussen** for travel within the town you have arrived in and **streekbussen (het streekvervoer** 'regional transport') leave from the same spot.

---

1 Although **het spoor** literally means 'the rails', the Dutch refer to trains leaving from **spoor 1**, **spoor 2**, etc. whereas the passengers stand on **het perron**. Thus only in the sense that a train leaves from platform 1 can **spoor** translate as 'platform'.

> Beware: a return ticket for train travel within the Netherlands must be used on the day of purchase; only international returns remain valid beyond that day. The larger airline-style ticket you get when travelling by train outside the country, or by plane, is called **het ticket**; the smaller, everyday ticket you get for internal travel or in a bus is called **het kaartje**.

Exercise 1

What follows is a page from **het spoorboekje**. The Dutch are masters at interpreting the hieroglyphics of this ubiquitous publication, which they read avidly on trains and buses. This is the timetable for the bus from Den Helder, in the north or North Holland (**de kop van Noorholland**) to the station (Havenhoofd) of the ferry which takes you across to the island of Texel,[2] 't Horntje being the name of the ferry station on the island. The first horizontal line is the time of departure (**de vertrektijd**) and the one beneath it is the time of arrival (**de aankomsttijd**). See if you can answer the following questions by deciphering the cryptic information given.

🚌 / ⛴ / **Den Helder** / **Texel**

112 a   Stadsdienst Den Helder (🚌 3)/TESO (⛴)

Den Helder	🚌	6 16	🚌	7 16	8 16	9 16	10 16	11 16	12 16	13 16	14 16	15 16
Den Helder, Havenhoofd **A**	❶	6 22	❷	7 22	8 22	9 22	10 22	11 22	12 22	13 22	14 22	15 22
Den Helder, Havenhoofd ⛴	❶	6 35	❷	7 35	8 35	9 35	10 35	11 35	12 35	13 35	14 35	15 35
Texel, 't Horntje ⛴ **A**	❶	6 55	❷	7 55	8 55	9 55	10 55	11 55	12 55	13 55	14 55	15 55

> vervolg >

Den Helder	16 16	17 16	18 16	19 16	20 16	❸ 21 16	
Den Helder, Havenhoofd **A**	16 22	17 22	18 22	19 22	20 22	❸ 21 22	
Den Helder, Havenhoofd ⛴	16 35	17 35	18 35	19 35	20 35	❸ 21 35	
Texel, 't Horntje ⛴ **A**	16 55	17 55	18 55	19 55	20 55	❸ 21 55	< einde <

❶ niet op zon- en feestdagen en niet op 30 apr en 25 mei

❷ van 29 mei – 24 sep en van 24 apr – 27 mei dagelijks; van 25 sep – 23 apr, echter niet op zon- en feestdagen
❸ niet op 31 dec

---

2 Usually pronounced **Tessel** but those with a Frisian orientation may pronounce the **x** as an **x**.

1 Ik wil op koninginnedag (30 april) naar Texel. Wanneer kan ik dus niét vertrekken?
2 Ik wil op 31 december zo laat mogelijk naar Texel gaan. Hoe laat vertrekt de boot vanuit Havenhoofd?
3 Ik moet om 12.00 uur een vriend op Texel ontmoeten en ik wil zo laat mogelijk vertrekken. Hoe laat gaat de bus van Den Helder?

Transitive and intransitive verbs

If a verb is used with an object it is said to be transitive; and if it can't take an object, it is intransitive. English is often not as fussy about the distinction as Dutch is. The verb **vertrekken** in dialogue 1 is a good example of the concept. A good Dutch–English dictionary will use a symbol (usually 'vi.') to indicate that this is not a transitive verb ('vt.'). This means that although **vertrekken** can be used to render 'The train left at 10.00' (**De trein is om tien uur vertrokken**), it is not the correct word in 'He left the house at 10.00', which contains an object, 'the house'. In this case you say **Hij heeft het huis om tien uur verlaten**. You must be on the lookout for this distinction when learning vocabulary – take note of the symbols your dictionary uses to help you choose the right word. Here are some more intransitive/transitive couplets like **vertrekken/ verlaten**:

branden/verbranden 'to burn'
Dit papier brandt niet makkelijk. This paper doesn't burn easily.
Ik heb het verbrand. I burnt it.

smaken/proeven 'to taste'
Deze appel smaakt heerlijk. This apple tastes delicious.
Proef deze appel. Taste this apple.

Note that all verbs that take **zijn** in the perfect are intransitive, and all transitive verbs take **hebben**, but many intransitive verbs also take **hebben**:

Hij is thuisgekomen. He came home. (vi.)
Hij is overleden. He has passed away. (vi.)
Ik heb het in de stad gekocht. I bought it in town. (vt.)
Wij hebben heel hard gelachen. We laughed heartily. (vi.)

Dialogue 2 ▣

Pauline is angry with Marius

PAULINE: Verdorie! Marius, heb jij de koekjes die ik pas vanochtend gekocht heb, al opgegeten?[3]

MARIUS: Ikke? Nee, hoor!

PAULINE: En de frisdrank die in de kast naast het aanrecht stond. Heb je die opgedronken? En het ijs dat in het vriesvak zat?

MARIUS: Ik niet, hoor! Waarom geef je mij altijd de schuld?

PAULINE: Omdat jij het altijd bent die zulke dingen doet zonder eerst te vragen of het mag.

PAULINE: *Oh damn! Marius, did you eat the biscuits I bought only this morning?*

MARIUS: *Who, me? No, I didn't.*

PAULINE: *And the soft drink that was in the cupboard next to the sink. Did you drink that? And the icecream that was in the freezer?*

MARIUS: *Not me! Why do you always blame me?*

PAULINE: *Because it is always you who does such things without first asking if it's alright.*

Language points

Relative pronouns

Relative pronouns: The biscuits *that* were in the cupboard.
                         The man *who* lives next door.

In English there is a range of words that act as relative pronouns. In the first example above we can use either *which* or *that* and in the sentence *The man whom I met in town yesterday is coming here tonight*, *whom* could be replaced by *who* or *that* or simply omitted. The situation in Dutch is much simpler. The Dutch say 'that' in all cases and as there are two words for 'that', **die** or **dat** (see page 80), you have to be sure you choose the right one. **Die** is used when the noun that precedes, and to which it relates, is either

---

3 **Opgegeten** and **opgedronken**, rather than simply **gegeten** and **gedronken**, express that the items have been totally consumed.

common gender or plural and **dat** is used when that noun is neuter singular. In addition, **die** and **dat** as relative pronouns send the finite verb in their clause to the end of that clause and in so doing resemble subordinating conjunctions:

De man die hiernaast woont is erg rijk.
The man who lives next door is very rich.

De tafel die ik gekocht heb is erg mooi.
The table I bought is very nice.

De stoelen die hij geverfd heeft zijn lelijk.
The chairs he painted are ugly.

De kinderen die je hier ziet spelen, wonen hiernaast.
The kids (that) you see playing here live next door.

Het kind dat in de tuin speelt is mijn neef.
The child that is playing in the garden is my nephew.

Note 1: If a comma is used at all between the clauses, and one is not necessary if the sentence as a whole is short, you place one at the end of the relative clause, not before it, e.g.
Hij heeft de koekjes die ze pas vanochtend gekocht heeft, al opgegeten.
He's already eaten the biscuits which she bought only this morning.

Note 2: Whereas in English the relative and the noun it relates back to stand side by side, this does not have to be the case in Dutch, e.g.
Hij heeft de koekjes die ze pas vanochtend gekocht heeft, al opgegeten.
Hij heeft de koekjes al opgegeten die ze pas vanochtend gekocht heeft.
Ik heb de vaas die ze me cadeau gegeven heeft, weggegeven.
Ik heb de vaas weggegeven die ze me cadeau gegeven heeft.
I've given away the vase (that/which) she gave me as a present.

Exercise 2

Fill in **die** or **dat**.

1 De trein ___ later vertrekt, komt om 9.00 uur in Amsterdam aan.
2 Waar is het kaartje ___ je net gekocht hebt?
3 De tickets ___ hier liggen zijn voor de reis naar België.
4 Piet is iemand ___ iedereen aardig vindt.
5 De mensen ___ naast ons wonen, komen uit Hongarije.
6 Het koekje ___ je in je mond hebt, is niet vers.

Exercise 3

Join the following sentences with **die** or **dat** putting the verb in the relative clause at the end.

Example: Mijn opa is erg oud. Hij woont in Den Haag.
Mijn opa die in Den Haag woont, is erg oud.

1 De auto is rood. Hij heeft de auto gisteren gekocht.
2 De mevrouw is erg aardig. Zij was net hier.
3 Het boek is erg interessant. Jij hebt het aan mij cadeau gegeven.
4 Het kind is stout. Het kind woont hiernaast.
5 De schrijfmachine is stuk. Jij hebt hem aan haar verkocht.

Swearwords and exclamations

O, god!	Oh, Lord
(God/pot) verdorie!	Oh, gee/Damn!
(God) verdikkeme!	Oh, gee/Damn!
Godverdikkie!	Oh, gee/Damn!
Godverdomme!	Bugger/Bloody hell!
Gedverdemme/Jasses!	Oh, yuck!
O, jee!	Blimey/Gee/Lord!
Goeie hemel!	Good heavens!
Stommerd/sufferd!	Idiot!
Hou je mond!	Shut up!
Onzin	Nonsense/Rubbish!
Schei uit/hou op!	Stop it/Leave off!

The most common strong curse in Dutch is **godverdomme**, which you must not use in polite company. All the others given above are quite innocuous; **pot**, for example, is a euphemism for **god** but using **god!** on its own as an exclamation is exceedingly common in Dutch and offends nobody. Note that **gedverdemme**, although seemingly a thinly disguised variant of **godverdomme**, has quite a different meaning.

Use of laten with infinitives

Laten has several meanings in Dutch and is a very important verb. On page 96 you saw it being used to render 'let's'. It can also mean 'to leave', e.g. **Ik heb mijn portemonnaie thuis gelaten** 'I've left my purse at home'. In addition, it is commonly used as an auxiliary verb with infinitives, e.g. **laten liggen** 'to leave (behind)', **laten vallen** 'to drop', **laten zien** 'to show', e.g. **Laat de koffiepot alsjeblieft niet vallen** 'Please don't drop the coffee-pot'. In such combinations it occurs in double-infinitive constructions (see page 134) when used in the perfect tense, e.g.

Ik heb mijn geld ergens laten liggen.
I've left my money somewhere.

Zij heeft de kom toch laten vallen.
She dropped the bowl after all.

Hij heeft haar zijn horloge laten zien.
He showed her his watch.

But over and above this, **laten** is the auxiliary verb you require when you '*have* someone do something', i.e. in Dutch you *let* someone do it, e.g.

Ze laat haar man de afwas doen.
She has her husband do the washing-up.

Ik moet mijn schoenen laten repareren.
I must have my shoes repaired.

Ze heeft haar huis laten verven.
She's had her house painted.

Note the order of verbs when you put a sentence like **Ik moet mijn schoenen laten repareren** into the perfect and end up with four verbs, i.e. a finite verb in second position and *three* infinitives at the end:

Ik heb mijn schoenen moeten laten repareren.
I had to have my shoes repaired.

Exercise 4

Put all the following **laten** sentences into the perfect tense.

Example: Ik liet het boek vallen.
Ik heb het boek laten vallen.

1 Charlotte laat Marius haar nieuwe pop zien.
2 Ik laat elke week de auto wassen.
3 Waar laat je je auto staan? (*to park*)
4 We lieten de dokter komen. (*called the doctor*)
5 We moeten de dokter laten komen.
6 Je mag je auto niet hier laten staan.

Reading text 🎧

You have now reached a point in your learning of Dutch where you are capable of understanding quite complex structures. See how well you can understand this text, which contains longer, more intricate sentences than you have been exposed to so far.

Vocabulary

het vervoermiddel	means/mode of transport
nauwelijks	hardly, scarcely
voorkomen	to occur
het pontveer/de pont	the ferry
de autoweg	highway, freeway
niet per se	not necessarily
de afstand	the distance
voorrang hebben	to have right-of-way

Modes of transport

Nederland kent vervoermiddelen die nauwelijks voorkomen in andere landen. Een paar grotere Nederlandse steden hebben bijvoorbeeld trams⁴ en je ziet ook vaak boten varen op de kanalen tussen de steden. Nederland heeft ook zo veel rivieren, kanalen en grachten⁵ dat het soms op kleinere wegen nodig is om een pontveer te nemen om over een waterweg te komen. Je vindt natuurlijk langs

---

4 This word gets a pseudo-English pronunciation, i.e. **trem**, and is sometimes even written that way. Its plural in **s** is also a sign of its not being an indigenous Dutch word.
5 A **gracht** (c) runs through a town and has houses on either side of it, whereas a **kanaal** (n) runs between towns through the countryside. In English we call both types a *canal*.

de autowegen bruggen over de rivieren maar dat is niet per se het geval op kleinere wegen op het platteland. Langs bijna elke weg in het land, dus ook langs de autowegen die de steden met elkaar verbinden, vind je een fietspad. Fietspaden hebben hun eigen borden waarop de afstand per fiets naar de volgende stad of het volgende dorp staat. Bij kruispunten in de stad hebben de fietspaden zelfs hun eigen verkeerslichten. Een fiets heeft vaak voorrang. Het Nederlandse wegen- en spoorwegnet is ook fantastisch. Dat is mogelijk omdat het land piepklein is en toch meer dan vijftien miljoen inwoners heeft – en ze bezitten allemaal een fiets.

Language points

Some variations of word order

Look at the first two sentences in the reading text above. According to the word order rules learnt so far, you would expect the verbs **voorkomen** and **varen** to stand at the end of the sentence, i.e.

Nederland kent vervoermiddelen die nauwelijks in andere landen voorkomen.
Een paar grotere Nederlandse steden hebben bijvoorbeeld trams en je ziet ook vaak boten op de kanalen tussen de steden varen.

It is not in fact always necessary to relegate infinitives and past participles to the very end of the sentence, so long as what follows them is an adverbial expression that starts with a preposition, i.e. in the above cases it is thanks to *in* **andere landen** and *op de kanalen* that you have the option of applying the word order that was used in the reading text.

Exercise 5

Rewrite the following sentences putting the infinitive or the past participle in the only other possible position.

Example: Ik liet het boek vallen op de vloer.
Ik liet het boek op de vloer vallen.

1 Ze heeft jaren geleden al haar geld aan het Rode Kruis gegeven.
2 We zullen je hoogst waarschijnlijk zien in de loop van het weekend.

3 Ze heeft vroeger samen met haar ouders op het platteland gewoond.
4 Waar zijn jullie dit jaar geweest met vakantie?
5 Je kunt het horen aan haar stem.
6 Ze hebben vragen gesteld na de lezing.

12 Paulines ouders komen naar Nederland

Pauline's parents come to the Netherlands

In this lesson you will learn about:

- the pluperfect tense
- compound nouns
- relative pronouns with prepositions
- expressions associated with holidays

Reading text ▢▢

Vocabulary

verkeerd	wrong
belanden	to end up, land
wanhopig	desperate
het (auto)ongeluk	the (car) accident
halen	to fetch
het medelijden	the sympathy
afhalen	to pick up, fetch (people)

Pauline tells of her parents' first trip over from England

Mijn ouders hadden de nachtboot van Harwich genomen. Ze hadden de hele nacht niet geslapen. Ze waren 's ochtends heel vroeg in Hoek van Holland aangekomen, waren op de autoweg naar Amsterdam verkeerd gereden en in Utrecht beland. Ze hebben ons toen vanuit Utrecht opgebeld, helemaal wanhopig omdat ze net buiten Utrecht een ongeluk hadden gehad en niet verder konden. Wij hebben ze moeten afhalen. Ze waren hartstikke moe en hebben de hele dag geslapen. Ik had medelijden met ze.

Language points

The pluperfect tense

The pluperfect tense: He *had gone* when I arrived.

The pluperfect is the past in the past, and is expressed in English by *had* followed by the past participle. It is used to express that an event took place in the past prior to another event in the past as illustrated in the sample sentence above. The concept is identical in Dutch but entails one small complication.

You have already learnt how to construct the perfect tense in Dutch using either **hebben** or **zijn** with the past participle (see page 67). The pluperfect is constructed in exactly the same way but using the past tense of **hebben** and **zijn**, i.e. **had/hadden** and **was/waren** respectively. In the reading passage above, **hadden genomen**, **hadden niet geslapen**, **waren aangekomen**, **waren gereden**, **waren beland** and **hadden een ongeluk gehad** are all events that had occurred prior to their ringing Pauline, which is expressed in the perfect (**hebben opgebeld**). **Aankomen, rijden** and **belanden** are all verbs of motion and are thus used with **waren**; all the other verbs are not and thus require **hadden**.

Exercise 1

Put the verbs in parentheses into the pluperfect.

Example: Nadat ik (eten), dronk ik een pilsje.
Nadat ik gegeten had, dronk ik een pilsje.

1 Nadat hij (televisie kijken), ging hij naar bed.
2 Marius (doen) zijn huiswerk voordat hij ging spelen.
3 Wij (zien) hem niet omdat hij zich achter een boom (verbergen).
4 Zij (komen) thuis zonder dat wij haar (horen).

Compound nouns

A compound noun: The *church tower* is in disrepair.

In English it is not always obvious whether you write compound nouns as one word, two words or hyphenate them, e.g. frontdoor, front door, front-door. In Dutch such words are always written as one word, e.g. **de kerktoren**, **de voordeur**. They can consist of more than two words, e.g. **de afwasborstelhouder** 'washing-up brush holder'. When two or more nouns of different genders are compounded in this way, the new noun takes the gender of the final component, e.g.

het ontbijt + de tafel = de ontbijttafel   the breakfast table
de lucht + het kussen = het luchtkussen   the air cushion

It is not uncommon for **-e-**, **-en-** or **-s-** to be inserted between the two parts of compound nouns and unfortunately there are no rules as to when these are required; it is usually a matter of sound, a feeling for which comes only with experience and exposure to the language, e.g.

de zonneschijn 'sunshine'
het stadspark 'city park', but **het stadhuis**[1] 'town hall'
de boekenkast 'book case', but **de boekhandel** 'book shop'

As the **n** in the combination **en** is usually not pronounced in western Dutch (see page 7), the Dutch themselves are often unsure whether the medial sound in such compounds is written **-e-** or **-en-**. They apply the following rule, but it often leaves you in the lurch: if the first part of the compound has a plural connotation, **-en-** is written, and otherwise **-e-**. This explains, for example, why they write **hondehok** 'dog kennel' (i.e. for one dog) and **kippeëi** 'chicken egg' (i.e. from one chicken), but **kippenhok** 'chicken pen' (i.e. for several chickens). But a pear tree, which is **pereboom**, bears more than one pear! As mentioned above, there is no rule that can be followed to tell you that this compound is not ****peerboom**, for example.[2]

Exercise 2

Try making compounds from the following nouns making sure you give the article of the new word too. There are some surprises in store for you here.

---

1 The main stress is nearly always borne by the first part of the compound but in this word, quite exceptionally, the stress is on **huis**.
2 In late 1995 it was decided to reform this aspect of Dutch spelling, advocating use of **-en** in all but a few cases, regardless of whether there is a plural connotation or not, i.e. **handenhok**, **kippenei**, **perenboom**. It will be quite some time before people get used to the new rules and they are consistently applied in all printed matter.

1 de keuken + de deur
2 de wijn + het glas
3 de bol + het veld
4 de knoop + het gat
5 het rund + het vlees

6 het kussen + de sloop
7 de pruim + de boom
8 het lam + het vlees
9 het kind + de fiets
10 het schaap + het vlees

Dialogue 🔘

An early Christmas card has arrived in the mail

PIET: Van wie hebben we al een kerstkaart gekregen, schat?
PAULINE: Van de mevrouw bij wie we in Wenen gelogeerd hebben.
PIET: Bedoel je de mevrouw aan wie ik een hekel had?
PAULINE: Ja, die.
PIET: Zij was onuitstaanbaar. Ze had overal stoelen staan waar je niet op mocht zitten.
PAULINE: Ja, dat klopt maar ze was ook iemand waaraan je gehecht kon raken als je de tijd nam om haar een beetje te leren kennen.
PIET: Zoveel tijd had ik niet. Ik had tenslotte maar een maand vakantie.

PIET: *Who have we already received a Christmas card from, honey?*
PAULINE: *From the woman we stayed with in Vienna.*
PIET: *Do you mean the woman I loathed?*
PAULINE: *Yes, that one.*
PIET: *She was unbearable. She had chairs standing all over the place that you weren't allowed to sit on.*
PAULINE: *Yes, that's right but she was someone you could get attached to if you took the time to get to know her a bit.*
PIET: *I didn't have that much time. After all, I only had a month's holiday.*

Language points

Relative pronouns with prepositions

A relative pronoun with a preposition:
The girl *that/who/whom* I gave the book *to* is my niece.
The table *that/which* we are sitting *at* now is too low.

What you learnt about relative pronouns in lesson 11 is not all there is to know about relatives. Relative 'that', 'which', 'who' and 'whom' can be used in combination with a preposition, as illustrated above. Without a preposition, the relative in Dutch is **die** or **dat**, as we have seen, but in combination with a preposition you will need to make a choice between **wie** and **waar**.

When the antecedent, i.e. the noun which the relative refers or relates back to, is a person, **wie** is used and the preposition precedes it. In other words you literally say 'to whom', 'with whom', 'from whom', etc., e.g.

Het meisje aan wie ik het boek gegeven heb, is mijn nicht.
The girl I gave the book to (= to whom) is my niece.

De man met wie ik stond te praten, is mijn oom.
The man I was talking to (= to whom) is my uncle.

De mensen van wie wij onze auto gekocht hebben, waren erg aardig.
The people we bought our car from (= from whom) were very nice.

When the antecedent is a thing (i.e. non-personal), **waar-** + preposition is used. In other words you literally say 'whereon', 'wherein', etc., e.g.

De tafel waaraan wij nu zitten, is te laag.
The table we are now sitting at (= at which) is too low.

De boekenkast waarin de boeken nu staan, staat op de slaapkamer.
The bookcase the books are in (= in which) is in the bedroom.

But in spoken Dutch it is far more common to separate **waar** from the preposition in the following way:

De tafel waar wij nu aan zitten, is te laag.
De boekenkast waar de boeken nu in staan, staat op de slaapkamer.

In effect this is not greatly different from English: in Dutch you simply say 'where' instead of 'that' or 'which', leave the preposition where it stands in English and put the finite verb at the end of the clause, i.e.

The chair that   he was sitting on . was broken.
De   stoel waar   hij op zat,   was stuk.

English often omits the relative when it is used together with a preposition, e.g. *The girl I gave the book to* ... , *The chair he was sitting on* ... It can never be omitted in Dutch.

In spoken Dutch the above distinction between preposition + **wie** for people and **waar** + preposition for things is commonly ignored and the latter construction is used in both cases, e.g.

Het meisje waaraan ik het boek gegeven heb, is mijn nicht. *or*
Het meisje waar ik het boek aan gegeven heb, is mijn nicht.
De man waarmee[3] ik stond te praten, is mijn oom.
De man waar ik mee stond te praten, is mijn oom.
De mensen waarvan wij onze auto gekocht hebben, waren erg aardig.
De mensen waar wij onze auto van gekocht hebben, waren erg aardig.

Exercise 3

Rewrite the following sentences replacing the preposition + **wie** with **waar-** + preposition, leaving the latter as one word for the time being.

1 De mensen met wie ik stond te praten, komen uit Spanje.
2 Het meisje naast wie jij zit, is erg lief, hè?
3 De leraar aan wie ik een hekel had, heeft de school verlaten.
4 Zij is iemand op wie je je kunt verlaten.
5 Dat zijn de kinderen aan wie ik al mijn oude speelgoed gegeven heb.

Exercise 4

Rewrite the sentences you have just compiled for exercise 3 separating the preposition from **waar** and putting it in the correct place in the sentence.

---

3 **Met** when used in combination with **waar**, **hier/daar** (see page 172) or as a separable prefix is replaced by **mee**, e.g. **meegaan** 'to go along with'. Similarly **tot** is replaced by **toe**, e.g. **waartoe** 'to which', **toestaan** 'to permit'.

Exercise 5

Translate the following sentences using **waar** + preposition and separating the two.

1 The couch you are sitting on was a present from my grandma.
2 Those are the glasses we drank out of last night.
3 The grass that we're lying on is wet.
4 The knife which I'm cutting the meat with isn't sharp enough.
5 The vacation which we had been looking forward to was terrible.
6 The Meijers are people you can't rely on.

Expressions associated with holidays

de vakantie	the holidays, vacation
een vakantie aan zee	a holiday by the sea
een vakantie op het platteland	a holiday in the country
op/met vakantie	on holiday
prettige vakantie	enjoy your holidays
in het buitenland	abroad, in a foreign country
zich verheugen op	to look forward to
Ik verheug me op ...	I am looking forward to ...

Culture point

De Randstad (**de rand** 'edge, rim') is what the Dutch call the circle of cities in the west of the country consisting of (in clockwise direction) Amsterdam, Utrecht, Rotterdam, Delft, The Hague, Leiden and Haarlem. An inhabitant of this economic hub of the country is called a **Randstedeling**. It is the dialect of this part of the country, which more or less corresponds with **Holland** in the narrow sense, that provided the Netherlands with a basis for the standard form of the language, **ABN**. This is an abbreviation of **Algemeen Beschaafd Nederlands** (General Cultivated Dutch).[4] True dialect that non-locals may have trouble in understanding is spoken in the north, east and south of the country.

---

4 The term is used as follows: **'Ik ken niet' in plaats van 'ik kan niet' is geen ABN**. In non-standard Dutch **kennen** and **kunnen** are often confused, as are **liggen** 'to lie' and **leggen** 'to lay'; compare what many speakers of English do with *lie* and *lay*.

13 Pauline doet de was

Pauline is doing the washing

In this lesson you will learn about:

- how to say 'whose'
- how to ask questions with 'what' plus a preposition
- the passive

Dialogue 🔲

Pauline is sorting the washing

PAULINE: Van wie zijn deze sokjes, Charlotte? Van jou of van Marius?
CHARLOTTE: Ze zijn van mij.
PAULINE: En wie z'n trui is dit?
MARIUS: Dat is mijn trui. Ik wil hem nu aantrekken.
PAULINE: Waar is dat voor nodig? Het is zo warm.
CHARLOTTE: Waar doe je nou mijn sokjes in, mama? Ik kan ze nooit vinden.
PAULINE: Ik doe ze in de middelste la van je ladenkast. Mag dat?

PAULINE: *Whose socks are these, Charlotte? Yours or Marius'?*
CHARLOTTE: *They're mine.*
PAULINE: *And whose pullover is this?*
MARIUS: *That's mine. I want to put it on now.*
PAULINE: *What's the need for that? It's so hot.*
CHARLOTTE: *What are you putting my socks in, mummy? I can never find them.*
PAULINE: *I'm putting them in the middle drawer of your chest of drawers. Is that alright?*

Language points

'Whose?' and 'what?' + preposition

'Whose' in a question is expressed by **van wie**, e.g.

Van wie is dit potlood?   Whose pencil is this?

Of course **van wie** can also render 'from whom/who ... from':

Van wie heb je geen cadeau Who didn't you get a present
gekregen?   from?

Compare the above with the relative pronoun 'whose':

Hij is de man van wie ik de ladder geleend heb.
He's the man whose ladder I borrowed.

In colloquial Dutch interrogative 'whose' is commonly expressed
by **wie z'n**, e.g.

Wie z'n potlood is dit?   Whose pencil is this?

Strictly speaking, when 'whose' clearly refers to a female, **wie d'r**
is used but if the question is not gender specific, the masculine **wie
z'n** prevails, e.g.

Wie d'r b.h. is dit?   Whose bra is this?

When 'what' is used in combination with a preposition, it is
expressed by **waar-**, e.g.

Waarmee heb je het vlees   What did you cut the meat with?
gesneden?

But it is more usual in spoken Dutch to separate the preposition
from the **waar**, e.g.

Waar heb je het vlees mee gesneden?

Compare the above with a relative **waar-** + preposition:

**Het mes waarmee ik het vlees gesneden heb, was niet scherp
genoeg.**
**Het mes waar ik het vlees mee gesneden heb, was niet scherp
genoeg.**
The knife I cut the meat with was not sharp enough.

Exercise 1

Rewrite the following questions replacing **van wie** with **wie z'n/d'r** or vice versa, making all necessary changes to the sentence.

1 Wie z'n kinderen zijn dit?
2 Van wie is dit overhemd?
3 Wie d'r slipje is dat? (*panties*)
4 Van wie zijn de postzegels die op tafel liggen?[1]
5 Wie z'n fiets mag ik lenen?

Exercise 2

Rewrite the following questions separating **waar** from the preposition.

1 Waarmee kan ik de aardappels schillen?
2 Waarnaar zitten jullie te kijken?
3 Waarop zit je nu?
4 Waaruit gaan we deze heerlijke wijn drinken?
5 Waarvoor heb je dat nodig?

Reading text 🔲

Vocabulary

bekend	well-known
de middeleeuwen	the Middle Ages
verhogen	to raise
zogenaamd	so-called
de verdediging	the defence
het gevaar	the danger
dikwijls = vaak	often
de Afsluitdijk	the Great Enclosing Dam
overstromen	to flood
droogleggen	to reclaim
bewoonbaar	inhabitable
de landbouw	the agriculture
bewaken	to guard

---

1 'On the table' is usually rendered by **op tafel** with omission of the definite article.

de dijkwacht   the dike watch
in dit opzicht   in this respect

Dikes

Nederland is bekend om zijn dijken. De eerste dijken werden in de middeleeuwen gebouwd maar ze worden nog steeds gebouwd en oude dijken worden verhoogd. Je vindt dijken niet alleen langs de kust maar ook in het binnenland waar de kust misschien vroeger liep. Soms is zo'n zogenaamde binnendijk gebouwd als extra verdediging tegen stormen waardoor de buitendijken vroeger dikwijls braken en het land overstroomde. In 1932 werd de Afsluitdijk geopend. Door de bouw van die dijk is de vroegere Zuiderzee het IJsselmeer[2] geworden en later zijn achter die dijk verdere dijken gebouwd om polders te maken. Een polder is een stuk land dat drooggelegd is en dus bewoonbaar geworden is of voor de landbouw gebruikt kan worden. De dijken van Nederland moeten bewaakt worden. Dat wordt door de dijkwacht gedaan. Nederland is in dit opzicht een uniek land.

Language points

The passive

The passive: The meat *is being cut* with a sharp knife.

The concept 'passive' is the same in both English and Dutch, but the Dutch express it in a slightly different way. Sometimes, for stylistic reasons, we choose not to mention who or what is performing an action, i.e. 'The door was opened' instead of 'He opened the door'; the former construction is called the passive and the latter the active. The doer of the action can also be mentioned in the passive if required, i.e. 'The door was opened by him'.

In English the passive is formed by using the verb 'to be' plus a past participle. In Dutch you use **worden** (lit. 'to become') plus the past participle. Here are the various tenses of the passive in Dutch and English:

---

2 When a word starts with **ij**, both letters are capitalised. **IJ** is also one key on a Dutch typewriter. Even the letter **y** of the alphabet is often pronounced **ij** and in most people's handwriting **ij** is a **y** with dots on it. But dictionaries regard the sound as **i** + **j**.

De deur wordt (door hem) geopend.	The door is (being) opened (by him).
De deur werd (door hem) geopend.	The door was (being) opened (by him).
De deur is (door hem) geopend.	The door has been opened (by him).
De deur was (door hem) geopend.	The door had been opened (by him).
De deur zal geopend worden.	The door will be opened.
De deur moet/kan geopend worden.	The door must/can be opened.
De deur zal geopend moeten worden.	The door will have to be opened.
De deur zal geopend zijn.	The door will have been opened.

There are two traps you have to beware of.

1 **Is geopend** translates 'has been opened'. 'The door is shut' and 'The door has been shut' are both **De deur is gesloten**. In English the former describes the state of the door and the latter the result of the action of shutting the door, but to the Dutch mind this is one and the same thing.

2 As you have seen, 'The door has been opened' is **De deur is geopend**. The past tense of that in English is *The door had been opened* and thus the past in Dutch is **De deur was geopend**. Despite appearances, this construction does not mean 'was opened', which is rendered by **werd geopend**.

Earlier in this book, where the active was being dealt with, you learnt that the Dutch normally express themselves in the perfect tense. Thus 'He shut the door' is more usually **Hij heeft de deur gesloten** than **Hij sloot de deur**. The same preference for the perfect exists in the passive too. Thus, although 'The door was shut by him' is literally **De deur werd door hem gesloten**, it is more usual to say in spoken Dutch **De deur is door hem gesloten**.

Note that **De deur was gesloten** can express either 'The door was shut' (i.e. the state the door was in) or 'The door had been shut' (the action that had been performed on the door).

Exercise 3

How many examples of the passive are there in the reading text on dikes? Underline them, i.e. both the auxiliaries **worden** or **zijn** and the dependent past participle.

Exercise 4

Use the passive to answer the following questions.

Example: Waar wordt brood van gemaakt? (van meel)
Brood wordt van meel gemaakt.

1 Waar is dat mee geschreven? (met een vulpen)
2 Waar wordt de afwas mee gedaan? (met het afwasmiddel)
3 Waar werd dat mee schoongemaakt? (met zeep)
4 Door wie was hij geholpen? (door mij)
5 Door wie kan hij geholpen worden? (door niemand)
6 Door wie is het geld geschonken? (door mijn man)
7 Waar wordt Nederlands gesproken? (in Nederland en België)

Exercise 5

First read this set of regulations for visitors to a castle park, then answer the questions.

1 Het park is open dagelijks van 10 uur tot 15 uur.
2 Toegang tot het park is gratis.
3 Het is verboden op dit terrein te fietsen.
4 Honden mogen niet vrij rondlopen.
5 Het is verboden zich op het gras te begeven.
6 Het is verboden de dieren te voeden.
7 Het roken wordt in dit park niet toegelaten.
8 Het is verboden bloemen te plukken.
9 Auto's dienen[3] op het parkeerterrein rechts van het slot geparkeerd te worden.
10 Rolstoelen kunnen van het kantoor geleend worden.
11 WC's bevinden zich 100 meter vóór de ingang tot het slot.
12 Het restaurant is 's woensdags gesloten.

A young couple who come on their bicycles find point 3 on the list relevant to them. Which point or points are relevant to the following people?

(a) Een oudere dame die haar hondelijn vergeten heeft.
(b) Een vader met zijn kinderen die een bal meegebracht hebben.
(c) Een gezin dat geen geld bij zich heeft.

---

3 In this context **dienen** is an official-sounding synonym of **moeten** which is commonly used on signs.

(d) Een echtpaar dat oud brood meegenomen heeft voor de eenden.
(e) Een oude man die heel graag een pijp rookt als hij wandelt.
(f) Een moeder met een klein kind dat dringend moet.
(g) Een paar jonge mensen die net na drie uur 's middags opdagen.
(h) Een dame die iets zou willen meenemen voor de vaas op haar koffietafel thuis.
(i) Een jonge man die zijn vriendin uitgenodigd heeft om op woensdag in het park te gaan eten.
(j) Een meisje dat haar oma, die slecht ter been is, een bezoek aan het park beloofd heeft.

Exercise 6

Which of the eleven regulations in exercise 5 contain clear passives? Those which start **Het is verboden ...** describe a state rather than an action and are thus not examples of true passives.

Culture point

Running through the middle of the province of Utrecht, from north to south, is the so-called **Waterlinie**. To the west of this line, the Netherlands lie below sea level, and to the east of it they gradually rise above it. The main defence against the sea in the west is first the sand-dunes along the coast, and second a system of dikes which are the result of over a thousand years of diligence on the part of the Dutch. Many Dutch windmills are living reminders of the early technology used to reclaim land. The completion of the Afsluitdijk in 1932 and the subsequent reclamation of much of the land behind it, was a landmark in the history of the country. But since then the Delta Works (**de Deltawerken**) have been completed in the province of Zeeland. This project, inaugurated in the late 1980s, has created vast reservoirs of fresh water and was intended to prevent a recurrence of a flood on the scale of the 1953 one, when the dikes in that region were breached.

14 Er zijn eekhoorns in de tuin

There are squirrels in the garden

In this lesson you will learn about:

- the meanings of the Dutch word **er**
- expressing the progressive or continuous form of verbs
- how to express actions that started in the past and are still continuing

---

Dialogue 1 🔲

Pauline and Piet have discovered squirrels in their garden

PAULINE: Piet, er zit een eekhoorn in de eikenboom achter in de tuin.

PIET: Er zijn er eigenlijk twee. Ik ben net gaan kijken en er zat er nog een in de notenboom van de buurman.

PAULINE: De eekhoorn die ik gezien heb, ziet er niet zo gezond uit, vind je niet?

PIET: Ja, en er ligt ook iets akeligs op de grond, braaksel of zo.

PAULINE: Ze schijnen van die eikenboom te houden, hè, want vorig jaar om deze tijd zaten er ook eekhoorns in, weet je nog?

PIET: Ja, dat klopt. Ik heb er op een dag een stuk of vijf geteld.

PAULINE: *Piet, there's a squirrel in the oak tree at the end of the garden.*

PIET: *There are two in fact. I just went and had a look and there was another one sitting in the neighbour's walnut tree.*

PAULINE: *The squirrel I saw doesn't look too healthy, don't you reckon?*

PIET: *Yes, and there is something yucky lying on the ground too, vomit or something like that.*

PAULINE: *They seem to like that oak tree, don't they, because last year at this time there were also squirrels in it, do you remember?*

PIET: *Yes, that's right. One day I counted about five of them.*

Language points

The meanings of the Dutch word er

Er is used highly idiomatically in Dutch. Some of its meanings have direct equivalents in English and others do not. It has been used on many occasions already in this book but its most idiomatic usages have been avoided till now. All its various uses must be mastered.

The basic meaning of **er** is 'there'. It is in fact an unemphatic form of **daar**. It has four functions:

1 *Dummy subject er.* Indefinite subjects are commonly placed after the verb in Dutch with **er** introducing the verb, which stands either in the singular or the plural depending on the number of the subject:

Er loopt een hond achter het hek.
There's a dog walking behind the fence.

Er zijn twee dingen die ik zeggen moet.
There are two things I have to say.

In the examples above, **er** corresponds exactly to English usage but this is certainly not always the case. Such constructions with a dummy subject **er** are much more common in Dutch than in English, e.g.

Toen kwam er een pastoor aan. Then a priest arrived.
Wat is er gebeurd? What (has) happened?
Wie is er vandaag jarig? Whose birthday is it today?

As you have seen, **er is/zijn** renders 'there is/are' but the Dutch have several other ways of expressing this. **Er ligt/liggen, er zit/zitten** and **er staat/staan** are often used instead of **er is/zijn** when the action of these verbs is appropriate to what is being referred to, e.g.

Er zit een muis in de hoek.
There is a mouse in the corner.

Er liggen twee kranten op tafel.
There are two papers (lying) on the table.

Er staan twee banken achter de schuur.
There are two benches (standing) behind the shed.

The following use of these three verbs should be noted in passing as it is related to the above. Here they also simply render 'to be':

Waar ligt Utrecht? Where is Utrecht? (e.g. while pointing to a map)
De koffie staat klaar. The coffee is ready.
Mijn broer zit in Japan/thuis. My brother is in Japan/at home.

Er is commonly used in combination with the passive, e.g.

Er wordt aan de deur geklopt. There's a knock at the door.
Er wordt in Italië veel wijn A lot of wine is drunk in Italy.
gedronken.

2 *Partitive er*. **Er** is used with numerals and adverbs of quantity (i.e. 'enough', 'too much', 'too few'). This usually has no parallel in English. Its literal meaning is something like 'of it/them', e.g.

Hoeveel heb je er? How many (of them) do you have?
Ik heb er drie. I have three (of them).
Hij heeft er genoeg. He has enough (of it/them).

The sentence **Er zijn er eigenlijk twee** in dialogue 1 contains both a dummy subject **er** and a partitive **er**.

3 *Pronominal er.* 'On it', 'in it', 'from it', etc. (i.e. a preposition + the pronoun 'it') is expressed in Dutch by **erop**, **erin**, **ervan**, etc.; *op het, *in het, *van het, etc. are not possible, e.g.

Dit is een stoel. Ik zit erop.   This is a chair. I'm sitting on it.

Neem deze pen en schrijf de boodschappenlijst ermee.
Take this pen and write the shopping list with it.

As with **waar-** + preposition etc. (see page 168), it is usual to separate **er** from the preposition, placing the **er** immediately after the finite verb and the preposition at the end of the clause, e.g.

Schrijf er de boodschappenlijst mee.	Write the shopping list with it.
Ik heb er het brood mee gesneden.	I cut the bread with it.
Hij gaat er een boot van bouwen.	He's going to build a boat from it.

Er + preposition not only translates 'on/in/from it', etc. but also 'on/in/from them', etc., when 'them' refers to non-personal objects, e.g.

We kijken er graag naar.   We like looking at it (a photo).
or
We like looking at them (photos).

Note that analogous to **erop** 'on it/them', etc., whether written as one word or two, are **daarop** 'on that/those', etc. and **hierop** 'on this/these', etc. Being emphatic forms, unlike **er**, they usually stand at the front of the sentence, e.g.

Daaraan moet je mij herinneren.	You must remind me of that.
Daar moet je mij aan herinneren.	You must remind me of that.
Hierop ga ik niet zitten.	I'm not going to sit on this/these.
Hier ga ik niet op zitten.	I'm not going to sit on this/these.

Compare:

Ik ga er niet op zitten.   I'm not going to sit on it/them.

4 *Locative er.* Locative simply means place and thus this **er** means 'there' indicating a place, i.e. an unemphatic **daar**.[1] **Daar**, because

---

1 Because **er** is in origin an unemphatic **daar**, it is commonly pronounced **d'r**.

it is usually emphatic, commonly stands at the beginning of a sentence – remember that fronting is one way that Dutch emphasises, e.g.

Ben je in Berlijn bekend?   Do you know your way around Berlin?

Ja, daar heb ik vroeger gewoond.   Yes, I used to live there.

Ja, ik heb er vroeger gewoond.   Yes, I used to live there.

The difference is not one of meaning but of emphasis, and because **er** is unstressed, locative **er**, like partitive and pronominal **er**, follows the finite verb.

Exercise 1

Rewrite the following sentences replacing the expressions in italics with **er** + preposition. Separate **er** from the preposition where possible.

Example: De jongens zitten niet *op de sofa.*
              De jongens zitten er niet op.

1   De hond ligt niet *op de grond.*
2   Ik weet niets *van dat ongeluk.*
3   Zij heeft het *uit de krant* geknipt.[2]
4   We hebben urenlang *in die auto* rondgereden.
5   Ik loop de hele dag *aan die film* te denken.
6   We kijken *naar een interessant televisieprogramma.*

Exercise 2

Rewrite the above sentences replacing the italicised expressions with **daar** + preposition. Separate **daar** from the preposition where possible.

Example: De jongens zitten niet *op de sofa.*
              Daar zitten de jongens niet op.

Exercise 3

Answer the following questions.

---

2 Contrary to the rule that pronominal **er** always follows the finite verb, when there is an object **het** in the sentence, **het** occupies that position and **er** follows **het**.

Example: Wat is dit en wat doe je ermee?

Het is een golfbal en je speelt er golf mee.

1 een viool (muziek maken)   2 tv (kijken naar)

3 tandenborstel (tanden poetsen)   4 zaag (hout zagen)

5 teddybeer (spelen)   6 hamer (spijkers hameren)

Expressing the progressive or continuous form of verbs

The progressive or continuous form of a verb: He *is/was talking.*

Earlier in this book the point was made that a verb like **ik lees/las** not only translates 'I read/read' (i.e. present and past), but also 'I am/was reading'. Although that is so, the Dutch are able to express the ongoing action of a verb if they consider it necessary in a given context.

'I am reading a book about the (German) occupation' can be expressed in four ways in Dutch:

1 Ik lees op het ogenblik een boek over de bezetting.
2 Ik ben op het ogenblik een boek over de bezetting aan het lezen.[3]
3 Ik ben op het ogenblik bezig een boek over de bezetting te lezen.
4 Ik zit op het ogenblik een boek over de bezetting te lezen.

Sentence 1 is neutral and is the form you have previously learnt. It is never incorrect. Sentences 2, 3 and 4 are examples of three different ways of expressing the continuous action of the verb, but are essentially synonymous with 1. For 4 to be appropriate you need to be sitting and performing the action at the time of speaking, whereas the other three can be uttered even if you are not actually reading at the time of speaking.

Because 4 is specific to the position of the body while performing the action, **liggen** and **staan** are also used in this construction, e.g.

Hij ligt te slapen. Maak hem niet wakker.
He's asleep. Don't wake him.

Ze staat buiten met de buurvrouw te praten.
She's outside talking to the neighbour.

All the above progressive forms are in the present, but they can also be expressed in the imperfect:

Ik was een boek over de bezetting aan het lezen.
Ik was bezig een boek over de bezetting te lezen.
Ik zat een boek over de bezetting te lezen.

---

3 In this construction **het** is sometimes written **'t**, e.g. **aan 't lezen**.

Progressives of the type **aan het lezen zijn** and **liggen/staan/zitten te** also commonly occur in the perfect but **bezig te** does not, e.g.

Ik ben de hele middag aan het tuinieren geweest.
I have been/was gardening all afternoon.

Ik heb een boek over de bezetting zitten lezen.
I have been/was reading a book about the occupation.

Hij heeft liggen slapen.   He has been (lying down) sleeping.

Take note of what happens with **liggen**, **staan** and **zitten** when used in the perfect, i.e. they require a double-infinitive construction (see page 134).

Exercise 4

Put the following sentences into the three forms of the progressive. In the third option use either **liggen**, **staan** or **zitten** depending on which is most appropriate to the action being performed.

Example: Charlotte speelt met haar pop.
Charlotte is met haar pop aan het spelen.
Charlotte is bezig met haar pop te spelen.
Charlotte zit met haar pop te spelen.

1 Marius doet zijn huiswerk.
2 Ze eten.
3 Piet maait het gras. (*third way not possible*)
4 Pauline doet de afwas.
5 Ze drinken allemaal koffie.

Exercise 5

Put the third option of the sentences in exercise 4 in the perfect tense

Example: Charlotte zit met haar pop te spelen.
Charlotte heeft met haar pop zitten spelen.

Dialogue 2 ▭

Pauline and Piet are talking about Pauline's eccentric uncle

PIET: Wat zit je te doen, Pauline?

PAULINE: Ik ben een brief aan het schrijven.
PIET: Aan wie?
PAULINE: Aan Oom Paul.
PIET: Hij had jarenlang geen telefoon. Heeft hij er nog altijd geen?
PAULINE: Jawel, hij heeft al een jaar een telefoon maar hij is doof geworden en kan hem niet meer gebruiken.
PIET: Hoe lang woont hij al in dat oude huis?
PAULINE: Hij woont er al een jaar of vijftig,[4] meen ik.
PIET: Niet te geloven! Hij heeft al die tijd zonder telefoon[5] geleefd en dan koopt hij er een als hij doof wordt. Wat een gekke vent!
PAULINE: Niet lelijk praten[6] over mijn lievelingsoom, hoor!

PIET: *What are you doing, Pauline?*
PAULINE: *I'm writing a letter.*
PIET: *Who to?*
PAULINE: *To Uncle Paul.*
PIET: *He didn't have a phone for years. Has he still not got one?*
PAULINE: *Yes, he has. He's had one for a year but he's gone deaf and can't use it any more.*
PIET: *How long has he lived in that old house?*
PAULINE: *He's lived there for about fifty years, I think.*
PIET: *Incredible! He lived all that time without a phone and then he buys one when he goes deaf. What a crazy guy!*
PAULINE: *Don't knock my favourite uncle now!*

---

4 On page 178 the expression **een stuk of vijf** 'approximately five', was used. **Een jaar of vijftig** 'about fifty years' is an extension of this idiom. Similarly you can say **een week/maand of drie** 'about three weeks/months' and **een man of tien** 'about ten people'. These expressions are all synonymous with **ongeveer** 'about, approximately' and are particularly common in the spoken language.

5 **Zonder** is never followed by the indefinite article in Dutch, e.g. **Hij is zonder hoed naar buiten gegaan** 'He went out without a hat on'.

6 Imperatives (see page 100) are sometimes expressed by infinitives, e.g. **Niet roken** 'No smoking', **Opstaan allemaal** 'All get up'.

Language points

How to express actions that started in the past and are still continuing

On page 129 you were given the rule 'A perfect in English is always a perfect in Dutch'. There is one notable exception to this rule: when an action that started in the past continues on into the present (i.e. it is still not completed) Dutch uses the present tense whereas English uses the perfect. These constructions in English usually contain an expression of time introduced by 'for', e.g.

Ik leer al twee jaar Nederlands.
I have been learning Dutch for two years.

Dutch uses the adverb **al** rather where English uses the preposition *for*; what the Dutch is in effect saying is 'I have been learning and am still in the process of learning' and thus a perfect tense, which indicates a completed action in Dutch, cannot be used, e.g.

Ik heb twee jaar in Duitsland gewoond.
I lived in Germany for two years.

Compare the following sentences from dialogue 2 which illustrate the concept:

Hoe lang woont hij al in dat oude huis?
How long has he been living in that old house (for)?

Hij woont er al een jaar of vijftig.
He's been living there for about fifty years.

Exercise 6

Make sentences from the following words expressing that the action of the verb has been ongoing for the period of time given, and translate the completed sentences into English using the correct tense.

Example: **Pauline, werken, vijf jaar, in Den Haag.**
Pauline werkt al vijf jaar in Den Haag.
Pauline has been working in The Hague for five years.

1 Piet, lesgeven, acht jaar, op een middelbare school.
2 Hij, leren, een hele tijd, Duits.

3 Charlotte, spelen, langer dan een uur, in de tuin.
4 Oom Paul, zijn, jaren, doof.
5 Haar broer zitten, een week of drie, in Griekenland.

Culture point

The Dutch tend to do their shopping (**boodschappen doen**) on a daily basis rather than buying in bulk for the week or the month. Dutch kitchens are usually very small and the fridge is a small bar fridge, just big enough to accommodate the day's shopping plus a few longer-lasting items like butter and cheese. Cool drinks and beer are not necessarily stored in the refrigerator but in the cellar or under the stairs, where they are kept cool but not cold; this is in keeping with local tastes and also partly explains why they can make do with such a small fridge. Besides, the Dutch believe that icy cold drinks are no better for you than are draughts in the loo.

Exercise 7

Here's a puzzle to increase your vocabulary. Working from left to right, fill in vertically the Dutch names of the following animals. (Remember that **ij** is regarded as one letter in Dutch.) When looking up the words, make sure you note what gender they are. If you get them right, the name of a well-known Dutch town will appear across the top line. What province is this town in and what is it famous for?

duck	octopus	hippopotamus	badger	hawk
elephant	butterfly	hedgehog	rhinoceros	

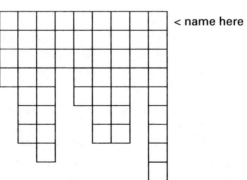

< name here

15 Wat heb je met de kerstkaarten gedaan?

What have you done with the Christmas cards?

In this lesson you will learn about:

- **al**, **alle(n)** and **allemaal**
- **beide(n)** and **allebei**
- **alles**, **iets**, **niets** and **niemand**
- the conditional and conditional perfect tenses
- saying 'should (have)' and 'could (have)'
- the weather

Dialogue 🔲

Piet has thrown away the Christmas cards

PAULINE: Wat heb je met al de kerstkaarten gedaan die we dit jaar gekregen hebben?
PIET: Die heb ik allemaal weggegooid. Wat moet je ermee?
PAULINE: Ik bewaar altijd alle kaarten tot volgend jaar om te weten aan wie ik dan een kerstgroet moet sturen.
PIET: Dat wist ik niet.
PAULINE: Dat is niets nieuws. Dat doe ik al jaren. Jij bent zo onoplettend.
PIET: Ik kan niet alles weten wat jij doet en denkt.

PAULINE: *What did you do with the Christmas cards that we got this year?*
PIET: *I threw them all away. What use are they?*
PAULINE: *I always keep all cards till next year so that I know who I have to send greetings to.*
PIET: *I never knew that.*

PAULINE: *That's nothing new. I've been doing that for years. You're so unobservant.*

Piet: *I can't know everything you think and do.*

Language points

Al, alle(n) **and** allemaal

'All' is expressed in three ways in Dutch, i.e. **al, alle, allemaal**. There is no difference in meaning between the three but the sentence structure can differ depending on which of the three is used:

> **Al de kinderen zijn boven aan het spelen.**
> **Alle kinderen zijn boven aan het spelen.**
> **De kinderen zijn allemaal boven aan het spelen.**
> All the children are upstairs playing.

Note that an **allemaal** referring to the subject always stands immediately after the finite verb and that **alle kinderen** can mean either 'all children' or 'all the children'. In addition to meaning 'all', **al**, as we have seen so often before, also means 'already', but context always makes it clear what is meant, e.g.

> **Ik ben al vergeten hoe hij heet.**
> I have already forgotten what his name is.

> **Ik ben al hun namen vergeten = Ik ben hun namen allemaal vergeten.**[1]
> I have forgotten all their names.

Alle can be used independently, i.e. not followed by a noun, as both a subject and an object, but sounds rather stilted; in all the following examples the alternatives with **allemaal** are more commonly heard, e.g.

> **Wat is er met de kopjes gebeurd? Alle zijn stuk. (= Ze zijn allemaal stuk.)**
> What's happened to the cups? They're all broken.

---

1 Although there is a complicated grammatical rule that determines whether you use **hebben** or **zijn** as the auxiliary of **vergeten** in the perfect, in practice the Dutch use **zijn** in all cases. In this case **allemaal** does not follow the verb as it refers to the object of the sentence.

Zij heeft ze alle (or **allemaal**) **kapot gemaakt.**
She broke them all.

When **alle** is used independently and refers to people, it takes an **n**, but in speech this **n** is often not heard, e.g.

Allen zijn naar de bioscoop gegaan. (= **Ze zijn allemaal gegaan.**)
They have all gone to the movies.

Hij heeft ze allen (or **allemaal**) **zien weggaan.**
He saw them all leaving.

Generally speaking, the most common forms heard in speech are those with **allemaal**, so get used to using this form.

Note that 'all' in expressions of time is expressed by **de/het hele**, e.g.

de hele dag/week/maand/zomer all day/week/month/summer
het hele jaar all year

Exercise 1

Rewrite the following sentences replacing **al** and **alle(n)** with **allemaal**.

Example: Ik heb al de kinderen in de tuin gezien.
Ik heb de kinderen allemaal in de tuin gezien.

1 Hij kent ze allen.
2 Al mijn familieleden zijn naar het feest gekomen.
3 Alle zijn uitverkocht.
4 Alle leerlingen mochten thuis blijven.
5 Pauline heeft al Piets overhemden gestreken.

Beide(n) **and** allebei

Beide(n) and **allebei** mean 'both' and as the usage of the two forms runs parallel with that of **alle(n)** and **allemaal**, it is worth looking at them here.

Beide, like **alle**, can stand before a noun or independently, taking an **n** in the same instances as where **alle** does and **allebei** stands in the same position in the sentence as **allemaal**, e.g.

Beide kinderen zijn boven aan het spelen.
De kinderen zijn allebei boven aan het spelen.
Both (the) children are upstairs playing.

Beiden zijn naar de bioscoop gegaan. (= Ze zijn allebei gegaan.)
Both have gone to the movies.

Hij heeft ze beiden (or **allebei**) **zien weggaan.**
He saw them both leaving.

Wat is er met de kopjes gebeurd? Beide zijn stuk. (= Ze zijn allebei stuk.)
What happened to the cups? Both are broken/They're both broken.

Zij heeft ze beide (or **allebei**) **kapot gemaakt.**
She broke them both.

Note:

Ik ken ze geen van beiden niet. I don't know either of them.

As with **alle/allemaal**, generally speaking, the most common form heard in speech is **allebei**.

Alles, iets, niets **and** niemand

Alles, **iets**, **niets** and **niemand** mean 'everything', 'something', 'nothing' and 'nobody' respectively. It is a peculiarity of English that in questions and after negatives *something* and *nothing* are replaced by *anything* and *somebody* and *nobody* by *anybody*, e.g.

1 He has something in his hand.
2 Has he got anything in his hand?
3 He hasn't got anything in his hand.
4 He knows nobody.
5 Doesn't he know anybody?
6 He doesn't know anybody.

Dutch makes no such distinction in questions and negated sentences:

1 Hij heeft iets in zijn hand.
2 Heeft hij iets in zijn hand?
3 Hij heeft niets in zijn hand.
4 Hij kent niemand.
5 Kent hij niemand?
6 Hij kent niemand.

Alles, **iets** and **niets** can be followed by a relative clause and, when they are, the relative pronoun required is **wat**,[2] e.g.

---

2 **Die** or **dat**, the usual relatives, cannot be used here because **alles**, **iets** and **niets** are not nouns with a gender by which to determine whether to use **die** or **dat**. It should be noted, however, that **dat** is used by some speakers instead of **wat**.

Niets wat jij zegt is waar.   Nothing (that) you say is true.

Ik heb iets voor je dat je heel leuk zal vinden.
I have something for you which you'll really like.

Iets (as well as colloquial **wat**) and **niets** can be followed by an adjective, in which case the adjective takes an **s** ending, e.g.

Ik heb iets/wat sleuks voor je. I have something nice for you.
Ik heb niets lekkers in huis.   I haven't got anything nice to eat in the house.

Exercise 2

Translate the following.

1 She's bought something expensive for his birthday.
2 There was nothing interesting for sale (**te koop**).
3 He gave me something he found under the cupboard.
4 I have nothing new to report (**berichten**).
5 There's something green lying on the floor.

Reading text 1 ▣

The following text is written in structurally much more difficult Dutch than you have had to cope with so far, but once you have worked through the grammar dealt with in this lesson, you should have no trouble with it. With the help of the vocabulary in the back of the book see how much you understand of it now and then come back and reread it when you have completed the lesson.

Charles V

Nederland had deel van Duitsland kunnen zijn. Tot het midden van de zestiende eeuw maakte het land deel uit van het Heilige Romeinse Rijk. In 1555 deed Karel de Vijfde, een Habsburger die ook koning van Spanje was, afstand van de troon van zijn rijk. Aan zijn broer gaf hij het Heilige Romeinse Rijk en aan zijn zoon, Filips de Tweede, gaf hij Spanje. Hij had besloten dat als zijn zoon alles zou erven, het voor hem moeilijk zou kunnen zijn om dat reuzerijk onder controle te houden. Karel had er tenslotte zelf moeite mee gehad. Hij had bijvoorbeeld in Nederland en Duitsland met de Hervorming te kampen gehad. Zou het niet verstandiger zijn, dacht

Karel, om de bezittingen te verdelen? Als hij het opstandige deel
van zijn rijk aan zijn broer zou geven, dan zou hij zijn hele energie
daaraan kunnen besteden. Als zijn zoon alleen maar Spanje zou
moeten regeren, en Spanje was bovendien ook rijker dan de rest
van het rijk vanwege zijn kolonies, zou dat diens[3] leven wat verge-
makkelijken. Maar de traditionele vijanden van Spanje waren
Frankrijk en Engeland. Zou het dus niet nuttig kunnen zijn voor
de koning van Spanje, dacht Karel, om landbezit in het noorden
van Europa te hebben voor het geval er oorlog zou uitbreken
tussen Spanje en die twee landen? Daarom besloot hij om de
Nederlanden te scheiden van de rest van het rijk en die aan zijn
zoon, de koning van Spanje, te geven. Vanaf dat ogenblik waren
Nederland en Duitsland politiek gescheiden. Als keizer Karel dat
niet gedaan had, had de geschiedenis van Europa heel anders
kunnen uitvallen.

Language points

The conditional tenses

The conditional tense: He *would help* you.
The conditional perfect tense: He *would have helped* you.

Conditionals are expressed by **zou/zouden** 'would'. An 'if' clause,
introduced by **als** in Dutch, may or may not follow or precede, e.g.

Hij zou me helpen. He'd help me.
Hij zou me helpen als hij de He'd help me if he had the time.
tijd had.
Als hij de tijd had, zou hij If he had the time, he'd help me.
me helpen.[4]

The verb in the **als** clause can be left in the imperfect, as done
above, or you can express the hypothetical nature of that verb by
replacing it by **zou/zouden** + infinitive; the force of a **zou/zouden**
in that clause is then similar to English 'was/were to', e.g.

---

3 This word tends to be limited to higher style. It means 'his' and is used when
zijn could be ambiguous; in this case it means Philip's, not Charles's, life.
4 It's not a bad idea to get into the habit of always using a comma when you start
a sentence with a subordinate clause, as it separates the finite verbs of the two
clauses. (See page 123).

Als hij de tijd had/zou hebben, zou hij me helpen.
If he had (= were to have) the time he'd help me.

Ze zou het kopen als je haar het geld gaf/zou geven.
She'd buy it if you gave (= were to give) her the money.

Although this use of 'was/were to' is rather high style in English, the equivalent construction with **zou/zouden** in Dutch is not at all formal; it merely emphasises the if and when of the situation.

Zou/zouden zijn and **zou/zouden hebben** are very commonly contracted to **was/waren** and **had/hadden,** but the presence of an **als** clause always makes it clear what the correct interpretation is, e.g.

Als hij niet zo veel rookte/zou roken, zou hij nu rijk zijn
Als hij niet zo veel rookte/zou roken, was hij nu rijk.
If he didn't smoke so much he would be rich now.

Als we niet zo'n grote tuin hadden, zouden we meer tijd hebben.
Als we niet zo'n grote tuin hadden, hadden we meer tijd.
If we didn't have such a big garden we would have more time.

Exercise 3

Join the following sentences using **als** to introduce the second. Do it both with and without **zou/zouden.**

Example: Ik zou je het geld geven. Ik had het.
Ik zou je het geld geven als ik het had.
Ik zou je het geld geven als ik het zou hebben.

1 Ik zou de planten water geven. Het was warm.
2 Ze zou graag een bad willen nemen. Er was warm water.
3 Ze zou boodschappen gaan doen. Ze had genoeg geld.
4 Nederland zou nog deel van Duitsland zijn. Het was niet losgebroken.
5 Hij zou je haar adres geven. Hij wist het.

Exercise 4

Write out the sentences in the previous exercise starting with the **als** clause.

Example: Ik zou je het geld geven. Ik had het.
Als ik het had, zou ik je het geld geven.
Als ik het zou hebben, zou ik je het geld geven.

The conditional perfect tense

Conditional perfect is the term given to 'would have' + past participle constructions. These can be translated literally, keeping in mind that 'have' will be either **hebben** or **zijn** depending on the auxiliary that the verb concerned takes in the perfect tense, e.g.

Perfect
Zij heeft een nieuw bankstel gekocht.
She bought a new lounge suite.

Zij is onmiddellijk naar huis gegaan.
She went home immediately.

Conditional perfect
Zij zou een nieuw bankstel gekocht hebben als ze genoeg geld gehad had.
She would have bought a new lounge suite if she had had enough money.

Hij zou onmiddellijk naar huis gegaan zijn als hij dat geweten had.
He would have gone home immediately if he had known that.

As you can see, the verbal constructions in these sentences are quite complicated but correspond word for word with their English translations. To reduce the number of verbs from three to two in conditional perfects like **Zij zou een nieuw bankstel gekocht hebben als ...** and **Hij zou onmiddellijk naar huis gegaan zijn als ...** , it is possible to contract **zou ... hebben** and **zou ... zijn** to **had** and **was** as explained earlier in this lesson (see page 195), e.g.

Zij had een nieuw bankstel gekocht als ...
Hij was onmiddellijk naar huis gegaan als ...

Saying 'should (have)' and 'could (have)'

The past tense of 'can', 'could/was able', was dealt with on page 134. But 'could' has two meanings in English: there is the imperfect or past tense, which is **kon** in Dutch, and the conditional, which is **zou kunnen**, i.e. *could* which means 'would be able', e.g.

Hij kon me gisteren niet helpen.
He couldn't help me yesterday.

Hij zou me niet kunnen helpen zelfs als hij tijd had.
He couldn't help me even if he had the time.

'Could have', a so-called conditional perfect, is expressed as follows:

Hij had me kunnen helpen.   He could have helped me.

Nederland had deel van Duitsland kunnen zijn.
The Netherlands could have been part of Germany.

The same sort of construction with **moeten** renders 'should have'

Hij had me moeten helpen.   He should have helped me.

Moeten, which so far we have learnt as meaning 'must/have to', is also used to express 'should'. There are parallels here with the use of **kunnen** as described above. 'Should' is strictly speaking **zou moeten**, but both **moest** and occasionally even **moet** are used too, e.g.

Je zou je vrouw heel wat meer moeten helpen.
Je moest/moet je vrouw heel wat meer helpen.
You should help your wife a great deal more.

Exercise 5

Translate the following into English.

1 Pauline had Marius van school kunnen halen als ze de auto gehad had.
2 Pauline vindt dat Piet Marius naar school zou moeten brengen.[5]
3 Pauline vond dat Piet Marius naar school had moeten brengen.
4 Ze was op tijd geweest als ze dat geweten had.
5 Ze zou op tijd geweest zijn als ze dat geweten had.
6 De kinderen hadden langer buiten gespeeld als het niet donker geworden was.
7 Als je elke dag met je hond ging wandelen, zou hij niet zo lastig zijn.
8 Als hij meer verdiende, zou hij een groter huis kopen.
9 Als hij meer zou verdienen, zou hij kunnen sparen.
10 Hij zou elk jaar op reis gegaan zijn als hij meer had verdiend.
11 Als hij meer verdiend had, was hij elke zomer op reis gegaan.

---

5 Note that 'to take' someone somewhere requires **brengen** not **nemen**.

Reading text 2 ▣

Het KNMI, the Royal Dutch Meteorological Institute, is based in
a small village to the east of Utrecht, De Bilt. The name of this
town is synonymous with the weather.

Vocabulary

opnieuw	again
de neerslag	precipitation, rainfall
enkele	several
de bui	shower
guur	bleak
af-/toenemen	to decrease/increase
tamelijk	rather
aanhouden	to last
naderen	to approach
de storing	depression
vrijwel	almost
zacht	mild
oplopen	to rise

behoorlijk	quite, very
flink wat	quite a lot of
wisselvallig	changeable
waaien	to blow (only of wind)
stevig	strongly

A weather report

De Bilt, dinsdag

Morgen valt opnieuw veel neerslag. Het regent dan langdurig, terwijl in het noorden ook natte sneeuw voor kan komen. Voor het zover is, hebben we vandaag nog een dag met zon, enkele buien en een gure westenwind.

Later vandaag neemt de wind af en wordt het droog. Dat is het eerst het geval in Zeeland; in Groningen kunnen de buien nog tamelijk lang aanhouden. Al snel nadert van het zuidwesten uit een nieuwe storing. Vóór middernacht neemt de bewolking opnieuw toe en woensdagochtend regent het in vrijwel het hele land.

Woensdag overdag ligt de temperatuur in het noorden enkele graden boven nul. Op hetzelfde moment stroomt in het zuidwesten de zachte lucht binnen; daar wijst de thermometer woensdag-middag mogelijk 10 graden aan. Later op de dag wint de zachte lucht verder terrein en loopt de temperatuur ook in het noorden langzaam op.

Na woensdag blijft het behoorlijk wisselvallig. De ene storing na de andere trekt over het land en er valt van tijd tot tijd flink wat regen. Ook waait het af en toe stevig. De temperatuur blijft daarbij steeds boven het vriespunt.

Language points

The weather

The following are useful expressions associated with weather:

het weerbericht	weather report
de weersverwachting	weather forecast
Het regent/hagelt/sneeuwt.	It is raining/hailing/snowing.
Het dondert/bliksemt.	It is thundering/lightning.
Het onweert.	There is a thunderstorm.
Het motregent.	It's drizzling.

Het dooit.	It's thawing.
15 graden boven/onder het vriespunt	15 degrees above/below freezing[6]
zonnig	sunny
bewolkt	cloudy, overcast
opklaren	to clear up
Wat is/was het voor weer?	What is/was the weather like?
Het is vandaag mooi/slecht weer.	The weather is lovely/awful today.

Exercise 6

On the next page is the weather map (**de weerkaart**) for Saturday, 14 January (**zaterdag veertien januari**) 1995. Answer questions 1–5 by referring to the small map of the Netherlands and questions 6–12 by referring to the larger map of Europe.

1 Hoe warm gaat het in Zeeland worden?
2 In welke twee Nederlandse provincies gaat het regenen?
3 In welke provincie loopt de temperatuur alleen maar tot vijf graden op?
4 Hoeveel graden is het in Utrecht? En op de Waddenzee?
5 Wat is de weersverwachting voor de Randstad?

6 In welk Europees land wordt het zonnig?
7 In welke drie Skandinavische landen gaat het vriezen?
8 Waar gaat het misten?
9 Waar in Zuidoost-Europa gaat het sneeuwen?
10 Komt er een hoge- of een lagedrukgebied boven de Noordzee voor?
11 Wat is de temperatuur in IJsland?
12 Wat is het voor weer in Marokko?

---

6 'Above/below freezing' can also be expressed as **boven/onder nul**.

ZATERDAG 14 JANUARI 1995 2

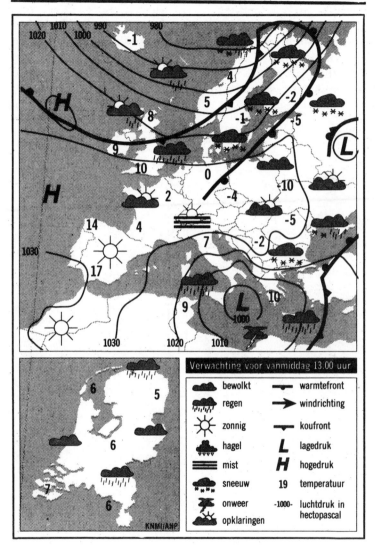

Verwachting voor vanmiddag 13.00 uur

bewolkt		warmtefront	
regen		windrichting	
zonnig		koufront	
hagel		*L*	lagedruk
mist		*H*	hogedruk
sneeuw		19	temperatuur
onweer		-1000-	luchtdruk in hectopascal
opklaringen			

KNMI/ANP

Exercise 7

Here's a puzzle to increase your vocabulary. Starting from the left
of the grid, fill in vertically the Dutch names of the following birds.
They are all common gender. If you get them right, the name of
yet another type of bird will appear across the middle of the puzzle.
What is the English name of this bird?

peacock   swan   starling   budgerigar
heron   swallow   crow   ostrich

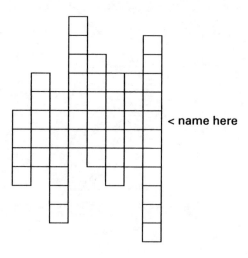

< name here

16 Piet is op school

Piet is at school

In this lesson you will learn about:

- negation and the position of **niet/nooit**
- prepositions
- verbs with prepositional objects
- the separating of prefixes from infinitives and past participles
- how to use the verb **hoeven** 'to need'

Dialogue 1

Piet's having a conversation with a colleague at school

PIET:	Waarom was je gisteren niet op school, Theo?
COLLEGA:	Ik voelde me niet lekker en wilde liever thuis blijven. Maar ik ben niet de hele dag in bed blijven liggen, hoor.
PIET:	Waarom niet?
COLLEGA:	Mijn vrouw was niet thuis en ze had het huis niet opgeruimd.
PIET:	En wat dan nog?
COLLEGA:	Nou ja, we kregen gisteravond eters en dus moest iemand het doen. Ik had me anders dood-geschaamd.
PIET:	Ga weg! Ik wou dat ik met jou getrouwd was in plaats van met Pauline.

PIET:	*Why weren't you at school yesterday, Theo?*
COLLEAGUE:	*I didn't feel well and preferred to stay at home. But I didn't stay in bed all day, you know.*
PIET:	*Why not?*

COLLEAGUE: *My wife wasn't home and she hadn't tidied up the house.*

PIET: *And what else?*

COLLEAGUE: *Well, we were having people for dinner and thus somebody had to do it. I would have died of shame otherwise.*

PIET: *Go on! I wish I was married to you instead of to Pauline.*

Language points

Negation and the position of niet/nooit

The position of the negative **niet** (as well as **nooit**) varies quite a lot but there are underlying rules, some of which are illustrated in dialogue 1. The rules are as follows:

Niet follows
1 expressions of time, e.g. **Hij komt vandaag niet** 'He's not coming today';
2 definite direct objects, e.g. **Hij kan de/die/zijn sleutel niet vinden** 'He can't find the/that/his key';
3 pronominal objects, e.g. **Ik ken hem niet** 'I don't know him'.

Niet precedes
1 expressions of time only when emphasising, e.g **Hij komt niet maandag (maar dinsdag)** 'He's not coming on Monday (but Tuesday)';
2 expressions of manner and place, e.g.

Ik rij niet hard.	I don't drive fast.
Hij woont niet hier.	He doesn't live here.

3 prepositions and prepositional objects and phrases, e.g.

Ik heb niet naar het programma gekeken.	I didn't watch the programme.
Ik heb er niet naar gekeken.	I didn't watch it.
Ze heeft het niet aan mij gegeven.	She didn't give it to me.
Hij woont niet in Engeland.	He doesn't live in England.

4 predicative adjectives, e.g. **Hij is niet arm** 'He is not poor';
5 indefinite direct objects, e.g.

Ze heeft niet genoeg geld bij zich.	She didn't have enough money on her.

| **Ze heeft nooit een brief geschreven.** | She has never written a letter. |

(Compare **Ze heeft de brief nooit geschreven** with a definite direct object.)

Niet either precedes or follows
complements of the verb **zijn**, e.g.

| **Hij is niet mijn vader.** | He is not my father. |
| **Hij is mijn vader niet.** | He is not my father. |

The following sample sentences illustrate and even combine several of the above rules. Look at them closely and relate them back to the rules:

Ik heb het niet aan haar gegeven.[1]	I didn't give it to her.
Ik heb het haar niet gegeven.	I didn't give it to her.
Hij heeft nooit een auto gehad.	He's never had a car.
Ik zou hem mijn auto nooit lenen.	I would never lend him my car.
Ik heb hem vandaag niet op school gezien.	I didn't see him at school today.
Ze heeft er niet aan gedacht.	She didn't think of it.

Remember that 'not a/any' is rendered by **geen**, e.g.

| **Hij heeft geen auto.** | He doesn't have a car. |
| **Hij heeft geen geld.** | He hasn't any money/He has no money. (see page 33) |

The following handy expressions are also negated with **geen**:

dorst hebben 'to be thirsty', e.g. **Ik heb geen dorst** 'I'm not thirsty';
honger hebben 'to be hungry', e.g. **Ik heb geen honger** 'I'm not hungry';
haast hebben 'to be in a hurry', e.g. **Ik heb geen haast** 'I'm not in a hurry';
slaap hebben 'to be sleepy', e.g. **Ik heb geen slaap** 'I'm not sleepy'.

Note the following couplets that are relevant to negation:

---

1 This sentence is synonymous with the next. Note that the use of **aan** 'to' with indirect objects, and the resulting word order, are more or less as in English:

| **Ze heeft een brief aan hem geschreven.** | She wrote a letter to him. |
| **Ze heeft hem een brief geschreven.** | She wrote him a letter. |

iets	something	**ergens**	somewhere
niets	nothing	**nergens**	nowhere
iemand	someone/-body	**ooit**	ever
niemand	no-one/-body	**nooit**	never

'Not . . . either' is expressed by **ook niet/geen**, e.g.

Hij komt ook niet.	He's not coming either.
Hij heeft ook geen geld.	He hasn't got any money either.
Hij heeft er ook geen.	He hasn't got one/any either.

'Not . . . until' (= only) is expressed by **pas**, e.g.

Hij komt pas maandag.	He's not coming until Monday.

Exercise 1

Negate the following sentences by putting **niet** in the right place or using **geen** where appropriate.

1 Ze heeft erge dorst.
2 De kinderen gaan vandaag naar school.
3 Pauline werkt in Utrecht.
4 Piet rijdt te langzaam.
5 Hij gaat met de tram naar zijn werk.
6 Dit jaar hebben de mussen een nest in de garage gebouwd.
7 De vloer is schoon.
8 Thijs is mijn oom.
9 Dit boek is in het Nederlands geschreven.
10 Ik heb het hem verteld.
11 Ik heb het aan hem verteld.
12 Hij koopt een nieuwe fiets voor Pauline.

Exercise 2

Translate the following sentences.

1 She hasn't any time to help you.
2 We don't start till next week.
3 She couldn't find her purse (**de portemonnaie**).
4 There's not a single (**enkel**) tree in front of the house.
5 She's not my mother but my aunt.
6 They are not coming tonight but Friday night.

Culture point

A **strippenkaart** (c) is a public transport ticket in the form of an elongated piece of cardboard consisting of horizontal bars (**strippen**) which can be inserted into an automatic ticket machine in buses and trams etc. for cancellation. They are sold in two lengths, the longer ticket ultimately working out cheaper. The number of zones being travelled across determines the number of **strippen** to be stamped. **Strippenkaarten** can be bought in any post-office, bus depot or **sigarenwinkel** prior to taking a bus or tram, thus reducing the delay caused in a bus, for example, by those who have not pre-purchased a ticket. Shorter, more expensive **strippenkaarten** can be obtained from the driver but you save money by buying in advance. **Strippenkaarten** have the added advantage of being valid on public transport (but not trains) throughout the country.

Dialogue 2 🎧

Piet is looking for his torch

PIET: Marius, heb jij weer zitten spelen met mijn zaklantaarn?
MARIUS: Nee, papa. Ik heb hem bij de koelkast in de keuken zien liggen.
PIET: Waar dan? Op, onder, voor, achter of naast de koelkast?
MARIUS: Ernaast, tussen de koelkast en het aanrecht.
PIET: Elke keer dat ik hem nodig heb, moet ik er eerst naar gaan zoeken. Ik word er gek van.
PAULINE: Zeur niet, Piet. Het is je eigen schuld. Je zet hem nooit weer terug op dezelfde[2] plaats.

---

2 In **dezelfde/hetzelfde** 'the same' the article and the adjective are written together as one word. **Hetzelfde** is used to express 'And the same to you', e.g. **Prettige vakantie, Joop. Hetzelfde, Piet.**

PIET:	*Marius, have you been playing with my torch again?*
MARIUS:	*No, daddy. I saw it lying near the fridge in the kitchen.*
PIET:	*Where? On, under, in front of, behind or next to the fridge?*
MARIUS:	*Next to it, between the fridge and the sink.*
PIET:	*Every time I need it, I first have to go looking for it. It drives me crazy.*
PAULINE:	*Stop grumbling, Piet. It's your own fault. You never put it back in the same place.*

Language points

Prepositions

You have been using prepositions since lesson 1. They are the (usually) little words that show the relationship of nouns and pronouns to each other, e.g. *He got a bike from his uncle on his birthday*. They are to be found in almost every Dutch and English sentence. The problem with prepositions is that they are often used very idiomatically, e.g.

Ik woon bij mijn tante.	I live with my aunt.
Waarom zit je bij het raam?	Why are you sitting near the window?
Ze heeft het bij V en D gekocht.	She bought it at V&D (a large store).

It is impossible to describe all the various uses of prepositions systematically. You will have to observe how they are used. What follows is a list of the most common prepositions with their primary meaning:

aan	on (vertical), at, to (people; compare **naar**)[3]
achter	behind
behalve	except (for)
bij	near, by, at
binnen	within, in(side)
boven	above, over
buiten	outside (of)
gedurende	during

3 **Aan** and **op** are two of the most ubiquitous and idiomatic of all prepositions, whose varied uses you should observe closely.

in	in, into
langs	along, past
met	with, by
na	after
naar	to (places)
naast	next to
om	around
ondanks	in spite of, despite
onder	under
op	on (horizontal), at
over	over, about (i.e. concerning)
sinds	since
tegen	against
tegenover	opposite
tijdens	during
tot	until
tussen	between
uit	out (of), from
van	from, of, off
vanwege	because of, on account of
volgens	according to
voor	for
vóór	in front of, before
zonder	without

Occasionally some prepositions are placed after the noun to express a motion in a given direction, e.g.

Hij is de gracht in gevallen.	He fell into the canal.
Ik reed de brug over.	I drove over the bridge.
Hij reed de hoek om.	I drove around the corner.
Gaat u die kant uit!	Go in that direction/that way (pointing)!
Ik ga de stad in.	I'm going (in)to town.

Compare the following two sentences to get some idea of what is being expressed by putting the preposition after the noun:

We liepen het bos door.
We walked through the forest (i.e. from one side to the other).

We liepen door het bos.
We walked through the forest (i.e. in the forest).

Heen is used in combination with some prepositions, with the preposition standing in front of the noun and **heen** after it. It expresses 'right through/around/over', etc., e.g.

Hij rende door de menigte heen.	He ran through the crowd.
Hij keek om zich heen.	He looked around him.
De kinderen renden om de tafel heen.	The children ran around the table.
Het vliegtuig vloog over de stad heen.	The plane flew over the city.

A preposition plus **heen** can occasionally have a figurative meaning, e.g.

We hebben langs elkaar heen gepraat.	We were speaking at cross purposes.
Ik heb eroverheen gelezen.	I missed it (while I was reading).

Another peculiarity of some prepositions is that they can be used in combination with another. Certain prepositional couplets stand either side of the noun and others precede the noun, e.g.

Hij is tegen een muur aan gereden.	He drove into a wall.
Hij is tegen een boom op gereden.	He drove into a tree.
Ik ging onder de brug door.	I went on under the bridge.
de eikenboom achter in de tuin	the oak tree down the back of the garden
midden in het bos	in the middle of the forest
boven op de kast	on top of the cupboard

There are too many such combinations to list. The reader is advised to observe how prepositions are used in Dutch because unfortunately grammatical rules do not go very far in helping you to master them.

Exercise 3

Fill in the appropriate preposition referring to the list given earlier in this lesson.

1 Zullen we (*before*) het avondeten even gaan wandelen?
2 Hij heeft zijn vader (*since*) de oorlog niet gezien.

3 (*After*) haar operatie lag ze nog twee weken in het ziekenhuis.
4 We zaten allemaal nog (*at*) tafel.
5 Hij heeft (*during*) de film zitten praten.
6 (*According to*) mijn moeder is hij een schurk.
7 We blijven vandaag (*on account of*) het weer thuis.
8 Ik lees op het ogenblik een boek (*about*) Australië.
9 We rijden nu (*past*) het postkantoor.
10 Hij woont (*opposite*) het station.

Reading text 🔲

Vocabulary

links/rechts	on the left/right
aan de linkerkant/	on the left/right
rechterkant	
rechtdoor	straight ahead
linksaf/rechtsaf	to the left/right

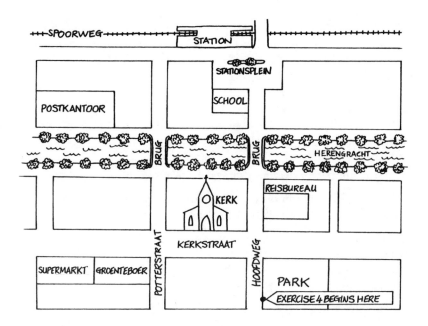

het plein	the square
oversteken	to cross
Bent u hier bekend?	Do you know the area? Are you from around here?

U staat vóór de supermarkt in de Kerkstraat. Rechts van u is de groenteboer. U wilt via het reisbureau naar het station. U gaat langs de Kerkstraat tot de Hoofdweg. Daar gaat u linksaf. U bezoekt het reisbureau aan de rechterkant. U gaat dan bij de Herengracht de brug over en loopt rechtdoor langs de school naar het Stationsplein. U steekt het plein over en komt bij het station aan.

Note: The adverbs **links** and **rechts** drop their **-s** and add an **-er** ending when used adjectivally in front of a noun and are usually written together with the noun as one word.

Exercise 4

Look at the street map on p. 211. You are in the park. Write the dialogue.

Stranger:	Says excuse me and asks you if you know the area.
You:	Answer yes and ask what the stranger wants to know.
Stranger:	Says he is looking for the post-office.
You:	Tell him how to get there by taking Kerk and Potter Streets and end by saying the post-office is on the right.

Language points

Verbs with prepositional objects

A verb with a prepositional object: I am thinking *of you.*

Many verbs are commonly used in combination with a given preposition and thus need to be learnt as follows:

denken aan	to think of
herinneren aan	to remind of
kijken naar	to look at
luisteren naar	to listen to
zich verheugen op	to look forward to
wachten op	to wait for

zeggen tegen	to say to
zoeken naar	to look for

There are too many to list so these should be observed and learnt as you meet them in texts.

Exercise 5

Translate the following sentences looking up the verbs in the back of the book to find the appropriate preposition.

1 Wat heeft hij (*to*) zijn moeder gezegd?
2 Ik geloof niet (*in*) god.
3 Ik verkies zijn broer (*to*) zijn zus.
4 Hij denkt (*about*) zijn vakantie na.
5 Hij heeft me (*for*) geld gevraagd.
6 Zij lijkt sprekend (. . .) haar moeder. (*to look like*)
7 Hij trouwde toen (*to*) haar. (*got married to*)
8 Ze glimlachte (*at*) het kind.
9 Het boek bestaat (*of*) twintig hoofdstukken.
10 De hond heeft (*at*) de kinderen geblaft.

The separating of prefixes from infinitives and past participles

Separable verbs like **opbellen** 'to ring up' and **thuiskomen** 'to come home' were dealt with on page 102. An optional word order commonly occurs with these verbs which has not been mentioned so far but with which you will have to become familiar.

Where the past participle of a separable verb occurs in a subordinate clause, i.e. at the end of the clause together with the auxiliary verb it is dependent on (see also page 124), the following variations of word order are possible:

1 **Wist je dat hij me gisteravond opgebeld heeft?**
2 **Wist je dat hij me gisteravond heeft opgebeld?**
3 **Wist je dat hij me gisteravond op heeft gebeld?**
Did you know that he rang me up last night?

1a **Ik geloof niet dat die boom gaat omvallen.**
2a **Ik geloof niet dat die boom om gaat vallen.**
I don't think that tree is going to topple over.

The alternative word order illustrated in sentences 3 and 2a, i.e. where the finite verb stands between the separable prefix and the past participle or infinitive, is something that occurs more commonly in speech than in writing and thus is more likely to be heard than seen.

A similar thing occurs colloquially in double-infinitive constructions (see page 134) where the first of the two infinitives can be placed between the prefix and its verb, e.g.

Ik heb hem willen opbellen.
Ik heb hem op willen bellen.
I wanted to ring him up.

Ze heeft mij zien weggaan.
Ze heeft mij weg zien gaan.
She saw me leaving.

> MOEDERS gevr. (A'dam en omg.), 25 tot plm. 30 jaar, die mee willen doen aan een marktonderzoek. U krijgt hier een vergoeding voor. Inl. 020-6654447.

Note: Key to the abbreviations used in the above classified advertisement:

gevr. = **gevraagd**	wanted	**plm.** = **plus minus** approximately
A'dam = **Amsterdam**		**Inl.** = **inlichtingen** information
omg. = **omgeving**	vicinity	

Exercise 6

Rewrite the following sentences applying the alternative word order described above.

1 Ik geloof dat hij wat later zal opdagen.
2 Ik zei tegen hem dat ik haar zou opbellen.
3 Hij heeft niet kunnen opstaan.
4 Weet je hoe laat zij aangekomen is?
5 Weet je wie al de koekjes heeft opgegeten?

How to use the verb hoeven 'to need'

The usual negative of *must* in English is *don't have to* or *don't need to*, e.g. *You must get up early* but *You don't have to get up early/You don't need to get up early.* The latter two forms are expressed by **hoeven** in Dutch, e.g. **Jij moet vroeg opstaan** and **Jij hoeft niet vroeg op te staan.** 'You mustn't get up early', where the meaning is somewhat different because it is a type of order, is in Dutch simply **Jij moet niet vroeg opstaan.**

Hoeven is a modal verb but differs from the other modals (see page 108) in requiring a **te** before the infinitive that follows; but in the perfect tense, where a double-infinitive construction is required, **te** is optional, e.g.

Ik heb hem niet hoeven (te) helpen. I didn't have to help him.

Durven 'to dare', which you would not normally see as a modal, behaves in a similar fashion, e.g.

Hij durft/durfde mij niet te helpen.
He doesn't/didn't dare to help me.

Hij heeft me niet durven (te) helpen.
He didn't dare help me.

Exercise 7

Negate the following sentences using **hoeven** while preserving the same tense as **moeten**. Remember too that **een** changes to **geen** when negating.

1 Je moet hem een tientje geven.
2 Ik moest een brief aan haar schrijven.
3 Ik heb een brief aan haar moeten schrijven.
4 De studenten moeten in het weekend een opstel schrijven.
5 De studenten hebben in het weekend een opstel moeten schrijven.

17 Marius wil gaan spelen

Marius wants to go and play

In this lesson you will learn about:

- independent use of modals
- present participles
- verbal nouns
- how to express ailments
- parts of the body

Dialogue 📼

Marius wants to go out to play but Pauline is putting her foot down

MARIUS: Mamma, ik wil in het park om de hoek gaan fietsen. Mag dat?

PAULINE: Nee, dat mag niet. Jij moet eerst je kamer opruimen.

MARIUS: Ach, nee. Moet dat?

PAULINE: Ja, dat moet.

MARIUS: En moet ik ook mijn treinstel inpakken?

PAULINE: Nee, dat hoeft niet. Dat kun je laten staan, maar je moet wel[1] al je kleren in de kast ophangen. (*er wordt aan de deur geklopt*)

PAULINE: Dat zal wel je vriendje zijn waar je mee gaat fietsen.

MARIUS: Dat denk ik ook.

PAULINE: Niets aan te doen. Je ruimt eerst je kamer op, hoor!

MARIUS: *Mummy, I want to ride my bike in the park around the corner. Is that okay* (= permitted)*?*

PAULINE: *No, it's not* (= that's not permitted). *First you have to tidy your room up.*

---

1 See page 50 for the explanation of the function of this **wel**.

MARIUS: *Oh, no. Do I have to* (= is that necessary)*?*
PAULINE: *Yes, you do* (= it is necessary).
MARIUS: *And do I have to pack my train set away too?*
PAULINE: *No, that's not necessary. You can leave that, but you will have to hang all your clothes up in the wardrobe.*
(there is a knock at the door)
PAULINE: *Is that your friend you're going cycling with?*
MARIUS: *It probably is.*
PAULINE: *That can't be helped. First you tidy your room up, do you hear?*

Language points

Independent use of modals

Hoeven, **kunnen**, **moeten**, **mogen** and **zullen** are commonly used alone, without an infinitive following, and with **dat** or **het** as the subject to express, e.g.:

Dat hoeft niet.	That's not necessary.
Dat moet.	That is necessary/must be done.
Dat kan.	That's possible.
Dat kan niet.	That is impossible.
Dat mag.	That is permissible/You may.
Dat mag niet.	That is not permissible/You may not.
Dat zal wel.	That's probably the case.

Zullen in this sense is always used with **wel**, e.g.

Piet zal wel thuis zijn, denk je niet?
Piet's probably at home, don't you think?
Ja, dat zal wel.
Yes, probably.

Present participles

A present participle: The child came in *crying.* The *crying* child.

Back on page 18 you learnt that as part of a verb Dutch does not have the equivalent of the English *-ing* form, i.e. 'The child is crying' is simply **Het kind huilt**. On page 184 you were introduced to possible ways of expressing this progressive if need be, i.e. **Het kind is aan het huilen, Het kind zit te huilen**.

The literal translation of 'crying' is **huilend**, i.e. this is the present participle, which is formed by simply adding **-d** or **-de** (usually optional) to the infinitive. But this form can only be used as an adverb or as an adjective standing before a noun in Dutch, e.g.

Het kind kwam huilend/huilende binnen.
Het huilende kind.

Verbal nouns

The '-ing' form in a sentence like 'Boiling vegetables is an art' is not rendered by the form described above. The Dutch say here 'The boiling of vegetables is an art', using a noun: **Het koken van groente is een kunst.** These so-called verbal nouns in Dutch are expressed by infinitives, which are regarded as neuter nouns where an article is required, e.g.

Ik ben niet in de wieg gelegd voor het vroege opstaan.
I'm not cut out for getting up early.

Studeren is niet makkelijk.   Studying is not easy.
Waar heeft hij het schilderen geleerd?
Where did he learn painting?

The last two examples can be expressed with a verb too, in which case they correspond to 'It isn't easy to study' and 'Where did he learn to paint?', e.g.

Het is niet makkelijk om te studeren.
Waar heeft hij leren schilderen? *or* Waar heeft hij geleerd om te schilderen?

How to express ailments

Ik heb pijn in mijn ...   My ... is hurting.
Mijn ... doet zeer/pijn.   My ... is hurting.
Ik heb hoofd-/kies-/buikpijn. I have a headache/toothache/
                                   stomach ache.

Note that 'a' is not translated in Dutch in the last example. Note too the use of the hyphen in that sentence. Where you list nouns compounded from the same root word, it is not necessary to repeat that noun, e.g.

Op zon- en feestdagen gesloten Closed on holidays and Sundays

Parts of the body

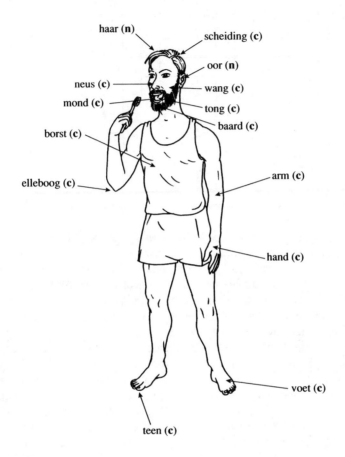

haar (**n**)

scheiding (**c**)

oor (**n**)

neus (**c**)

wang (**c**)

mond (**c**)

tong (**c**)

baard (**c**)

borst (**c**)

elleboog (**c**)

arm (**c**)

hand (**c**)

voet (**c**)

teen (**c**)

Exercise 1

Insert the Dutch words for the following parts of the body vertically into the grid below, starting from the left of the grid. If you
get them all right, the name of a Dutch city will appear across the
middle. Of which province is it the capital city?

breast, hand, foot, arm, toe, tongue, cheek, elbow, mouth, beard,
ear, nose, parting, hair

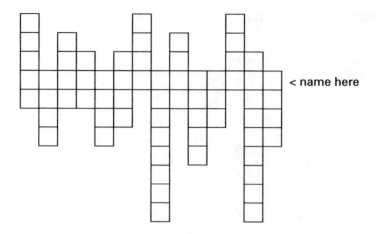

< name here

Culture point

A uniquely Dutch festivity is **Sinterklaas**, St Nicholas' Day, the sixth of December. The name **Sinterklaas** is a synonym of **Sint Nikolaas**, who, by tradition, arrives in the Netherlands from Spain by boat. He is accompanied by a blackamoor called **Zwarte Piet**. **Sint**, as he is known for short, is attired in red bishop's garb and wears a mitre and carries a staff. He has a book in which the good and bad deeds of the children over the last year have been recorded. Piet is there to punish the bad ones and hand out **pepernootjes** (small buttons of ginger bread) to the good ones. Sinterklaas and Father Christmas (compare the name *Santaclaus*) are clearly closely related. Until the post-war period the Sinterklaas tradition, complete with gift giving, far outweighed that of Christmas, except as far as the latter was of significance to practising Christians, of course, but Christmas is gradually overshadowing Sinterklaas, certainly when it comes to gift giving. Sinterklaas is not a public holiday, but everybody gets into the spirit of it whether at work or at home. Sint visits on the evening of the fifth. Gifts, whether brought by Sint personally or deposited anonymously in your letter box or on your desk (all cards are signed by Sint or Sint and Piet) are accompanied by a rhyme, often miniature works of art, which usually has a dig at you from the point of view of the writer. You look for clues in the verse as to who it might be from. The gifts are usually quite modest, often consisting of any one of numerous delicacies which are associated with the festivity, e.g. **speculaas** (a sort of ginger bread), **taai-taai** (aniseed-flavoured ginger bread), **marsepein** and **chocoladeletters**. It's a wonderful tradition and one which all Dutch people regard with great fondness.

Key to the exercises

Lesson 1

Piet talks about his family

My name is Piet and I live in Amsterdam. I am married to Pauline. She is English, but she speaks Dutch. I am a teacher at a secondary school in Amsterdam but Pauline works in The Hague. She goes to work by train every day. She is a secretary in a travel agency. We have two children, a son and a daughter. His name is Marius and hers is Charlotte.

Exercise 1

Ik heet Piet en ik woon in Amsterdam. Ik ben getrouwd met Pauline. Zij is Engels, maar ze spreekt Nederlands. Ik ben leraar op een middelbare school in Amsterdam maar Pauline werkt in Den Haag. Ze gaat elke dag met de trein naar haar werk. Zij is secretaresse bij een reisbureau. Wij hebben twee kinderen, een zoon en een dochter. Hij heet Marius en zij heet Charlotte.

Exercise 2

Country	Inhabitant (male)	Language/Nationality
Duitsland	Duitser	Duits
Engeland	Engelsman	Engels
Frankrijk	Fransman	Frans
Nederland	Nederlander	Nederlands
Zweden	Zweed	Zweeds
België	Belg	Belgisch

Exercise 3

	Voornaam <u>Otto</u>
	Familienaam <u>Schmidt</u>
	Leeftijd <u>30</u>
	Lengte <u>1.86 m</u>
	Nationaliteit <u>Duits</u>
Beroep	<u>Bakker</u>
Ogen	<u>Blauw</u>
Haar	<u>Lichtbruin</u>
Adres	<u>Europaweg 5</u>
	<u>Hamburg</u>
	<u>Bondesrepubliek Duitsland</u>

Exercise 4

Lisa Houghton is 31 jaar oud. Zij is lerares. Zij is één meter zeventig lang en heeft groene ogen en zwart haar. Zij is Engels/Engelse en zij woont in Nederland.

Exercise 5

Piet is a teacher. He is Dutch/a Dutchman and he is married to Pauline. Pauline is English/an English woman. She is a secretary and she works in The Hague. She speaks English and Dutch.

Exercise 6

Ik <u>heet</u> Piet en ik <u>woon</u> in Amsterdam. Ik <u>ben</u> getrouwd met Pauline. Zij <u>is</u> Engels, maar ze <u>spreekt</u> Nederlands. Ik <u>ben</u> leraar op een middelbare school in Amsterdam maar Pauline <u>werkt</u> in Den Haag. Ze <u>gaat</u> elke dag met de trein naar haar werk. Zij <u>is</u> secretaresse bij een reisbureau. Wij <u>hebben</u> twee kinderen, een zoon en een dochter. Hij <u>heet</u> Marius en zij <u>heet</u> Charlotte.

Exercise 7

lopen/loop/loopt   vertalen/vertaal/vertaalt

antwoorden/antwoord/antwoordt   vragen/vraag/vraagt
naaien/naai/naait   beloven/beloof/belooft

Exercise 8

Zij naait.	Zij lopen.
Ik woon in Londen.	Zij heeft een zoon en een dochter.
Hij vertaalt een boek.	Zij wonen in Engeland.
Ik vraag.	Jij belooft.

Exercise 9

Jᴜ:	Goeie morgen!
Vʀɪᴇɴᴅ:	Goeie morgen!
Jᴜ:	Het is leuk om je weer te zien. Hoe gaat het (met je/jou)?
Vʀɪᴇɴᴅ:	Het gaat slecht. Hoe gaat het met jou?
Jᴜ:	Het gaat (heel) goed/prima/uitstekend.
Vʀɪᴇɴᴅ:	Hoe gaat het met Pauline?
Jᴜ:	Het gaat goed met haar.
Vʀɪᴇɴᴅ:	Hoe gaat het met jouw vrouw?
Jᴜ:	Ook goed. Ze is in Den Haag.

Lesson 2

Exercise 1

1 Groningen ligt in de provincie Groningen, in het noordoosten van Nederland. 2 Zwolle ligt in de provincie Overijssel, in het oosten van Nederland. 3 Leiden ligt in de provincie Zuid-Holland, in het westen van Nederland. 4 Utrecht ligt in de provincie Utrecht, in het midden van Nederland. 5 Middelburg ligt in de provincie Zeeland, in het zuidwesten van Nederland. 6 Tilburg ligt in de provincie Noord-Brabant, in het zuiden van Nederland.

Exercise 2

1 Leiden is een stad in het westen van Nederland. 2 Den Haag is een stad in het westen van Nederland/van het land. Het is de zetel van de regering en de hoofdstad van Zuid-Holland. 3 Noord-Holland is een provincie van Nederland/een Nederlandse provincie. 4 Berlijn is de hoofdstad van Duitsland. 5 Kopenhagen is de

hoofdstad van Denemarken. 6 Brussel is de hoofdstad van België. 7 Londen is de hoofdstad van Engeland/Groot-Brittanië. 8. Parijs is de hoofdstad van Frankrijk. 9 Nederland is een land in het noordwesten van Europa. 10 België ligt in het noordwesten van Europa, ten zuiden van Nederland.

Exercise 3

(1 De man) in (2 de keuken) is (3 de vader) of (4 het kind). She lives next-door to (5 een leraar). I don't know where (6 de vrouw) works. (7 Het huis) is for sale. Belgium is (8 een land) to the south of the Netherlands. (9 De school) is at (10 het einde) of (11 de straat).

Exercise 4

1 Frans; 2 de oom; 3 het bord; 4 het zout.

Exercise 5

1 Helaas ben ik leraar. 2 Hier wonen wij. 3 Engeland ken ik niet. 4 Elke dag gaat Pauline naar Den Haag. 5 Nu zet Ineke koffie.

Exercise 6

1 Onze zoon is niet ziek. 2 Gelukkig woon ik niet in Rusland. 3 Ze rijden niet elke dag naar Leiden. 4 Morgen ga ik niet met de tram.

Exercise 7

1 Mijn collega heeft geen leuke vrouw. 2 Hij woont niet in dit land. 3 Zij werkt niet in ander land. 4 Het huis heeft geen zolder. 5 Ik heb geen tweede fiets.

Exercise 8

1 65; 2 49; 3 92; 4 41; 5 83; 6 55; 7 78; 8 37.

Exercise 9

twee gulden vijfendertig, één gulden vijfentachtig, negenenzestig cent, driehonderd vierenzestig gulden vijfentwintig cent, twaalfhonderd vierendertig gulden, vijfentwintig cent, honderd vijf gulden, vijfentwintig mark, tachtig pond, vijfenvijftig dollar.

Lesson 3

Exercise 1

1 de bananen; 2 de leraren; 3 de vaders; 4 de vrouwen; 5 de mannen; 6 de landen; 7 de scholen; 8 de dochters; 9 de zetels; 10 de hoofdsteden; 11 de regeringen; 12 de kinderen; 13 de Duitsers; 14 de ogen; 15 de jaren; 16 de aardappels; 17 de uien; 18 de treinen

Exercise 2

1 druiven; 2 bananen; 3 uien; 4 peren; 5 aardappels; 6 mannen; 7 lammeren; 8 bladeren; 9 kinderen; 10 landen; 11 Nederlanders; 12 steden; 13 golven; 14 eieren; 15 auto's.

Exercise 3

1 het oog; 2 het schip; 3 de golf; 4 het kalf; 5 de peer; 6 de vrouw 7 de weg; 8 de stad; 9 de druif; 10 de gans; 11 de tafel; 12 de schoen; 13 het pad; 14 de kat; 15 het meisje.

Exercise 4

JIJ:	Wat/hoeveel kosten de bananen?
GROENTEBOER:	Die/ze kosten drie gulden per kilo.
JIJ:	Ik wou graag vier bananen. Heeft u ook druiven?
GROENTEBOER:	Ik heb helaas geen druiven.
JIJ:	Wat/hoeveel kosten de peren?
GROENTEBOER:	Die/ze kosten vier (gulden) vijftig per kilo.
JIJ:	Ik wou graag een kilo peren.
GROENTEBOER:	Anders nog iets?
JIJ:	Dat was het.
GROENTEBOER:	Dat is zeven gulden vijfenzeventig alles bij elkaar.
JIJ:	Ik heb geen kleingeld. Kunt u honderd gulden wisselen?
GROENTEBOER:	Dat kan, mevrouw/meneer.
JIJ:	Alstublieft.

GROENTEBOER: Alstublieft. Tot ziens.

Exercise 5

1 Zijn grootvader heet (prins) Bernhard 2 Hij komt uit Duitsland
3 Zijn moedertaal is Duits 4 Het woont/zij wonen in Den Haag
5 Zij was de koningin van Nederland 6 De kop van de koningin/
Beatrix staat op alle Nederlandse munten.

Exercise 6

1 Wonen jullie in Amsterdam/Rotterdam enz.?[1] 2 Spreekt zij/uw
vrouw Engels? 3 Is Den Haag de hoofdstad van Nederland?
4 Werkt Pauline in Amsterdam? 5 Rij jij/rijdt u altijd zo hard?
6 Hou jij/houdt u van haar?

Exercise 7

1 Ja. 2 Ja. 3 Ja. 4 Jawel. 5 Nee. 6 Jawel.

Exercise 8

1 Kerstmis valt in december. 2 Nieuwjaarsdag valt in januari. 3 Ik
heb vakantie in juni. 4 Pinksteren valt in mei. 5 Koninginnedag is
altijd in april. 6 Ik ben in [your birthday] jarig. 7 Pasen valt bijna
altijd in april. 8 In Nederland begint de zomer in juni.

Exercise 9

1 Dertig april. 2 [your birthday]. 3 Vijf mei. 4 Op 25 december.
5 Eén januari.

Lesson 4

Exercise 1

YOU: Met Paul.
CALLER: Is Joop thuis?

---

1 **Enz.** is the abbreviation of **enzovoorts** 'and so on', and as such is the equivalent
of 'etc.'.

You:	Ja, hij is thuis. Met wie spreek ik?
Caller:	Met André de Schutter. Kan ik met Joop praten?
You:	Wilt u even wachten!
Joop:	Hallo, met Joop.
Caller:	Ik ben het, Joop, André.
Joop:	Ik ken u niet. U bent verkeerd verbonden.

Exercise 2

```
             1G
       2V E R T A A L D
          W                        3G
          O                4G       E
 5G E R O O K T        6G E L E E F D
    E   N          7G   E        A  O
    Z   D        8G E T E L D    N  O
    E              E    Z    O   T  D
 9G E T R O U W D  E    O        W
    D         A    T    F        O
       10B E D A N K T  D        O
             S          O        R
    11G E B L A F T  12B E L O O F D
```

Exercise 3

1 ontmoet/ontmoet; 2 wek/gewekt; 3 herhaal/herhaald; 4 blaf/geblaft; 5 verf/geverfd; 6 bloos/gebloosd; 7 praat/gepraat; 8 huur/gehuurd.

Exercise 4

1 Ik heb vandaag gewerkt. 2 Hij heeft de hele week gewerkt. 3 Zij hebben de hele dag gewerkt. 4 Ik heb hem gisteravond ontmoet. 5 Piet heeft een boek vertaald. 6 Zij heeft vanmorgen/vanochtend gebeld. 7 Hij heeft niets gezegd. 8 Heb je gewerkt? 9 Zij heeft de muur geverfd. 10 Wij hebben een huis gehuurd.

Exercise 5

```
      ¹G  E  D  A  A  N
       E                      ²G
       W        ³G         ⁴G  E  G  E  V  E  N
 ⁵G  E  V  O  N  D  E  N        K
   E      N        S       ⁶G  E  Z  O  C  H  T
   K      N        N   ⁷G   E         C
   E      E    ⁸G   E  W  E  E  S  T   H
   K      N        D   H   L          T
   E               E   A   A
   N               N   D  ⁹G  E  D  A  C  H  T
                           E
          ¹⁰G  E  K  O  M  E  N
```

Exercise 6

1 Zij heeft het boek aan mij gegeven. 2 Hij heeft een reis naar Griekenland gewonnen. 3 Ik heb Hilde in de stad gezien. 4 Piet heeft te veel bier gedronken. 5 We hebben het gevonden.

Exercise 7

1 Ik heb boodschappen gedaan. 2 Ik heb brood gebakken. 3 Ik heb de auto gewassen. 4 Ik heb overhemden gestreken. 5 Ik heb mijn moeder gebeld. 6 Ik heb aardappels geschild.

Exercise 8

1 De computer is verdwenen. 2 Heeft Marius het genomen? 3 Is Pauline al thuisgekomen? 4 Zij is naar Amsterdam gereden. 5 Piet is naar huis gegaan. 6 Ze heeft koffie gedronken. 7 Is Lien al verhuisd? 8 Heb je Hilde gebeld? 9 Ze heeft ja gezegd. 10 We zijn de hele dag thuis gebleven.

Exercise 9

1 Ik ben naar huis gereden. 2 Ik heb nooit een Mercedes gereden. 3 Heb je ooit in de Noordzee gezwommen? 4 Ik ben een keer van Frankrijk naar Engeland gezwommen. 5 We zijn gisteren naar Den Helder gefietst. 6 Heb jij nooit gefietst?

Exercise 10

1 Ik kan ze vergeten. 2 Ik kan naar België verhuizen. 3 Ik kan weer bellen/terugbellen. 4 Ik kan het licht uitdoen. 5 Ik kan ja zeggen. 6 Ik kan een auto aanhouden. 7 Ik kan naar huis gaan. 8 Ik kan een kaars aansteken.

Exercise 11

Je kan met een potlood schrijven. Je kan met een kwast verven. Je kan met een schaar knippen. Je kan met een naald naaien. Je kan met een lepel roeren. Je kan met een schop graven. Je kan met een pen tekenen.

Exercise 12

PAULINE: Charlotte, heb jij de koekjes gezien?
CHARLOTTE: Ja, ik heb twee koekjes opgegeten en Marius heeft ook twee koekjes opgegeten.
PAULINE: Nu hebben we geen koekjes voor vanavond.
CHARLOTTE: Sorry/het spijt me dat ik de koekjes opgegeten heb.

Exercise 13

PIET: Hebben jullie op mij gewacht?
PAULINE: Ja, waar ben je gebleven?
PIET: Ik heb de auto gewassen.
PAULINE: Heb je honger?
PIET: Ja, ik heb razende honger. Het spijt me dat ik zo laat ben.
PAULINE: Het geeft niet. Jaap heeft gebeld.
PIET: Hoe gaat het met Jaap/hem?
PAULINE: Goed/Het gaat goed met hem.

Lesson 5

Exercise 1

1 Hij heeft haar in de stad gezien. 2 Heb je hem gezien? 3 Ik heb ze/hen bij de buren gezien. 4 Hij woont bij ons. 5 Ik heb het aan ze/hen gegeven. 6 Zij kennen me niet. Ken jij ze/hen? 7 Ik zoek jou/je. 8 Ik heb ze gevonden.

Exercise 2

1 Wat een auto! Waar heb je hem gekocht? 2 Mijn oom heeft een marmot. Hij heet Rob. Wil je hem zien? 3 Ik heb een konijn. Het heet Lies. Wil je het aaien?

Exercise 3

1 Ken je zijn vader? 2 Nee, maar ik ken haar moeder. 3 Onze ouders en hun ouders kennen elkaar. 4 Heb je je huiswerk gedaan? 5 Heeft u uw auto gewassen?

Exercise 4

1 Ken je die man? 2 Die ken ik niet, maar deze wel. 3 Dat is mijn broer. 4 Dit is mijn zus. 5 Dit zijn zijn boeken. 6 Ik wil deze stoelen verven. 7 Ken je die mensen? Het zijn mijn buren. 8 Die boom is te groot voor deze tuin maar die is niet te groot.

Exercise 5

deze/die koelkast, deze/die lamp, deze/die appels, dit/dat fornuis, dit/dat bed, deze/die bedden, deze/die vogel, deze/die honden, deze/die ooms.

Exercise 6

1 Ik woon in een groot huis. Hoe groot is dat van jou? 2 Mijn kinderen heten Marius en Charlotte. Hoe heten die van jou? 3 Ken je die van mij niet? 4 Ik heb een mooie handtas gekocht maar die van haar was duurder. 5 Die hond is van hen maar die van ons is veel leuker, vind je niet?

Exercise 7

1 Paulines schoonouders, de schoonouders van Pauline, Pauline d'r schoonouders; 2 Piets kinderen, de kinderen van Piet, Piet z'n kinderen; 3 de hond van de buurman, de buurman z'n hond; 4 De kat van de buren, de buren hun kat; 5 Lien en Jaaps ouders, de ouders van Lien en Jaap, Lien en Jaap hun ouders; 6 de hoofdstad van het land; 7 het gezicht van de kat.

Exercise 8

1 zijn schoondochter; 2 zijn schoonzoon 3 zijn kleinzoon; 4 zijn kleindochter 5 zijn achterkleinzoon; 6 zijn achterkleindochter 7 zijn vader; 8 zijn moeder 9 zijn schoonvader; 10 zijn schoonmoeder 11 zijn zwager; 12 zijn schoonzuster 13 zijn neef; 14 zijn nicht 15 zijn grootvader; 16 zijn grootmoeder 17 zijn oom; 18 zijn tante 19 zijn neef; 20 zijn nicht 21 zijn overgrootvader; 22 zijn overgrootmoeder 23 zijn betovergrootvader; 24 zijn betovergrootmoeder.

Exercise 9

1 Grote bomen zijn soms gevaarlijk. 2 Ik heb rode èn groene appels gekocht. 3 Wat een brede weg! 4 Ik heb geen Nederlands geld. 5 Welke boeken heb je me geleend? 6 Het dikke over Shakespeare en dat dunne over de oorlog. 7 Was het een goedkope of een dure fiets? 8 Ik heb geen wit overhemd en ook geen witte broek. 9 Hij komt elke dag/elk jaar. 10 Ze heeft de vieze vloer geveegd.

Lesson 6

Exercise 1

1 Met wie werkt je vader? 2 Van wie is deze kat? 3 Waar komen de buren vandaan? 4 Hoeveel heb je voor je nieuwe jurk betaald, Pauline? 5 Wie woont naast julllie? 6 Waar ga je vanavond naartoe? 7 Welke jurk ga je dragen? 8 In wat voor een huis wonen jouw ouders?

Exercise 2

1 Ik ga morgen Tante Lies bezoeken/bij Tante Lies op visite. 2 Ik doe morgen boodschappen. *or* Ik ga morgen boodschappen doen. 3 Waar zal ze wonen? *or* Waar gaat ze wonen? 4 Marius zal nu naar bed moeten gaan. 5 Ik doe het voor je. *or* Ik zal het voor je doen. 6 Ze komen volgende week.

Exercise 3

1 Zullen we televisie kijken? 2 Zullen we naar Duitsland rijden? 3 Zullen we koffie drinken? 4 Zullen we een ijsje kopen? 5 Zullen we Oma bezoeken/bij Oma op visite gaan?

Exercise 4

1 Laten we televisie kijken! 2 Laten we naar Duitsland rijden! 3 Laten we koffie drinken! 4 Laten we een ijsje kopen! 5 Laten we Oma bezoeken/bij Oma op visite gaan!

Exercise 5

1 Op het ogenblik kunnen we niet komen. 2 Morgen moet je me komen helpen. 3 Vandaag is Marius op school. 4 Elke middag spelen de kinderen in het park. 5 Vijftien jaar geleden heeft hij in Utrecht gewoond.

Exercise 6

1 Charlotte heeft hem vanochtend aan haar vriendin gegeven. 2 Piet heeft haar gisteren in de stad gezien. 3 Hij gaat hem nu lezen. 4 Ze hebben het vorige week verkocht. 5 Ze zit het op het ogenblik te doen. 6 De kinderen hebben ze dit jaar gekregen.

Lesson 7

Exercise 1

klop – kloppen 'to beat'; maak – maken 'to make'; bak – bakken 'to fry'; leg – leggen 'to lay/put'; keer – keren 'to turn'.

Exercise 2

Ik heb van het meel, het ei, de melk en een snufje zout een mooi glad beslag gemaakt. Ik heb hiervan in de hete boter in de koekenpan op een niet te groot vuur pannenkoeken gebakken. Ik heb tijdens het bakken dunne schijfjes appel in het deeg gelegd. Ik heb de pannenkoeken gekeerd toen[2] de bovenzijde droog was.

Exercise 3

1 Sta onmiddellijk op! 2 Nodig je broer uit! 3 Eet de appel op! 4 Neem het geld aan! 5 Kom alsjeblieft binnen! 6 Doe het raam open! 7 Geef het geld uit!

Exercise 4

1 opgestaan; 2 uitgenodigd; 3 opgegeten; 4 aangenomen; 5 binnengekomen; 6 opengedaan; 7 uitgegeven.

Exercise 5

1 Hij is onmiddellijk opgestaan. 2 Ik heb je broer uitgenodigd. 3 Marius heeft een appel opgegeten. 4 Pauline heeft het geld niet aangenomen. 5 Hij is niet binnengekomen. 6 Zij heeft het raam opengedaan. 7 Zij heeft het geld uitgegeven.

Exercise 6

1 Sta (even) op! Wil je (even) opstaan? Zou je (even) willen opstaan? 2 Bel me morgen (even) op! Wil je me morgen (even) opbellen? Zou je me morgen (even) willen opbellen? 3 Steek de kaars (even) aan! Wil je de kaars (even) aansteken? Zou je de kaars (even) willen aansteken? 4 Kom (even) binnen! Wil je (even) binnenkomen? Zou je (even) willen binnenkomen? 5 Lees die brief (even) voor! Wil je die brief (even) voorlezen? Zou je die brief (even) willen voorlezen? 6 Doe die rommel (even) weg! Wil je die rommel (even) wegdoen? Zou je die rommel (even) willen wegdoen?

---

2 See page 124 for an explanation of why **wanneer** changes to **toen** in the past tense.

Exercise 7

Beste Alistair,

We zijn nu in Amsterdam. We blijven twee dagen hier. Twee dagen is niet erg lang maar we moeten (op) woensdag in Londen zijn. We zouden graag het Rijksmuseum (willen) bezoeken maar we hebben niet genoeg tijd. We kunnen helaas niet alles doen. En we hebben ook niet veel geld over.
    Wat ga jij in/van de zomer doen? Zullen we samen naar Athene gaan? Laten we ons geld voor die reis sparen!
    Ik moet naar het postkantoor. Doe de groeten aan je ouders!

Hartelijke groeten,

Johan

Exercise 8

1 Hij belt je op om je voor een feest uit te nodigen. 2 Pauline heeft geprobeerd om Marius te helpen. 3 We waren te moe om zo vroeg op te staan. 4 Hij wenst om langer in Duitsland te blijven. 5 Het is niet gemakkelijk om Lunteren op de kaart te vinden. 6 Ik vind het moeilijk om Frans te spreken. 7 Ze had heel veel om te doen. 8 Het is voor haar niet mogelijk om thuis te komen.

Lesson 8

Exercise 1

Piet: Eet smakelijk!
Pauline: Smakelijk eten! Geef me alsjeblieft de ham, Piet!
Piet: Zeker. Alsjeblieft.
Pauline: Dank je. Mag ik nog een glaasje wijn?
Piet: Je hebt nog wat.
Pauline: Ach, ja. Proost! Geef me de boter alsjeblieft!
Piet: Maar je hebt nog geen brood.
Pauline: Ach, ja. Wat stom van me! Mag ik het brood!
(een tijdje later)
Piet: Het was heerlijk/verrukkelijk maar ik heb genoeg gehad.
Pauline: Ik ook. Laten we de afwas doen!

Exercise 2

1 Het heet De Poort ('the gateway'). 2 Het staat in Utrecht. 3 Op dinsdag en vrijdag. 4 Niet op woensdag. (**de zalm** 'salmon') 5 Twee gulden goedkoper. 6 Aardappelgarnituur (potatoes of one kind or another), groente en salade.[3] 7 (Franse) frites,[4] aardappelpuree ('mashed potatoes') en krieltjes ('new potatoes'). 8 Elke avond tussen vijf en negen uur.

Exercise 3

het vadertje, het broertje, het kastje, het huisje, het dakje, het stoeltje, het deurtje, het lepeltje, het sigaretje, het blaadje, het bedje, het kussentje, het rekeningetje.

Exercise 4

de schoentjes, twee lampjes, drie appeltjes, deze peertjes, die twee boekjes, die mannetjes, de kraantjes, de hondjes, de sterretjes, de belletjes.

Exercise 5

1 het vlees; 2 de boter; 3 de uien; 4 de koffie; 5 het bier; 6 het zout.

Exercise 6

1 Hij komt pas overmorgen. 2 Wat doe je vanavond? 3 Wat heb je gisteravond gedaan? 4 Ik heb hem vanmorgen/vanochtend in de stad gezien. 5 Mijn vader komt overmorgenavond/woensdagavond terug.

Exercise 7

1 Morgen is het vrijdag vijf april/Het is morgen vrijdag vijf april. 2 Overmorgen is het zaterdag zes april. 3 Gisteren was het

---

3 **De sla** is a more common word for salad and lettuce.
4 Potato chips or French fries are usually called **patat** in the Netherlands but in Belgium they're called **frites**, also spelt **friet**, which reflects the pronunciation of the word.

woensdag drie april. 4 Eergisteren was het dinsdag twee april. 5 Afgelopen maandag was het één april. 6 Aanstaande zondag is het zeven april.

Lesson 9

Exercise 1

1 Hij heeft gezegd dat Pauline in Den Haag werkt. 2 Hij heeft gezegd dat Pauline in Engeland geboren is. 3 Hij heeft gezegd dat Piet vroeg wil thuiskomen. 4 Hij heeft gezegd dat de kinderen moeten opstaan. 5 Hij heeft gezegd dat Paulines moeder haar opgebeld heeft/heeft opgebeld.

Exercise 2

1 Wanneer ga je naar Engeland? 2 Als hij thuis komt, ga ik boodschappen doen. 3 Marius heeft de schaar teruggegeven toen hij klaar was. 4 Wanneer Piet zijn buurman op straat tegenkwam, heeft hij hem altijd gegroet.

Exercise 3

1 Toen ik thuiskwam, was hij al thuis. 2 Hoewel Pauline hem gewaarschuwd had, heeft Piet het toch gedaan. 3 Terwijl de kinderen televisie kijken, kookt Pauline. 4 Als het gaat regenen, willen we morgen niet gaan.

Exercise 4

1 Waar werkt Piet nu? 2 Wie heeft het kopje gebroken? 3 Hoeveel verdient ze? 4 Wat heeft ze gezegd?

Exercise 5

1 Hij kwam elke dag erg laat thuis. 2 Pauline werkte in Den Haag. 3 Marius ging maandag niet naar school. 4 Charlotte kreeg een tientje voor haar verjaardag van haar opa. 5 De kinderen speelden gezellig met elkaar in de tuin. 6 Die hond beet iedereen. 7 Mijn zus praatte te veel. 8 Mijn ouders werkten te hard.

Exercise 6

Wim had een prachtige auto en hij kocht elke drie jaar een nieuwe. Zijn auto's waren altijd rood. Hij hield van auto's en hij reed graag hard. Hij parkeerde zijn auto achter zijn huis. Hij waste hem elke week en gaf hem één keer in de maand een servicebeurt. Zijn vrouw vond het lastig dat hij altijd met zijn auto bezig was. Om de drie jaar kreeg zij een nieuwe fiets van Wim. Wim verwende zijn vrouw niet.

Exercise 7

1 Wat doe je donderdags? 2 Waar werk je 's woensdags? 3 Wat doe je aanstaande vrijdag? 4 Waar was je afgelopen/varige maandag? 5 Waar ga je in het weekend naartoe? 6 Het gras groeit zo snel/hard in de lente. 7 Ik ga van de zomer naar Italië.

Exercise 8

1 Het spijt me, meneer, maar dinsdag ben ik op de universiteit. 2 Het spijt me, meneer, maar donderdag ben ik in Groningen, in het noorden van het land. 3 Het spijt me, meneer, maar vrijdag ben ik in het buitenland. 4 Het spijt me, meneer, maar in het weekend ben ik in Engeland. 5 Het spijt me, meneer, maar volgende week ben ik in Parijs. 6 Het spijt me, meneer, maar volgende maand ben ik terug in Nederland.

Lesson 10

Exercise 1

1 Pauline moest met de trein naar Den Haag (gaan). 2 De kinderen konden vandaag niet buiten spelen. 3 Ze mochten ook niet boven spelen. 4 Piet wilde/wou niet naar school (gaan). 5 Ik ging mijn tante bezoeken. 6 Hij kwam ons elk jaar met Kerstmis bezoeken. 7 Ik zag hem in de tuin werken. 8 Zij hoorde mij altijd binnenkomen.

1 Pauline heeft met de trein naar Den Haag moeten gaan. 2 De kinderen hebben vandaag niet buiten kunnen spelen. 3 Ze hebben ook niet boven mogen spelen. 4 Piet heeft niet naar school willen gaan. 5 Ik ben mijn tante gaan bezoeken. 6 Hij is ons elk jaar met

Kerstmis komen bezoeken. 7 Ik heb hem in de tuin zien werken. 8 Zij heeft mij altijd horen binnenkomen/binnen horen komen. (The separation of 'binnen' from 'komen' is explained on page 213.)

Exercise 2

1 Twee keer per dag, om acht uur 's avonds en om acht over een 's nachts. 2 Op het tweede net/op Nederland Twee. 3 Om twaalf voor zeven 's avonds op Nederland Twee. 4 'Overal en nergens' om elf voor acht op Nederland Twee. 5 Om negen voor zeven 's avonds op Nederland Twee. 6 Om vier voor half vier (Nieuws voor slechthorenden). 7 De AVRO en hij begint om elf over half twaalf 's avonds.

Exercise 3

1 De kinderen vervelen zich. 2 Marius heeft zich erg slecht gedragen. 3 De kinderen moeten zich gedragen. 4 U vergist zich. 5 Ik schaam me. 6 De kinderen hebben zich niet kunnen gedragen. 7 Herinner je je waar hij woont? 8 We verheugen ons op de reis. 9 Hij heeft zich voorgesteld.

Exercise 4

S G R A V E N H A G E < name here

's-Gravenhage, which is called **Den Haag** for short, is the capital city of the province of South-Holland.

Exercise 5

1 Men spreekt Fries in Friesland. In Friesland spreekt men Fries. 2 Zij noemen zich Friezen. 3 Er zijn/wonen omtrent vijfhonderdduizend Friezen in Nederland. 4 Veel borden in Friesland zijn in het Fries en in het Nederlands.

Exercise 6

1 Nee, Italië is warmer dan Nederland. Nee, Nederland is niet zo warm als Italië. 2 Nee, Duitsland heeft meer inwoners dan België. Nee, België heeft niet zoveel inwoners als Duitsland. 3 Nee, mensen zijn intelligenter dan dieren. Nee, dieren zijn niet zo intelligent als mensen. 4 Nee, de Atlantische Oceaan is groter dan de Noordzee. Nee, de Noordzee is niet zo groot als de Atlantische Oceaan. 5 Nee, een Engels pond is meer waard dan een Amerikaanse dollar. Nee, een Amerikaanse dollar is niet zo veel waard als een Engels pond.

Exercise 7

1 Deze bananen zijn rijper dan die. 2 Dit zijn de lekkerste appels. 3 Wanneer zijn aardappels het duurst? 4 Deze peren zijn net zo duur als die/even duur als die. 5 De jongens zijn net zo braaf als de meisjes. 6 Hij heeft nog harder gesproken maar niet zo hard als zij. 7 Dit is het interessantste gebouw in de stad. 8 Hij was succesvoller dan ik. 9 Mijn oom is de armste van de twee.

Lesson 11

Exercise 1

1 Niet om 6 uur 16. 2 De laatste boot op 31 december vertrekt om 20 uur 35. 3 De bus vertrekt om 11 uur 16.

Exercise 2

1 De trein die later vertrekt, komt om 9.00 uur in Amsterdam aan. 2 Waar is het kaartje dat je net gekocht hebt? 3 De tickets die hier liggen zijn voor de reis naar België. 4 Piet is iemand die iedereen aardig vindt. 5 De mensen die naast ons wonen, komen uit Hongarije. 6 Het koekje dat je in je mond hebt, is niet vers.

Exercise 3

1 De auto die hij gisteren gekocht heeft, is rood. 2 De mevrouw die net hier was, is erg aardig. 3 Het boek dat jij aan mij cadeau gegeven hebt, is erg interessant. 4 Het kind dat hiernaast woont, is stout. 5 De schrijfmachine die jij aan haar verkocht hebt, is stuk.

Exercise 4

1 Charlotte heeft Marius haar nieuwe pop laten zien. 2 Ik heb elke week de auto laten wassen. 3 Waar heb je je auto laten staan? 4 We hebben de dokter laten komen. 5 We hebben de dokter moeten laten komen. 6 Je hebt je auto niet hier mogen laten staan.

Exercise 5

1 Ze heeft jaren geleden al haar geld gegeven aan het Rode Kruis. 2 We zullen je hoogst waarschijnlijk in de loop van het weekend zien. 3 Ze heeft vroeger samen met haar ouders gewoond op het platteland. 4 Waar zijn jullie dit jaar met vakantie geweest? 5 Je kunt het aan haar stem horen. 6 Ze hebben na de lezing vragen gesteld.

Lesson 12

Exercise 1

1 Nadat hij televisie gekeken had, ging hij naar bed. 2 Marius had zijn huiswerk gedaan voordat hij ging spelen. 3 Wij hadden hem niet gezien omdat hij zich achter een boom verborgen had. 4 Zij waren thuisgekomen zonder dat wij haar gehoord hadden.

Exercise 2

1 de keukendeur; 2 het wijnglas; 3 het bollenveld; 4 het knoopsgat; 5 het rundvlees; 6 de kussensloop; 7 de pruimeboom (new spelling: pruimenboom); 8 het lamsvlees; 9 de kinderfiets; 10 het schapevlees (new spelling: schapenvlees).

Exercise 3

1 De mensen waarmee ik stond te praten, komen uit Spanje. 2 Het meisje waarnaast jij zit, is erg lief, niet waar? 3 De leraar waaraan ik een hekel had, heeft de school verlaten. 4 Zij is iemand waarop je je kunt verlaten. 5 Dat zijn de kinderen waaraan ik al mijn oude speelgoed gegeven heb.

Exercise 4

1 De mensen waar ik mee stond te praten, komen uit Spanje. 2 Het meisje waar jij naast zit, is erg lief, niet waar? 3 De leraar waar ik een hekel aan had, heeft de school verlaten. 4 Zij is iemand waar je je op kunt verlaten. 5 Dat zijn de kinderen waar ik al mijn oude speelgoed aan gegeven heb.

Exercise 5

1 De bank waar jij op zit, was een cadeau van mijn oma. 2 Dat zijn de glazen waar we gisteravond uit gedronken hebben. 3 Het gras waar wij op liggen, is nat. 4 Het mes waar ik het vlees mee snij, is niet scherp genoeg. 5 De vakantie waar wij ons op verheugd hadden, was verschrikkelijk. 6 De Meijers zijn mensen waar je je niet op verlaten kunt.

Lesson 13

Exercise 1

1 Van wie zijn deze kinderen? 2 Wie z'n overhemd is dit? 3 Van wie is dat slipje? 4 Wie z'n postzegels liggen op tafel? 5 Van wie mag ik de fiets lenen?

Exercise 2

1 Waar kan ik de aardappels mee schillen? 2 Waar zitten jullie naar te kijken? 3 Waar zit je nu op? 4 Waar gaan we deze heerlijke wijn uit drinken? 5 Waar heb je dat voor nodig?

Exercise 3

Where **is geworden** is in bold, this is not the passive but the perfect tense of **worden** 'to become'.

Nederland is bekend om zijn dijken. De eerste dijken <u>werden</u> in de middeleeuwen <u>gebouwd</u> maar ze <u>worden</u> nog steeds <u>gebouwd</u> en oude dijken <u>worden</u> <u>verhoogd</u>. Je vindt dijken niet alleen langs de kust maar ook in het binnenland waar de kust misschien vroeger liep. Soms <u>is</u> zo'n zogenaamde binnendijk <u>gebouwd</u> als extra verdediging tegen stormen waardoor de buitendijken vroeger dikwijls braken en het land overstroomde. In 1932 <u>werd</u> de Afsluitdijk <u>geopend</u>. Door de bouw van die dijk **is** de vroegere Zuiderzee het IJsselmeer **geworden** en later <u>zijn</u> achter die dijk verdere dijken <u>gebouwd</u> om polders te maken. Een polder is een stuk land dat <u>drooggelegd</u> <u>is</u> en dus bewoonbaar **geworden is** of voor de landbouw <u>gebruikt</u> kan <u>worden</u>. De dijken van Nederland moeten <u>bewaakt</u> <u>worden</u>. Dat <u>wordt</u> door de dijkwacht <u>gedaan</u>. Nederland is in dit opzicht een uniek land.

Exercise 4

1 Dat is met een vulpen geschreven. 2 De afwas met wordt het afwasmiddel gedaan. 3 Dat werd met zeep schoongemaakt. 4 Hij was door mij geholpen. 5 Hij kan door niemand geholpen worden. 6 Het geld is door mijn man geschonken. 7 Nederlands wordt in Nederland en België gesproken.

Exercise 5

(a) point 4; (b) point 5; (c) point 2; (d) point 6; (e) point 7; (f) point 11; (g) point 1; (h) point 8; (i) point 12; (j) point 10.

Exercise 6

7 Het roken wordt in dit park niet toegelaten. 9 Auto's dienen op het parkeerterrein rechts van het slot geparkeerd te worden. 10 Rolstoelen kunnen van het kantoor geleend worden.

Lesson 14

Exercise 1

1 De hond ligt er niet op. 2 Ik weet er niets van. 3 Zij heeft het eruit geknipt. 4 We hebben er urenlang in rondgereden. 5 Ik loop er de hele dag aan te denken. 6 We kijken ernaar.

Exercise 2

1 Daar ligt de hond op. 2 Daar weet ik niets van. 3 Daar heeft zij het uit geknipt. 4 Daar hebben wij urenlang in rondgereden. 5 Daar loop ik de hele dag aan te denken. 6 Daar kijken we naar.

Exercise 3

1 Het is een viool en je maakt er muziek mee. 2 Het is een tv en je kijkt ernaar. 3 Het is een tandenborstel en je poetst er je tanden mee. 4 Het is een zaag en je zaagt er hout mee. 5 Het is een teddybeer en je speelt ermee. 6 Het is een hamer en je hamert er spijkers mee.

Exercise 4

1 Marius is zijn huiswerk aan het doen. Marius is bezig zijn huiswerk te doen. Marius zit zijn huiswerk te doen. 2 Ze zijn aan het eten. Ze zijn bezig te eten. Ze zitten te eten. 3 Piet is het gras aan het maaien. Piet is bezig het gras te maaien. 4 Pauline is de afwas aan het doen. Pauline is bezig de afwas te doen. Pauline staat de afwas te doen. 5 Ze zijn allemaal koffie aan het drinken. Ze zijn allemaal bezig koffie te drinken. Ze zitten allemaal koffie te drinken.

Exercise 5

1 Marius heeft zijn huiswerk zitten doen. 2 Ze hebben zitten eten. 3 (not possible) 4 Pauline heeft de afwas staan doen. 5 Ze hebben allemaal koffie zitten drinken.

Exercise 6

1 Piet geeft al acht jaar les op een middelbare school/op een middelbare school les. Piet has been teaching at a secondary school for eight years. 2 Hij leert al een hele tijd Duits. He's been learning German for quite a while/quite some time. 3 Charlotte speelt al langer dan een uur in de tuin. Charlotte has been playing in the garden for more than an hour. 4 Oom Paul is al jaren doof. Uncle Paul has been deaf for years. 5 Haar broer zit al een week of drie in Griekenland. Her brother has been in Greece for about three weeks.

Exercise 7

E	I	N	D	H	O	V	E	N	< name here
E	N	IJ	A	A	L	L	O	E	
N	K	L	S	V	I	I	E	U	
D	T	P		I	F	N	L	S	
	V	A		K	A	D		H	
	I	A		N	E			O	
	S	R		T	R			O	
		D						R	
								N	

Eindhoven is in North Brabant and is the home of Philips, the famous Dutch electronics concern.

Lesson 15

Exercise 1

1 Hij kent ze allemaal. 2 Mijn familieleden zijn allemaal naar het feest gekomen. 3 Ze zijn allemaal uitverkocht. 4 De leerlingen mochten allemaal thuis blijven. 5 Pauline heeft Piets overhemden allemaal gestreken.

Exercise 2

1 Ze heeft iets duurs voor zijn verjaardag gekocht. 2 Er was niets interessants te koop. 3 Hij heeft me iets gegeven wat hij onder de kast gevonden heeft. 4 Ik heb niets nieuws te berichten. 5 Er ligt iets groens op de grond/vloer.

Exercise 3

1 Ik zou de planten water geven als het warm was. Ik zou de planten water geven als het warm zou zijn. 2 Ze zou graag een bad willen nemen als er warm water was. Ze zou graag een bad willen nemen als er warm water zou zijn. 3 Ze zou boodschappen gaan doen als ze genoeg geld had. Ze zou boodschappen gaan doen als ze genoeg geld zou hebben. 4 Nederland zou nog deel van Duitsland zijn als het niet losgebroken was. Nederland zou nog deel van Duitsland zijn als het niet losgebroken zou zijn/zou zijn losgebroken. 5 Hij zou je haar adres geven als hij het wist. Hij zou je haar adres geven als hij het zou weten.

Exercise 4

1 Als het warm was, zou ik de planten water geven. Als het warm zou zijn, zou ik de planten water geven. 2 Als er warm water was, zou ze graag een bad willen nemen. Als er warm water zou zijn, zou ze graag een bad willen nemen. 3 Als ze genoeg geld had, zou ze de boodschappen gaan doen. Als ze genoeg geld zou hebben, zou ze de boodschappen gaan doen. 4 Als het niet losgebroken was, zou Nederland nog deel van Duitsland zijn. Als het niet losgebroken zou zijn/zou zijn losgebroken, zou Nederland nog deel van Duitsland zijn. 5 Als hij het wist, zou hij je haar adres geven. Als hij het zou weten, zou hij je haar adres geven.

Exercise 5

1 Pauline could have fetched Marius from school if she had had the car. 2 Pauline thinks that Piet should take Marius to school. 3 Pauline thought that Piet should have taken Marius to school. 4 She would have been on time if she had known that. 5 She would have been on time if she had known that. 6 The children would have played outside longer if it hadn't got dark. 7 If you went for a walk with your dog every day he wouldn't be so bothersome. 8 If he earnt more he would buy a bigger house. 9 If he earnt more he could/would be able to save. 10 He would have gone on a trip/made a trip/gone travelling every year if he had earnt more. 11 If he had earnt more he would have gone on a trip/made a trip/gone travelling every summer.

Exercise 6

1 Het gaat 7 graden worden. 2 Het gaat in Groningen en Limburg regenen. 3 In Drenthe. 4 Het is 6 graden in Utrecht en ook op de Waddenzee. 5 Bewolkt.

6 In Spanje. 7 In IJsland, Zweden en Finland. 8 In Zwitserland. 9 In Bulgarije. 10 Een hogedrukgebied. 11 Minus één/één graad onder het vriespunt/onder nul. 12 Zonnig.

Exercise 7

< name here

Papegaai means 'parrot'.

Lesson 16

Exercise 1

1 Ze heeft geen erge dorst. 2 De kinderen gaan vandaag niet naar school. 3 Pauline werkt niet in Utrecht. 4 Piet rijdt niet te langzaam. 5 Hij gaat niet met de tram naar zijn werk. 6 Dit jaar hebben de mussen geen nest in de garage gebouwd. 7 De vloer is niet schoon. 8 Thijs is niet mijn oom/Thijs is mijn oom niet. 9 Dit boek is niet in het Nederlands geschreven. 10 Ik heb het hem niet verteld. 11 Ik heb het niet aan hem verteld. 12 Hij koopt geen nieuwe fiets voor Pauline.

Exercise 2

1 Ze heeft geen tijd om je te helpen. 2 We beginnen pas volgende week. 3 Ze kon haar portemonnaie niet vinden. 4 Er staat geen enkele boom vóór het huis. 5 Ze is niet mijn moeder maar mijn tante. 6 Ze komen niet vanavond maar vrijdagavond.

Exercise 3

1 Zullen we vóór het avondeten even gaan wandelen? 2 Hij heeft zijn vader sinds de oorlog niet gezien. 3 Na haar operatie lag ze nog twee weken in het ziekenhuis. 4 We zaten allemaal nog aan tafel. 5 Hij heeft gedurende de film zitten praten. 6 Volgens mijn moeder is hij een schurk. 7 We blijven vandaag vanwege het weer thuis. 8 Ik lees op het ogenblik een boek over Australië. 9 We rijden nu langs het postkantoor. 10 Hij woont tegenover het station.

Exercise 4

STRANGER: Pardon, meneer/mevrouw. Bent u hier bekend?
YOU: Ja, wat wilt u weten?
STRANGER: Ik zoek het postkantoor.
YOU: U gaat op de hoek linksaf. U gaat/loopt langs de Kerkstraat tot de Potterstraat/U gaat/loopt rechtdoor tot de Potterstraat. Daar gaat u rechtsaf en gaat/loopt tot de Herengracht. U gaat/loopt de gracht/brug over en gaat linksaf. Het postkantoor vindt u aan de rechterkant/rechts.
or
U gaat bij de Kerkstraat linksaf. Dan gaat u rechtdoor tot de Potterstraat. Daar gaat u rechtsaf en rechtdoor tot de Herengracht. U gaat/steekt de brug/gracht over en gaat linksaf en het postkantoor staat rechts/aan de rechterkant.

Exercise 5

1 Wat heeft hij tegen zijn moeder gezegd? 2 Ik geloof niet in god. 3 Ik verkies zijn broer boven zijn zus. 4 Hij denkt over zijn vakantie na. 5 Hij heeft me om geld gevraagd. 6 Zij lijkt sprekend op haar moeder. 7 Hij trouwde toen met haar. 8 Ze glimlachte

tegen het kind. 9 Het boek bestaat uit twintig hoofdstukken. 10 De hond heeft tegen de kinderen geblaft.

Exercise 6

1 Ik geloof dat hij wat later op zal dagen. 2 Ik zei tegen hem dat ik haar op zou bellen. 3 Hij heeft niet op kunnen staan. 4 Weet je hoe laat zij aan is gekomen? 5 Weet je wie al de koekjes op heeft gegeten?

Exercise 7

1 Je hoeft hem geen tientje te geven. 2 Ik hoefde geen brief aan haar te schrijven. 3 Ik heb geen brief aan haar hoeven (te) schrijven. 4 De studenten hoeven in het weekend geen opstel te schrijven. 5 De studenten hebben in het weekend geen opstel hoeven (te) schrijven.

Lesson 17

Exercise 1

```
B           W           N
O V         A   M       E
R O A  T    N   O       U S
S H E  R  T O G E N B O S C H   < name here
T A T  M  E N       L D A O   H A
  N       E G       L   A R   E A
  D       N E       E   R     I R
             B           D     D
             O                 I
             O                 N
             G                 G
```

's-Hertogenbosch, also called **Den Bosch** for short, is the capital of North Brabant. It is sometimes called by its French name in English, **Bois-le-Duc**.

Alphabetical list of irregular verbs

A † denotes a verb that always takes **zijn** in the perfect tense, whereas a + denotes that the verb can take either **zijn** or **hebben**, depending on the meaning. If the base verbs below take **zijn**, compounds formed from them might not, and vice versa, e.g. **staan** 'to stand' takes **hebben**, but **opstaan** 'to stand/get up' takes **zijn** **trekken** 'to pull' takes **hebben**, but **vertrekken** 'to depart' takes **zijn**.

bakken	**bakte**	**bakten**	**gebakken**	to bake
barsten†	**barstte**	**barstten**	**gebarsten**	to burst
bederven+	**bedierf**	**bedierven**	**bedorven**	to spoil
bedriegen	**bedroog**	**bedrogen**	**bedrogen**	to deceive
beginnen†	**begon**	**begonnen**	**begonnen**	to begin
begrijpen	**begreep**	**begrepen**	**begrepen**	to understand
bevelen	**beval**	**bevalen**	**bevolen**	to order
bewegen	**bewoog**	**bewogen**	**bewogen**	to move
bidden	**bad**	**baden**	**gebeden**	to pray
bieden	**bood**	**boden**	**geboden**	to offer
bijten	**beet**	**beten**	**gebeten**	to bite
binden	**bond**	**bonden**	**gebonden**	to bind
blazen	**blies**	**bliezen**	**geblazen**	to blow
blijken†	**bleek**	**bleken**	**gebleken**	to appear
blijven†	**bleef**	**bleven**	**gebleven**	to remain, stay
blinken	**blonk**	**blonken**	**geblonken**	to shine
braden	**braadde**	**braadden**	**gebraden**	to roast
breken	**brak**	**braken**	**gebroken**	to break
brengen	**bracht**	**brachten**	**gebracht**	to bring
brouwen	**brouwde**	**brouwden**	**gebrouwen**	to brew
buigen	**boog**	**bogen**	**gebogen**	to bend
delven	**delfde**	**delfden**	**gedolven**	to dig
denken	**dacht**	**dachten**	**gedacht**	to think

doen	deed	deden	gedaan	to do
dragen	droeg	droegen	gedragen	to carry
drijven⁺	dreef	dreven	gedreven	to float, drive
dringen⁺	drong	drongen	gedrongen	to push, crowd
drinken	dronk	dronken	gedronken	to drink
druipen	droop	dropen	gedropen	to drip
duiken⁺	dook	doken	gedoken	to dive
dwingen	dwong	dwongen	gedwongen	to force
eten	at	aten	gegeten	to eat
fluiten	floot	floten	gefloten	to whistle
gaan†	ging	gingen	gegaan	to go
gelden	gold	golden	gegolden	to be valid
genezen⁺	genas	genazen	genezen	to heal
genieten	genoot	genoten	genoten	to enjoy
geven	gaf	gaven	gegeven	to give
gieten	goot	goten	gegoten	to pour
glijden⁺	gleed	gleden	gegleden	to glide, slide
glimmen	glom	glommen	geglommen	to glimmer
graven	groef	groeven	gegraven	to dig
grijpen	greep	grepen	gegrepen	to seize, grab
hangen	hing	hingen	gehangen	to hang
hebben	had	hadden	gehad	to have
heffen	hief	hieven	geheven	to lift
helpen	hielp	hielpen	geholpen	to help
heten	heette	heetten	geheten	to be called
houden	hield	hielden	gehouden	to hold
jagen	joeg	joegen	gejaagd	to chase
	jaagde	jaagden	gejaagd	to hunt
kiezen	koos	kozen	gekozen	to choose
kijken	keek	keken	gekeken	to look
klimmen⁺	klom	klommen	geklommen	to climb
klinken	klonk	klonken	geklonken	to sound
knijpen	kneep	knepen	geknepen	to pinch
komen†	kwam	kwamen	gekomen	to come
kopen	kocht	kochten	gekocht	to buy
krijgen	kreeg	kregen	gekregen	to get, receive
krimpen⁺	kromp	krompen	gekrompen	to shrink
kruipen⁺	kroop	kropen	gekropen	to crawl, creep
kunnen	kon	konden	gekund	to be able
lachen	lachte	lachten	gelachen	to laugh[1]

---

1 But **glimlachen** 'to smile' is regular, i.e. **glimlachte, geglimlacht**.

laden	laadde	laadden	geladen	to load
laten	liet	lieten	gelaten	to let, leave
lezen	las	lazen	gelezen	to read
liegen	loog	logen	gelogen	to lie, tell lies
liggen	lag	lagen	gelegen	to lie
lijden	leed	leden	geleden	to suffer
lijken	leek	leken	geleken	to seem
lopen⁺	liep	liepen	gelopen	to walk, run
malen	maalde	maalden	gemalen	to grind
melken	molk	molken	gemolken	to milk
meten	mat	maten	gemeten	to measure
moeten	moest	moesten	gemoeten	to have to
mogen	mocht	mochten	gemogen	to be allowed to
nemen	nam	namen	genomen	to take
ontginnen	ontgon	ontgonnen	ontgonnen	to reclaim
(op)bergen	borg (op)	borgen (op)	(op)geborgen	to store
overlijden†	overleed	overleden	overleden	to pass away
prijzen	prees	prezen	geprezen	to praise
raden	raadde	raadden	geraden	to guess, advise
rijden⁺	reed	reden	gereden	to ride, drive
rijzen†	rees	rezen	gerezen	to rise
roepen	riep	riepen	geroepen	to call
ruiken	rook	roken	geroken	to smell
scheiden	scheidde	scheidden	gescheiden	to separate
schelden	schold	scholden	gescholden	to abuse
schenden	schond	schonden	geschonden	to violate
schenken	schonk	schonken	geschonken	to pour, donate
scheppen	schiep	schiepen	geschapen	to create
scheren	schoor	schoren	geschoren	to shear, shave
schieten	schoot	schoten	geschoten	to shoot
schijnen	scheen	schenen	geschenen	to seem, shine
schrijven	schreef	schreven	geschreven	to write
schrikken†	schrok	schrokken	geschrokken	to be frightened
schuiven⁺	schoof	schoven	geschoven	to push, shove
slaan	sloeg	sloegen	geslagen	to hit[2]
slapen	sliep	sliepen	geslapen	to sleep
slijpen	sleep	slepen	geslepen	to sharpen
sluipen	sloop	slopen	geslopen	to steal, sneak

---

2 **Slaan** should not be confused with the regular verb **slagen** 'to succeed; to pass an exam'. Note the past participle is **geslagen**, not **geslaan**.

sluiten	sloot	sloten	gesloten	to close
smelten⁺	smolt	smolten	gesmolten	to melt
smijten	smeet	smeten	gesmeten	to throw
snijden	sneed	sneden	gesneden	to cut
spannen	spande	spanden	gespannen	to stretch
spijten	speet	speten	gespeten	to be sorry
spinnen	spon	sponnen	gesponnen	to spin
splijten	spleet	spleten	gespleten	to split
spreken	sprak	spraken	gesproken	to speak
springen⁺	sprong	sprongen	gesprongen	to jump
spruiten†	sprot	sproten	gesproten	to sprout
staan	stond	stonden	gestaan	to stand
steken	stak	staken	gestoken	to stab
stelen	stal	stalen	gestolen	to steal
sterven†	stierf	stierven	gestorven	to die
stijgen†	steeg	stegen	gestegen	to rise, climb
stinken	stonk	stonken	gestonken	to stink, smell
stoten	stootte	stootten	gestoten	to push, shove
strijken	streek	streken	gestreken	to iron
treden†	trad	traden	getreden	to tread, step
treffen	trof	troffen	getroffen	to hit
trekken⁺	trok	trokken	getrokken	to pull
vallen†	viel	vielen	gevallen	to fall
vangen	ving	vingen	gevangen	to catch
varen⁺	voer	voeren	gevaren	to sail
vechten	vocht	vochten	gevochten	to fight
verbieden	verbood	verboden	verboden	to forbid
verdwijnen†	verdween	verdwenen	verdwenen	to disappear
vergelijken	vergeleek	vergeleken	vergeleken	to compare
vergeten⁺	vergat	vergaten	vergeten	to forget[3]
verliezen	verloor	verloren	verloren	to lose[4]
vermijden	vermeed	vermeden	vermeden	to avoid
verraden	verried	verrieden	verraden	to betray
verslijten⁺	versleet	versleten	versleten	to wear out
verslinden	verslond	verslonden	verslonden	to devour

---

3 The criteria for the use of **zijn** or **hebben** with **vergeten** are different from other verbs marked ⁺: when the meaning is 'to have left something behind' **hebben** may be used but when a fact etc. has been forgotten only **zijn** can be employed; in practice **zijn** is more commonly used in both cases, e.g. **Ik heb/ben mijn regenjas vergeten, Ik ben het woord nu vergeten**.
4 You will hear both **Ik ben mijn pen verloren** and **Ik heb mijn pen verloren** with no difference in meaning. See also **vergeten**.

verwijzen	verwees	verwezen	verwezen	to refer
verzinnen	verzon	verzonnen	verzonnen	to ponder
verzwelgen	verzwolg	verzwolgen	verzwolgen	to swallow up
vinden	vond	vonden	gevonden	to find
vlechten	vlocht	vlochten	gevlochten	to plait
vliegen[+]	vloog	vlogen	gevlogen	to fly
vriezen	vroor	vroren	gevroren	to freeze
vouwen	vouwde	vouwden	gevouwen	to fold
vragen	vroeg	vroegen	gevraagd	to ask
vreten	vrat	vraten	gevreten	to gorge, eat
waaien	woei	woeien	gewaaid	to blow (wind)
	waaide	waaiden	gewaaid	
wassen	waste	wasten	gewassen	to wash
wegen	woog	wogen	gewogen	to weigh
werpen	wierp	wierpen	geworpen	to throw
werven	wierf	wierven	geworven	to recruit
weten	wist	wisten	geweten	to know
weven	weefde	weefden	geweven	to weave
wijzen	wees	wezen	gewezen	to show, point
willen	wou/wilde	wilden	gewild	to want to
winden	wond	wonden	gewonden	to wind
winnen	won	wonnen	gewonnen	to win
worden†	werd	werden	geworden	to become
wreken	wreekte	wreekten	gewroken	to avenge
wrijven	wreef	wreven	gewreven	to rub
wringen	wrong	wrongen	gewrongen	to wring
zeggen	zei	zeiden	gezegd	to say
zenden	zond	zonden	gezonden	to send
zien	zag	zagen	gezien	to see
zijn†	was	waren	geweest	to be
zingen	zong	zongen	gezongen	to sing
zinken†	zonk	zonken	gezonken	to sink
zitten	zat	zaten	gezeten	to sit
zoeken	zocht	zochten	gezocht	to look for, seek
zouten	zoutte	zoutten	gezouten	to salt
zuigen	zoog	zogen	gezogen	to suck[5]
zuipen	zoop	zopen	gezopen	to booze
zullen	zou	zouden		'will'
zwelgen	zwolg	zwolgen	gezwolgen	to guzzle

---

5 But **stofzuigen** 'to vacuum clean' is regular, i.e. **stofzuigde**, **gestofzuigd**.

zwellen†	zwol	zwollen	gezwollen	to swell
zwemmen⁺	zwom	zwommen	gezwommen	to swim
zweren	zwoer	zwoeren	gezworen	to swear (oath)
	zweerde	zweerden	gezworen	to fester
zwerven	zwierf	zwierven	gezworven	to roam
zwijgen	zweeg	zwegen	gezwegen	to be silent

Glossary of grammatical terms

active	The active is the opposite of the passive. 'He is/was reading a book' is an example of a sentence in the active (i.e. the normal present/past tense) whereas the passive of this would be 'The book is/was being read by him'.
article	See 'definite article' and 'indefinite article'.
aspiration	Some consonants, notably **p**, **t** and **k**, are pronounced in English allowing a puff of air to escape from the mouth. This is called aspiration. These consonants are unaspirated in Dutch.
attributive	An attributive adjective is one that stands in front of a noun and in Dutch may require an **e**-ending, e.g. **een oude man**. The opposite to this is a predicative adjective which does not stand in front of a noun and consequently does not ever take an ending, e.g. **De man is erg oud**.
clause	A clause is that part of a sentence which contains its own subject and finite verb. A sentence may consist of either one or more clauses, e.g. 'I saw the man' (one clause), 'I saw the man who was stealing a car' (two clauses). (See 'main clause', 'coordinate clause', 'subordinate clause' and 'relative clause'.)
closed syllable	A closed syllable is one that ends in a consonant, e.g. **kat**, **kat-ten**; **man**, **man-nen**. (See 'open syllable'.)
comparative	The comparative of an adjective or adverb is that form which has '-er' added to it or is preceded by 'more', e.g. 'bigger', 'more interesting'.
compound noun	A compound noun is one that has been formed

by putting two nouns together, e.g. **stadhuis** 'town hall'.

conditional — The conditional is the tense of a verb formed with 'would', i.e. it expresses what you would do if a certain condition applied, e.g. 'I would go if I had enough time'.

continuous — The present or past continuous is another name for the present or past progressive. (See 'progressive'.)

coordinate clause — A coordinate clause is one which is introduced by a coordinating conjunction, i.e. one of the four joining words **en, maar, of** or **want** which coordinates its clause to the main clause (= makes it equal to), which is indicated by the finite verb in the coordinate clause not being relegated to the end of that clause, e.g. **Hij blijft vandaag thuis want hij voelt zich niet lekker**, where **want** is the coordinating conjunction and **want hij voelt zich niet lekker** the coordinate clause. (Compare 'subordinate clause'.)

definite article — 'The' is referred to as the definite article, as it refers to a definite object, as opposed to 'a', the indefinite article. The definite article varies in Dutch according to gender and whether a noun is singular or plural.

demonstrative — A demonstrative, as the word implies, is a word that points out or distinguishes. 'This/these' and 'that/those' are examples of demonstratives.

diphthong — When two adjacent vowels are pronounced together in such a way that they produce a new vowel sound, the new sound is called a diphthong, e.g. **e** + **i** = **ei**.

direct object — The direct object in a sentence is the object of the verb, i.e. the person or thing that is having the action of the verb performed on it, e.g. 'I can see the man/the ball'.

diminutive — A diminutive in Dutch is a noun which has had the suffix **-(t)je** added to it to render it small, e.g. **een huis/een huisje** 'a house/a little house'.

direct question — See 'indirect question'.

double infinitive — A double-infinitive construction is one where a clause in the perfect tense has two infinitives at the end of it, rather than a past participle and an infinitive, e.g. **Ik heb hem zien komen** and not *__**Ik heb hem gezien komen**__.

dummy subject   This refers to one of the functions of **er** where **er** stands in first position in the clause in the position normally occupied by the subject, e.g. **Er ligt een boek op de tafel**, which is a more usual way of expressing **Een boek ligt op de tafel**.

finite verb   A finite verb is one which has a subject and takes an ending, e.g. **Hij schrijft een boek**. The opposite to this is an 'infinitive', which is the basic form of a verb that has not been defined as to who is performing it, i.e. it does not have an ending, e.g. **Hij gaat een brief schrijven**, where **gaat** is a finite verb and **schrijven** an infinitive.

first person   The pronoun 'I' is referred to as the first person singular and 'we' as the first person plural.

fronting   Fronting refers to putting a word at the front or beginning of a sentence, e.g. **Hij komt morgen terug** can also be expressed as **Morgen komt hij terug** by applying fronting to **morgen**.

genitive   The genitive case in Dutch is a now archaic mechanism for showing either possession or rendering 'of' (**van**), e.g. **de heer des huizes** = **de heer van het huis** = the man of the house.

half-long vowel   Dutch distinguishes between short and long vowels but has three vowels (i.e. **eu**, **ie**, **oe**) which are pronounced longer than short vowels but not as long as long vowels, except when followed by **r**, when they too are pronounced long. (See 'short vowel'.)

imperfect tense   The imperfect tense, also called the simple past, is that tense of the verb expressed by a single word in Dutch, e.g. **schreef** 'wrote'. It contrasts with the 'perfect tense' or compound past which consists of two words, e.g. **Hij heeft geschreven** 'He has written'. (See 'perfect tense'.)

indefinite article   See 'definite article'.

indirect object   The indirect object in a sentence is the person or object the action of the verb is applied 'to', e.g. He gave the book (direct object) to the girl (indirect object).

indirect question	A direct question reproduces a question verbatim, e.g. 'Where does he live?' The indirect question form of this is 'where he lives', e.g. 'I do(n't) know where he lives'.
infinitive	See 'finite verb'.
interrogative	An interrogative is a question word, most of which start with 'wh' is English and **w** in Dutch, e.g. 'what', 'where', 'when', 'how'.
intransitive verb	See 'transitive verb'.
locative	A locative **er** is one that means 'there' with reference to place, e.g. **Ik heb er vroeger gewoond** 'I used to live there'. This is in contrast to other meanings of **er** which do not refer to place, e.g. **Er was eens een koning** 'Once upon a time there was a king'.
long vowel	See 'short vowel'.
main clause	A main clause, as opposed to a subordinate clause (see 'subordinate clause') is one which makes sense on its own, i.e. it has a subject and finite verb and is not introduced by a conjunction, e.g. **Hij blijft vandaag thuis omdat hij zich niet lekker voelt**, where **Hij blijft vandaag thuis** is the main clause in this compound sentence.
modal verb	A modal auxiliary verb is a verb which is always used in conjunction with an infinitive and which expresses the attitude of the subject of the action to be performed, i.e. volition (**willen** 'to want to'), obligation (**moeten** 'to have to/must'), permission (**mogen** 'to be allowed to/may'), ability (**kunnen** 'to be able to/can'). These verbs in both English and Dutch show many irregularities.
object	See 'direct object' and 'indirect object'.
open syllable	An open syllable is one that ends in a vowel, e.g. **maan** (closed) but **ma-nen** (first syllable open and second syllable closed). The **n** after **ma** is seen as belonging to the next syllable in Dutch. (See 'syllabification'.)
partitive	This refers to one of the functions of **er**, i.e. that which is used in combination with numerals and quantities, e.g. **Ik heb er tien gezien** 'I saw ten of them', **Ik heb er maar een kwart gebruikt** 'I

only used a quarter (of them/it)', where it refers to part of a greater whole.

passive See 'active'.

perfect tense The perfect tense in Dutch is a compound tense, i.e. one formed from more than one word, where the finite verb is a form of the verb **zijn** or **hebben** plus a past participle, e.g. **Hij heeft een brief geschreven, Hij is naar huis gegaan**.

pluperfect tense The pluperfect tense is that which consists of 'had' + a past participle in English and of **was/ waren** or **had/hadden** + a past participle in Dutch. It expresses the past in the past in both languages.

possessive Possessives are words such as 'my/mine', 'your/ yours' which indicate the possessor of a noun, e.g. 'This is my book/It is mine'.

predicative See 'attributive'.

progressive The present or past progressive is a variation of the present or past tenses that emphasises that an action is or was in the process of being performed, e.g. 'He is/was reading' is the progressive form of 'He reads/read'.

reflexive Reflexive pronouns are used with reflexive verbs. They indicate that the action of the verb is being performed on the subject of the verb (i.e. the action reflects back), e.g. **Hij scheert zich elke ochtend** 'He shaves [himself] every day' where **zich** is the third person singular of the reflexive pronoun and **zich scheren** is said to be a reflexive verb.

relative clause/ pronoun A relative pronoun connects a relative clause to a main clause, i.e. it relates back to a noun in the main clause, e.g. 'The man who gave me the money was very rich', where 'who' is a relative pronoun relating back to 'man' and 'who gave me the money' is the relative clause which in Dutch requires subordinate word order, i.e. the finite verb is sent to the end, e.g. **die mij het geld gegeven heeft**. (See 'subordinate clause'.)

schwa This is the name given by linguists to that nondescript vowel sound that we hear in the first syllable of 'again' or in the second syllable of 'father'. Those speakers of English who pronounce 'film' as 'filem' are inserting a schwa between the 'l' and the 'm' to facilitate pronunciation of the cluster 'lm'.

second person
: The pronoun 'you' is referred to as the second person. In Dutch there are two forms in the singular, **jij** and **u**, and two forms in the plural, **jullie** and **u** where English only has the one word for all functions.

separable
: A separable verb is one with a prefix (usually a preposition, e.g. **opbellen** 'to ring up') which separates from the verb and stands at the end of the clause in the present and imperfect tenses (e.g. **Hij belde mij op**) and which permits the **ge-** of the past participle to be inserted between it and the rest of the verb, e.g. **Hij heeft mij opgebeld**.

short vowel
: A short vowel is one which is pronounced short and thus contrasts with the same vowel pronounced long, e.g. **lat** (short), **laat** (long). See 'half-long vowel'. The stem is the root form of a verb once the **en** ending of the infinitive has been removed and the necessary spelling changes have been made, e.g. the stem of **lopen** is **loop** and of **schrijven** is **schrijf**.

subject
: The subject of a clause is the noun or pronoun that is performing the action of the finite verb in that clause, e.g. 'The man/he is reading a book'. It determines what the ending of the finite verb will be, e.g. **De man/hij leest een boek**, but **Wij lezen een boek**.

subordinate clause
: A subordinate clause is one that is introduced by a subordinating conjunction, i.e. a joining word that subordinates its clause to the main clause (= makes it secondary to), which is indicated by the finite verb in the subordinate clause being relegated to the end of that clause, e.g. **Hij blijft vandaag thuis omdat hij zich niet lekker voelt**, where **omdat** is the subordinating conjunction and **omdat hij zich niet lekker voelt** the subordinate clause. (See 'main clause' and 'coordinate clause'.)

superlative	The superlative of an adjective or adverb is that form which has 'st' added to it or is preceded by 'most', e.g. 'biggest', 'most interesting'.
syllabification	The rules for hyphenating words are different in Dutch from English where the derivation of the word is significant, e.g. 'be-long-ing', 'work-ed'. In Dutch words are always divided (syllabified) by starting each new syllable with a consonant, e.g. **kat-ten**, **ma-nen**, **be-doe-ling**, despite the fact that **en** and **ing** are derivational endings that have been attached to these words.
third person	The pronouns 'he', 'she' and 'it' are referred to as the third person singular and 'they' as the third person plural.
transitive verb	A transitive verb is one that can take an object, as opposed to an intransitive verb, which is one that cannot, e.g. 'He is reading a book' ('read' is transitive because of 'book'), but 'He is going to Germany' ('go' is intransitive because 'to Germany' is not the object of the verb, merely an adverb of place telling you where the action of the verb is to take place.)
verbal noun	A verbal noun is a verb (i.e. an infinitive) that is used as a noun, e.g. **het lezen van kookboeken** 'the reading of cookbooks'.

English–Dutch glossary

a	**een**	America	**Amerika**
abdicate	**afstand doen**	American	**Amerikaan** (c);
about	**omtrent,**		**Amerikaans**
	ongeveer; over	an	**een**
above	**boven**	and	**en**
abroad	**buitenland** (n)	angry	**boos**
accept	**aannemen**	animal	**dier** (n)
accident	**ongeluk** (n)	answer	**antwoord** (c);
according to	**volgens**		**antwoorden**
acquaintance	**kennis** (c)	anything	**iets**
actually	**eigenlijk**	appeal	**beroep** (n)
address	**adres** (n)	appear	**schijnen,**
aeroplane	**vliegtuig** (n)		**blijken**
afford	**zich veroorloven**	apple	**appel** (c)
affordable	**betaalbaar**	approximately	**ongeveer**
after	**na; nadat**	April	**april** (c)
afternoon	**middag** (c)	argument	**ruzie** (c)
this afternoon	**vanmiddag**	arm	**arm** (c)
again	**weer**	around	**om; circa,**
against	**tegen**		**ongeveer**
age	**leeftijd** (c)	arrive	**aankomen**
ago	**geleden**	art	**kunst** (c)
agriculture	**landbouw** (c)	article	**artikel** (n)
all	**allemaal; alles**	as	**als; zo**
allow	**toelaten**	as if	**alsof**
almost	**bijna**	ask (for)	**vragen (om)**
alone	**alleen**	assistant	**bediende** (c)
along	**langs**	assume	**aannemen**
already	**al**	at	**aan, bij, op**
also	**ook; eveneens**	Atlantic	**Atlantische**
although	**(al)hoewel**		**Oceaan**

atmosphere	**sfeer** (c)	believe (in)	**geloven (in)**
attic	**zolder** (c),	bell	**bel** (c)
	vliering (c)	belt	**riem** (c)
August	**augustus** (c)	bench	**bank** (c)
aunt	**tante** (c)	between	**tussen**
Australia	**Australië**	bicycle	**fiets** (c)
Australian	**Australiër** (c),	bicycle garage	**fietsenstalling** (c)
	Australisch	bicycle path	**fietspad** (n)
autumn	**herfst** (c)	bicycle stand	**fietsenrek** (c)
average	**gemiddeld**	big	**groot**
awake	**wakker**	bilingual	**tweetalig**
bachelor	**vrijgezel** (c)	bill	**rekening** (c)
back	**terug**	bird	**vogel** (c)
bad	**slecht**	birthday	**verjaardag** (c)
badger	**das** (c)	it's my birthday	**ik ben jarig**
bake	**bakken**	biscuit	**koekje** (n)
baker	**bakker** (c)	biscuit barrel	**koekjestrommel**
bald	**kaal**		(c)
ball	**bal** (c)	bit	**beetje** (n)
banana	**banaan** (c)	bite	**bijten**
bank	**bank** (c)	black	**zwart**
bank teller	**bankbediende**	blame	**kwalijk nemen**
	(c)	I'm sorry	**Neem me niet**
bark (at)	**blaffen (tegen)**		**kwalijk**
bath	**bad** (n)	blanket	**deken** (c)
batter	**beslag** (n)	blast!	**jeetje!**
be	**zijn**	Bloody hell!	**(God)**
beard	**baard** (c)		**verdomme!**
beat	**kloppen; slaan**	blue	**blauw**
because	**omdat, want**	blush	**blozen**
because of	**wegens, vanwege**	boat	**boot** (c)
become	**worden**	book	**boek** (n)
bed	**bed** (n)	book	**reserveren**
bedroom	**slaapkamer** (c)	book case	**boekenkast** (c)
beer	**bier** (n), **pils** (c)	boot	**laars** (c) (pl.
before	**voor, voordat**		**laarzen**)
begin	**beginnen**	border	**grens** (c)
behave	**zich gedragen**	born	**geboren**
behind	**achter**	borrow	**lenen**
Belgian	**Belg** (c),	both	**beide, allebei**
	Belgisch	bowl	**kom** (c)
Belgium	**België**	box	**doos** (c)

Boxing Day	**Tweede Kerstdag** **(c)**	calendar	**kalender** (c)
		calf	**kalf** (n)
boy	**jongen** (c)	call	**noemen**
bra	**beha** (c)	be called	**heten**
bread	**brood** (n)	camp	**kamperen**
break	**breken**	can (to be	**kunnen**
break out	**uitbreken**	able to)	
breakfast	**ontbijt** (n); **ontbijten**	canal	**gracht** (c); **kanaal** (n)
breast	**borst** (c)	candle	**kaars** (c)
bridge	**brug** (c)	cap	**pet** (c); **muts** (c)
bring	**brengen**	capital city	**hoofdstad** (c)
bring along	**meebrengen**	car	**auto** (c)
broadcast	**uitzenden**	car park	**parkeerterrein**
broadcasting	**omroep** (c)		**(n)**
association		cat	**kat** (c)
broke	**blut**	cattle	**rund** (n)
broken	**stuk, kapot, gebroken**	cent	**cent** (c)
		century	**eeuw** (c)
broom	**bezem** (c)	certainly	**zeker, beslist**
brother	**broer** (c)	chance	**kans** (c)
brother-in-law	**zwager** (c)	change	**veranderen**
brown	**bruin**	change (clothes)	**zich omkleden**
brush	**borstel** (c)	change (money)	**kleingeld** (n)
budgerigar	**parkiet** (c)	change (e.g.	**wisselen**
bugger!	**(god-) verdomme!**	money)	
		change (e.g.	**overstappen**
building	**gebouw** (n)	trains)	
bulb	**bol** (c)	chapter	**hoofdstuk** (n)
burn	**branden, verbranden**	cheap	**goedkoop**
		cheek	**wang** (c)
bus	**bus** (c)	cheers!	**proost!**
busy	**bezig**	cheese	**kaas** (c)
but	**maar**	chest	**borst** (c)
butter	**boter** (c); **roomboter** (c)	chest of drawers	**ladenkast** (c)
		chicken	**kip** (c); **kuiken** (c)
butterfly	**vlinder** (c)	child	**kind** (n)
button	**knoop** (c)	chips	**patat** (c)
buy	**kopen**	chocolate	**chocola** (c)
for sale	**te koop**	choose	**kiezen**
by	**door, bij, met**	Christmas Day	**Eerste Kerstdag**
bye	**dáág**		**(c)**

Christmas	**Kerstmis** (c), **Kerstfeest** (n)	congratulate	**feliciteren**
		congratulations!	**Gefeliciteerd!**
Merry	**Gelukkig**	connect	**verbinden**
Christmas!	**Kerstfeest!**	consist of	**bestaan uit**
church	**kerk** (c)	construction	**bouw** (c)
cigar	**sigaar** (c)	control	**controle** (c)
cigarette	**sigaret** (c)	conversation	**gesprek** (n)
cinema	**bioscoop** (c)	cook	**koken**
circa	**omtrent**	corner	**hoek** (c)
city	**stad** (c)	cosiness	**gezelligheid** (c)
class (school)	**klas** (c)	cost	**kosten**
class (social)	**klasse** (c)	cosy	**gezellig**
clean	**schoon;** **schoonmaken**	cotton	**katoen** (n)
		country	**land** (n)
clean up	**opruimen**	countryside	**platteland** (n)
clear up	**opklaren**	couple	**paar** (c)
close	**dichtdoen**	course	**loop** (c)
clothes	**kleren** (pl.)	cousin	**neef** (c); **nicht** (c)
cloud	**wolk** (c)		
cloudy	**bewolkt**	cover	**deksel** (n), **sloop** (c)
coast	**kust** (c)		
coat	**jas** (c)	crazy	**gek**
coffee	**koffie** (c)	cross	**boos; kruis** (c)
instant coffee	**oploskoffie** (c)	crossroad	**kruispunt** (n)
coffeepot	**koffiepot** (c)	crow	**kraai** (c)
coin	**munt** (c)	crowd	**menigte** (c)
cold	**koud**	crown	**kroon** (c)
collar	**kraag** (c)	cruel	**wreed**
collect	**ophalen;** **verzamelen**	cry	**huilen**
		cup	**kopje** (n)
colony	**kolonie** (c)	cupboard	**kast** (c)
comb	**kam** (c)	cushion	**kussen** (n)
come	**komen**	customer	**klant** (c)
come along	**meekomen**	cut	**knippen; snijden**
come home	**thuiskomen**	cute	**lief**
come in	**binnenkomen**	cycle	**fietsen**
commemorate	**herdenken**	dad	**pa**
common	**gebruikelijk**	daily	**dagelijks**
compartment	**coupé** (c)	damn!	**(god-)**
computer	**computer** (c)		**verdikkeme!**
condolences!	**Gecondoleerd!**		**verdikkie!**
confectionery	**snoep** (c)		**verdorie!**

dance	**dansen**	dishwashing	**afwasmiddel** (n)
danger	**gevaar** (n)	liquid	
dangerous	**gevaarlijk**	distance	**afstand** (c)
dare	**durven**	divide	**verdelen**
dark	**donker**	divorced	**gescheiden**
darling	**lieveling, lieverd,**	do	**doen**
	schat	dog	**hond** (c)
daughter	**dochter** (c)	doll	**pop** (c)
daughter-in-law	**schoondochter** (c)	door	**deur** (c)
day	**dag** (c)	dough	**deeg** (n)
dead	**dood**	dove	**duif** (c)
deaf	**doof**	draw	**tekenen**
dear (in letters)	**beste; lieve;**	drawer	**la** (c)
	geachte	drawing	**tekening** (c)
dear	**lieveling, lieverd,**	dress	**jurk** (c)
	schat	dress	**zich aankleden**
December	**december** (c)	drink	**drinken**
decide	**besluiten**	drink up	**opdrinken**
defence	**verdediging** (c)	drive	**rijden**
defend	**verdedigen**	dry	**droog**
degree	**graad** (c)	dry dishes	**afdrogen**
delay	**vertraging** (c),	duck	**eend** (c)
	vertragen	dumb	**stom**
delicious	**lekker**	during	**gedurende;**
depart	**vertrekken**		**tijdens**
depend	**afhangen**	Dutch	**Nederlands** (n)
desperate	**wanhopig**	Dutchman	**Nederlander** (c)
despite	**ondanks**	Dutch-speaking	**Nederlandstalig**
dial	**draaien**	each	**elk, ieder**
dialect	**dialect** (n)	each other	**elkaar, mekaar**
die	**sterven**	ear	**oor** (n)
different	**verschillend**	early	**vroeg**
difficult	**moeilijk**	earn	**verdienen**
difficulty	**moeite** (c)	earthquake	**aardbeving** (c)
dig	**graven**	east	**oosten** (n)
dike	**dijk** (c)	Easter	**Pasen** (c)
dike watch	**dijkwacht** (c)	eastern	**oostelijk**
direct	**rechtdoor**	easy	**(ge)makkelijk**
dirty	**vies**	eat	**eten**
disappear	**verdwijnen**	eat up	**opeten**
dislike	**een hekel**	economic	**economisch**
	hebben aan	edge	**rand** (c)

egg	**ei** (n)	exciting	**spannend**
eight	**acht**	excuse me!	**pardon!; sorry!**
eighteen	**achttien**	exist	**bestaan**
eighty	**tachtig**	expect	**verwachten**
elbow	**elleboog** (c)	expensive	**duur**
elephant	**olifant** (c)	extremely	**hartstikke**
eleven	**elf**	eye	**oog** (n)
emperor	**keizer** (c)	fabulous	**prachtig**
end	**einde** (n)	face	**gezicht** (n)
enemy	**vijand** (c)	fact	**feit** (n)
energy	**energie** (c)	in fact	in feite
engineer	**ingenieur** (c)	fall	**vallen**
England	**Engeland**	fall out	**uitvallen**
English	**Engels**	fall over	**omvallen**
Englishman	**Engelsman** (c)	family	**familie** (c); **gezin**
enjoyment	**plezier** (n)		(n)
enough	**genoeg**	famous	**beroemd**
enter	**binnenkomen;**	fantastic	**fantastisch**
	instappen	far	**ver**
entirely	**heel, helemaal**	fast	**vlug, snel, hard**
entrance	**ingang** (c);	fat	**dik**
	toegang (c)	father	**vader** (c)
essay	**opstel** (n)	father-in-law	**schoonvader** (c)
evangelical	**evangelisch**	favourite	**lievelings-**
even	**zelfs**	February	**februari** (c)
evening	**avond** (c)	Federal Republic	**Bondsrepubliek**
this evening	**vanavond**	of Germany	(c)
evening meal	**avondeten** (n)	feed	**voeden**
ever	**ooit**	feel	**(zich) voelen**
every	**elk; ieder**	female	**vrouwelijk**
everyday	**alledaags**	feminine	**vrouwelijk**
everyone	**iedereen**	fence	**hek** (n)
everything	**alles**	ferry	**pont** (c),
everywhere	**overal**		**pontveer** (n)
exactly	**precies**	fetch	**halen**
example	**voorbeeld** (n)	few	**paar** (c); **weinig**
for example	**bijvoorbeeld**	field	**veld** (n)
excellent	**uitstekend**	fifteen	**vijftien**
except (for)	**behalve**	fifty	**vijftig**
exchange bureau	**wisselkantoor**	film	**film** (c)
	(n)	finally	**eindelijk**
exchange rate	**wisselkoers** (c)	find	**vinden**

finger	**vinger** (c)	freeze	**vriezen**
fire	**vuur** (n)	freezer	**vriesvak** (n)
firm	**firma** (c)	compartment	
first name	**voornaam** (c)	freezing point	**vriespunt** (n)
fish	**vis** (c)	French	**Frans** (n)
fit	**passen** (c)	Frenchman	**Fransman** (c)
five	**vijf**	French woman	**Française** (c)
flag	**vlag** (c)	fresh	**vers**
Flanders	**Vlaanderen**	Friday	**vrijdag** (c)
flat	**flat** (c)	friend	**vriend** (c)
flat	**vlak**	friendly	**vriendelijk**;
Fleming	**Vlaming** (c)		**aardig**
Flemish	**Vlaams**	from	**van, uit**
flood	**overstromen**	fruit	**fruit** (n)
floor	**vloer** (c)	frying pan	**koekenpan** (c)
floppy disk	**schijfje** (n)	full	**vol**
flour	**meel** (n)	funny	**grappig**
flower	**bloem** (c)	garage	**garage** (c)
fly	**vliegen**	garden	**tuin** (c)
fly (of trousers)	**gulp** (c)	garden	**tuinieren**
fog	**mist** (c)	garlic	**knoflook** (c)
food	**eten** (n)	gee!	**jee!** (c)
foot	**voet** (c)	German	**Duitser** (c),
for	**voor**		**Duits** (n)
forbid	**verbieden**	Germany	**Duitsland**
forecast	**weersver -**	get well soon!	**beterschap!**
	wachting (c)	get	**krijgen**
forest	**bos** (n)	get in	**instappen**
forget	**vergeten**	get out	**uitstappen**
forgive	**vergeven**	get up	**opstaan**
forgive me	**neem me niet**	gift	**cadeau** (n)
	kwalijk	gigantic	**reuze**
fork	**vork** (c)	girl	**meisje** (n)
fortunately	**gelukkig**	give	**geven**
forty	**veertig**	give (as a	**cadeau geven**
fountain pen	**vulpen** (c)	present)	
four	**vier**	give out	**uitgeven**
fourteen	**veertien**	given name	**voornaam** (c)
franc (Belgian)	**frank** (c)	glass	**glas** (n)
France	**Frankrijk**	glove	**handschoen** (c)
free	**gratis**; **vrij**	go	**gaan**
freeway	**autoweg** (c)	go away	**weggaan**

God	**God** (c)	ground	**grond** (c)
good	**goed**	guard	**bewaken**
good afternoon	**goeie middag**	guilder	**gulden** (c)
good evening	**goeien avond**	guilt	**schuld** (c)
good heavens!	**goeie hemel!**	guinea pig	**marmot** (c)
good morning	**goeie morgen**	guy	**vent** (c)
good night	**welterusten**	habit	**gewoonte** (c)
goodbye	**tot ziens**	hail	**hagel** (c),
goose	**gans** (c)		**hagelen**
govern	**regeren**	hair	**haar** (n)
government	**regering** (c)	half	**half**
grandchild	**kleinkind** (n)	ham	**ham** (c)
granddaughter	**kleindochter** (c)	hammer	**hamer** (c);
grandfather	**grootvader** (c)		**hameren**
grandma	**oma** (c)	hand	**hand** (c)
grandmother	**grootmoeder** (c)	handbag	**handtas** (c)
grandpa	**opa** (c)	handkerchief	**zakdoek** (c)
grandparents	**grootouders** (pl.)	hang up	**ophangen**
grandson	**kleinzoon** (c)	happen	**gebeuren**
grape	**druif** (c)	happy	**gelukkig**
grass	**gras** (n)	harbour	**haven** (c)
Great Enclosing	**Afsluitdijk** (c)	hardly	**nauwelijks**
Dam		hasten	**haast hebben;**
great-grandchild	**achterkleinkind**		**zich haasten**
	(n)	hat	**hoed** (c)
great-	**achterklein-**	have	**hebben**
granddaughter	**dochter** (c)	hawk	**havik** (c)
great-grandfather	**overgrootvader**	he	**hij**
	(c)	head	**hoofd** (n)
great-	**overgrootmoeder**	headline	**hoofdpunt** (n)
grandmother	(c)	health	**gezondheid** (c)
great-grandson	**achterkleinzoon**	healthy	**gezond**
	(c)	hear	**horen**
great-great-	**betovergroot-**	heartily	**hartelijk**
grandfather	**vader** (c)	hedgehog	**egel** (c)
great-great-	**betovergroot-**	help	**helpen**
grandmother	**moeder** (c)	her	**haar**
great	**prima**	herb	**kruid** (n)
green	**groen**	herself	**zich; zichzelf;**
greengrocer	**groenteboer** (c)		**zelf**
greeting	**groet** (c)	here	**hier**
grey	**grijs**	heron	**reiger** (c)

hi	hoi	I	ik
hide	verstoppen, verbergen	ice	ijs (n)
		icecream	ijs (n); ijsje (n)
high	hoog	if	als; of
high-pressure system	hogedrukgebied (n)	immediate(ly)	onmiddellijk
		important	belangrijk
highway	autoweg (c)	in	in; binnen
hill	heuvel (c)	in front of	vóór
him	hem	inhabitable	bewoonbaar
himself	zich; zichzelf; zelf	inhabitant	inwoner (c)
		inherit	erven
hippopotamus	nijlpaard (n)	inside	binnen
his	zijn	instead of	in plaats van
history	geschiedenis (c)	intelligent	intelligent
hit	slaan	interesting	interessant
hold	houden	into	in
hole	gat (n)	introduce	voorstellen
holiday	vakantie (c)	invite	uitnodigen
Have a nice holiday!	Prettige vakantie!	iron	strijken
		irritating	lastig
holy	heilig	island	eiland (n)
home	thuis	it	het
homework	huiswerk (n)	Italy	Italië
hope	hopen	its	zijn
hospital	ziekenhuis (n)	itself	zich; zelf
hot	heet	jacket	colbert (n)
hour	uur (n)	January	januari (c)
for hours	urenlang	jeans	spijkerbroek (c)
house	huis (n)	journey	reis (c)
housewife	huisvrouw (c)	July	juli (c)
housework	huiswerk (n)	jumper	trui (c)
how many	hoeveel	June	juni (c)
how much	hoeveel	junk	rommel (c)
hundred	honderd	just	eens; even; net
hunger	honger (c)	keep	houden; bewaren
to be hungry	honger hebben	key	sleutel (c)
		kill	doden
hurry	haast (c)	kilogram	kilo (c)
to be in a hurry	haast hebben	kind	soort (n)
		king	koning (c)
I'm in a hurry	Ik heb haast	kingdom	koninkrijk (n)
husband	man (c)	kiss	kus (c); kussen

kitchen	**keuken** (c)	lightning	**bliksem**
knife	**mes** (n)	like	**houden van,**
knock	**kloppen**		**aardig vinden**
know	**weten; kennen**	like	**net zo(als)**
labourer	**arbeider** (c)	list	**lijst** (c)
ladder	**ladder** (c)	listen (to)	**luisteren (naar)**
lamb	**lam** (n)	live	**wonen; leven**
land	**land** (n);	lock	**slot** (n)
	belanden	long	**lang**
landing	**overloop** (c)	look (at)	**kijken (naar)**
language	**taal** (c)	look like	**lijken op**
native language	**moedertaal** (c)	look for	**zoeken (naar)**
large	**groot**	look forward	**zich verheugen**
last	**vorig, verleden,**	(to)	**(op)**
	afgelopen	look out	**opletten,**
last	**duren**		**oppassen**
laugh	**lachen**	Lord!	**god!**
leaf	**blad** (n)	lose	**verliezen**
learn	**leren**	lot	**heleboel** (c)
leash	**hondelijn** (c)	loud	**hard**
leave	**weggaan, laten,**	lounge	**woonkamer** (c)
	verlaten,	lounge suite	**bankstel** (n)
	vertrekken	love	**houden van**
left	**links**	low	**laag**
to the left	**linksaf**	low pressure	**lagedrukgebied**
leg	**been** (n)	system	(n)
lend	**lenen**	lucky, to be	**boffen**
length	**lengte** (c)	Wasn't she	**Wat heeft zij**
less	**minder**	lucky!	**geboft!**
let	**laten**	madam	**mevrouw** (c)
letter	**brief** (c)	madhouse	**gekkenhuis** (n)
letterbox	**bus** (c)	magazine	**tijdschrift** (n)
liberate	**bevrijden**	mainland	**vasteland** (n)
Liberation Day	**Bevrijdingsdag**	make	**maken**
	(c)	make up	**opmaken**
licence	**rijbewijs** (n)	male	**mannelijk**
(driver's)		man	**man** (c)
lie	**liggen, leugen**	manager	**manager** (c),
life	**leven** (n)		**directeur** (c)
light	**aansteken**	map	**kaart** (c)
light	**licht** (n),	March	**maart** (c)
	lamp (c)	married	**getrouwd**

married couple	**echtpaar** (c)	morning	**morgen** (c),
marry	**trouwen**		**ochtend** (c)
to get	**trouwen met**	this morning	**vanmorgen,**
married to			**vanochtend**
masculine	**mannelijk**	most	**meest**
match	**lucifer** (c)	mostly	**meestal**
mature (of	**belegen**	mother	**moeder** (c)
cheese)		mother-in-law	**schoonmoeder** (c)
May	**mei** (c)	mountain	**berg** (c)
may (to be	**mogen**	mouse	**muis** (c)
allowed to)		mouth	**mond** (c)
me	**mij, me**	mouthful	**hapje** (n)
meal	**maaltijd** (c)	move	**bewegen;**
mean	**betekenen;**		**verplaatsen**
	bedoelen	move house	**verhuizen**
meat	**vlees** (n)	movies	**bioscoop** (c)
meet	**ontmoeten**	mow	**maaien**
meeting	**vergadering** (c)	Mr	**meneer** (c)
melt	**smelten**	Mrs	**mevrouw** (c)
menu	**menu** (n)	mum	**moe**
mess	**puinhoop** (c)	music	**muziek** (c)
message	**boodschap** (c)	must (to	**moeten**
Meuse	**Maas** (c)	have to)	
middle	**midden** (n),	my	**mijn**
	middel (n)	myself	**me; mezelf; zelf**
in the middle	**in het midden**	nail	**spijker** (c)
of	**van**	narrow	**smal**
Middle Ages	**middeleeuwen**	nationality	**nationaliteit** (c)
	(pl.)	naturally	**natuurlijk**
milk	**melk** (c)	naughty	**stout**
million	**miljoen** (n)	near	**bij**
minced meat	**gehakt** (n)	nearly	**bijna**
mistake	**zich vergissen**	neat	**netjes**
modern	**modern**	necessary	**nodig**
moment	**ogenblik** (n),	need	**nodig hebben**
	moment (n)	need to	**moeten; hoeven**
Monday	**maandag** (c)	You don't	**Je hoeft het**
money	**geld** (n)	need/have	**niet te doen**
monkey	**aap** (c)	to do it	
month	**maand** (c)	needle	**naald** (c)
more	**meer**	neighbour	**buurman,**
moreover	**bovendien**		**-vrouw** (c)

neighbourhood	**buurt** (c)	observant	**oplettend**
nephew	**neef** (c)	occupation	**beroep** (n)
nest	**nest** (c)	occupation	**bezetting** (c)
Netherlands	**Nederland**	occur	**voorkomen**
never	**nooit**	ocean	**oceaan** (c)
New Year's	**Nieuwjaarsdag**	October	**oktober** (c)
Day	(c)	octopus	**inktvis** (c)
Happy New	**Gelukkig**	of	**van**
Year!	**Nieuwjaar!**	of course	**natuurlijk**
new	**nieuw**	off	**van**
news	**nieuws** (n),	office	**kantoor** (n)
	journaal (n)	often	**dikwijls, vaak**
newspaper	**krant** (c)	old	**oud**
next	**volgend,**	on	**op, aan**
	aanstaande	one	**één**
next door	**hiernaast**	one (pronoun)	**men**
next to	**naast**	one and a half	**anderhalf**
nice	**leuk, prettig**	onion	**ui** (c)
niece	**nicht** (c)	only	**alleen maar**
night	**nacht** (c)	open	**open; opendoen,**
last night	**vannacht**		**openen**
nine	**negen**	operation	**operatie** (c)
nineteen	**negentien**	opposite	**tegenover**
ninety	**negentig**	or	**of**
noise	**herrie** (c)	orange	**oranje**
nonsense	**onzin** (c)	ostrich	**struisvogel** (c)
no one	**niemand**	other	**ander**
north	**noorden** (n)	otherwise	**anders**
North Sea	**Noordzee** (c)	our	**ons, onze**
northern	**noordelijk**	ourself	**ons; zelf**
nose	**neus** (c)	out	**uit, buiten**
not	**niet**	outside	**buiten**
note	**briefje** (n), **biljet**	over	**boven; over**
	(n)	oversleep	**zich verslapen**
nothing	**niets**	own	**bezitten**
November	**november** (c)	pack up	**inpakken**
now	**nu, nou**	pain	**pijn** (c), **zeer** (n)
now and then	**af en toe**	paint	**verven;**
nowhere	**nergens**		**schilderen**
number	**nummer** (n)	paintbrush	**kwast** (c)
nut	**noot** (c)	palace	**paleis** (n)
oak	**eik** (c)	pan	**pan** (c)

pancake	**pannenkoek** (c)	platform	**perron** (n);
panties	**slipje** (n)		**spoor** (n)
parents	**ouders** (pl.)	play	**spelen**
parents-in-law	**schoonouders**	please	**alsjeblieft,**
	(pl.)		**alstublieft**
Paris	**Parijs**	please	**bevallen**
park	**park** (n)	plum	**pruim** (c)
park	**parkeren**	pocket	**zak** (c)
parrot	**papegaai** (c)	polder	**polder** (c)
part	**deel** (n)	polish	**poetsen**
parting (in hair)	**scheiding** (c)	political	**politiek**
party	**feest(je)** (n)	poor	**arm**
pass (time)	**besteden**	popular	**populair**
pass away	**overlijden**	port	**haven** (c)
passport	**paspoort** (n)	possess	**bezitten**
past	**langs**	possession	**bezitting** (c)
pastries, cakes	**gebak** (n)	possible	**mogelijk**
(collective)		post-office	**postkantoor** (n)
pat	**aaien**	pot	**pan** (c)
path	**pad** (n)	potato	**aardappel** (c)
pay	**betalen**	pound	**pond** (n)
pea	**erwt** (c)	practical	**praktisch**
peacock	**pauw** (c)	prefer (to)	**verkiezen**
pear	**peer** (c)		**(boven)**
peasoup	**erwtensoep** (c)	prepare	**klaarmaken**
peel	**schillen**	present	**cadeau** (n)
pen	**pen** (c)	preserve	**bewaren**
pencil	**potlood** (n)	priest	**pastoor** (c)
Pentecost	**Pinksteren** (c)	prince	**prins** (c)
perhaps	**misschien**	princess	**prinses** (c)
permit	**toelaten**	probably	**waarschijnlijk**
person	**mens** (c)	programme	**programma** (n)
pick	**plukken**	promise	**beloven**
piece	**stuk** (n)	proud (of)	**trots (op)**
pigeon	**duif** (c)	province	**provincie** (c)
piggy bank	**spaarpotje** (n)	pub	**kroeg** (c), **café**
pineapple	**ananas** (c)		(n)
pinch of salt	**een snufje zout**	public	**openbaar**
pink	**rose**	public	**het openbaar**
pipe	**pijp** (c)	transport	**vervoer**
place	**plaats** (c)	publish	**uitgeven**
plate	**bord** (n)	purple	**paars, purper**

purse	**portemonnaie** (c)	repeat	**herhaling** (c),
put (horizontal)	**leggen**		**herhalen**
put (vertical)	**zetten**	report	**berichten**
put (in)	**stoppen**	rest	**rest** (c); **rust** (c)
put on	**aantrekken**	restaurant	**restaurant** (n)
put out	**doven**	return	**teruggaan**
(cigarette)		return ticket	**retour** (n)
quarter	**kwart** (n);	Rhine	**Rijn** (c)
	kwartier (n);	rhinoceros	**neushoorn** (c)
	kwartje (n)	rib	**rib** (c)
queen	**koningin** (c)	rice	**rijst**
Queen's	**Koninginnedag**	rich	**rijk**
Birthday	(c)	ride	**rijden**
quick	**vlug, snel, hard**	ridiculous	**belachelijk**
quiet	**stil**	right	**rechts**
rabbit	**konijn** (n)	to the right	**rechtsaf**
radio	**radio** (c)	ring	**bellen**
railway	**spoorweg** (c)	ring up	**opbellen**
rain	**regen** (c),	ripe	**rijp**
	regenen	river	**rivier** (c)
raise	**verhogen**	road	**weg** (c)
rather	**tamelijk, nogal,**	Roman	**Romeins**
	vrij	roof	**dak** (n)
read	**lezen**	room	**kamer** (c)
read aloud	**voorlezen**	round	**rond, om; circa,**
ready	**klaar**		**ongeveer**
real	**echt**	rubber	**rubber** (c)
rebellious	**opstandig**	run	**rennen**
receive	**krijgen,**	rural	**landelijk**
	ontvangen	Russia	**Rusland**
recommend	**aanbevelen**	sail	**zeilen**
recover	**herstellen**	salad	**sla** (c)
red	**rood**	salt	**zout** (n)
Reformation	**Hervorming** (c)	same	**dezelfde,**
refrigerator	**koelkast** (c)		**hetzelfde**
regret	**spijten**	Saturday	**zaterdag** (c)
reliable	**betrouwbaar**	sauce	**saus** (c)
remember	**zich herinneren**	sausage	**(rook)worst** (c)
remind (of)	**herinneren** (**aan**)	(smoked)	
rent	**huren**	save	**sparen**
repair	**repareren,**	savings book	**spaarboekje** (n)
	herstellen	saw	**zaag** (c), **zagen**

say (to)	**zeggen (tegen)**	shop	**winkel** (c)
scarcely	**nauwelijks**	go shopping	**boodschappen**
scarf	**sjaal** (c)		**doen**
scatter	**strooien**	shovel	**schop** (c)
school	**school** (c)	shut	**sluiten**
scissors	**schaar** (c)	shut up!	**hou je mond!**
scoundrel	**schurk** (c)	sick	**ziek**
scratch	**krabben**	side	**kant** (c)
scrub	**poetsen**	sign	**bord** (n)
sea	**zee** (c)	sign	**tekenen**
seat	**zitplaats** (c);	simple	**eenvoudig**
	zetel (c)	simplify	**vergemakke-**
secondary	**middelbaar**		**lijken**
(school)		since	**sinds**
secretary	**secretaresse** (c)	sing	**zingen**
see	**zien**	singer	**zanger** (c)
seem	**schijnen, lijken,**	single	**enkel**
	blijken	a single	**een enkele**
self	**zelf**	ticket	**reis**
self-raising	**zelfrijzend**	sink	**aanrecht** (n)
sell	**verkopen**	sir	**meneer** (c)
send	**sturen**	sister	**zus(ter)** (c)
sender	**afzender** (c)	sister-in-law	**schoonzuster** (c)
sensible	**verstandig**	sit	**zitten**
separate	**scheiden**	situation	**geval** (n)
separation	**scheiding** (c)	six	**zes**
September	**september** (c)	sixteen	**zestien**
serve	**dienen**	sixty	**zestig**
service	**dienst** (c)	size	**maat** (c)
seven	**zeven**	skirt	**rok** (c)
seventeen	**zeventien**	sleep	**slapen**
seventy	**zeventig**	be sleepy	**slaap hebben**
sew	**naaien**	sleep in	**zich verslapen;**
sharp	**scherp**		**uitslapen**
shave	**(zich) scheren**	slice	**schijfje** (n), **snee**
she	**zij, ze**		(c); **snijden**
shed	**schuur** (c)	slow	**langzaam**
sheep	**schaap** (n)	small	**klein**
ship	**schip** (n)	smile (at)	**glimlachen**
shirt	**overhemd** (n)		**(tegen/naar)**
shoe	**schoen** (c)	smoke	**roken**
shoelace	**veter** (c)	smooth	**glad**

snow	**sneeuw** (c), **sneeuwen**	status	**status** (c)
		stay	**blijven**; **logeren**
so	**dus**, **zo**	step	**stap** (c); **tree** (c)
so-called	**zogenaamd**	stocking	**(nylon)kous** (c)
soap	**zeep** (c)	stir	**roeren**
sock	**sok** (c)	stitch	**hechten**
sofa	**sofa** (c)	stomach	**buik** (c)
soft	**zacht**	stop	**stoppen,**
soft drink	**frisdrank** (c)		**aanhouden**
some	**wat**	storm	**storm** (n)
something	**iets**	storm	**onweren**
sometimes	**soms**	stove	**fornuis** (n)
somewhere	**ergens**	street	**straat** (c)
son	**zoon** (c)	strike	**staking** (c),
son-in-law	**schoonzoon** (c)		**staken**
soon	**straks**	struggle	**kampen**
sorry	**sorry**	study	**studeren**
sort	**soort** (n)	stupid	**stom**
soup	**soep** (c)	successful	**succesvol**
south	**zuiden** (n)	such	**zulk**
southern	**zuidelijk**	sugar	**suiker** (c)
Spain	**Spanje**	suggest	**voorstellen**
sparrow	**mus** (c)	suit	**pak** (n)
speak	**spreken**	summer	**zomer** (c)
special	**speciaal**	Sunday	**zondag** (c)
spell	**spellen**	sunny	**zonnig**
spelling	**spelling** (c)	sunshine	**zonneschijn** (c)
spend (money)	**uitgeven**	supermarket	**supermarkt** (c)
spend (time)	**besteden**	surname	**achternaam** (c),
spice, herb	**kruid** (n)		**familienaam**
spoil	**verwennen;**		(c)
	bederven	survive	**overleven**
spoon	**lepel** (c)	swallow	**zwaluw** (c)
spring	**lente** (c)	swan	**zwaan** (c)
squirrel	**eekhoorn** (c)	Swede	**Zweed** (c)
staircase	**trap** (c)	Sweden	**Zweden**
stamp	**postzegel** (c)	Swedish	**Zweeds** (n)
stand	**staan**	sweep	**vegen**
stand up	**opstaan**	sweet	**lief, zoet**
star	**ster** (c)	sweetie	**liefje** (n)
starling	**spreeuw** (c)	swim	**zwemmen**
station	**station** (n)	swimming pool	**zwembad** (n)

switch off	**uitdoen**	thirst	**dorst**
sympathy	**medelijden** (n)	to be thirsty	**dorst hebben**
table	**tafel** (c)	thirteen	**dertien**
take	**nemen**	thirty	**dertig**
take off	**uittrekken**	this	**dit, deze**
(clothes)		those	**die**
talk	**praten**	thousand	**duizend**
tap	**kraan** (c)	three	**drie**
taste	**proeven; smaken**	throne	**troon** (c)
tasty	**smakelijk**	throw (away)	**(weg)gooien**
taxi	**taxi** (c)	thunder	**donder** (c),
tea	**thee** (c)		**donderen**
teach	**lesgeven**	Thursday	**donderdag** (c)
teacher	**leraar** (c)	ticket	**kaartje** (n)
telephone	**telefoon** (c)	ticket	**ticket** (n)
television	**televisie** (c)	tidy up	**opruimen**
tell	**vertellen**	tie	**(strop)das** (c)
temperature	**temperatuur** (c)	tight	**strak**
ten	**tien**	time	**tijd** (c); **keer** (c)
terrace house	**rijtjeshuis** (n)	tiny	**piepklein**
terrible	**erg, vreselijk**	tired	**moe**
than	**dan**	to	**naar, aan; te**
thank	**bedanken**	today	**vandaag**
thank you	**dank je wel,**	toe	**teen** (c)
	dank u wel	together	**samen**
thanks	**bedankt**	toilet	**wc** (c)
that	**dat, die, wat**	tomato	**tomaat** (c)
the	**de, het**	tomorrow	**morgen** (c)
theatre	**schouwburg** (c)	tomorrow	**morgenmiddag**
their	**hun**	afternoon	
them	**ze, hun, hen**	tomorrow	**morgenavond**
themselves	**zich; zelf**	evening	
then	**dan, toen**	tomorrow	**morgenochtend**
there	**er, daar**	morning	
therefore	**daarom**	tongue	**tong** (c)
these	**deze**	tonight	**vannacht**
they	**zij, ze**	too	**ook; te**
thin	**dun**	tooth	**tand** (c), **kies** (c)
thing	**ding** (n)	top	**bovenzijde** (c)
think (about)	**nadenken**	topping (for	**beleg** (n)
	(over/om)	bread)	
think of	**denken aan**	tot (e.g. of gin)	**borrel** (c)

tourist bureau	**VVV** (c)	unfortunately	**helaas**
town hall	**stadhuis** (n)	unique	**uniek**
town	**stad** (c)	unobservant	**onoplettend**
toys	**speelgoed** (n)	unreliable	**onbetrouwbaar**
traditional	**traditioneel**	until	**tot**
traffic	**verkeer** (n)	upstairs	**boven**
traffic light	**verkeerslicht** (n)	urgent	**dringend**
train	**trein** (c)	us	**ons**
train set	**treinstel** (n)	use	**gebruiken**
tram	**tram** (c)	useful	**nuttig**
translate	**vertalen**	usually	**gewoonlijk**
transport	**vervoer** (n)	vacation	**vakantie** (c)
public	**het openbaar**	various	**verschillend**
transport	**vervoer**	vase	**vaas** (c)
travel	**reizen**	vegetables	**groente** (c)
travel agency	**reisbureau** (n)	vegetarian	**vegetariër** (c);
traveller's	**reischeque** (c)		**vegetarisch**
cheque		very	**erg, heel, zeer**
tree	**boom** (c)	view	**opzicht** (n)
trousers	**broek** (c)	village	**dorp** (n)
true	**waar, echt**	violin	**viool** (c)
trust	**vertrouwen**	visit	**bezoek** (n),
try	**proberen**		**visite** (c);
try on	**aanpassen**		**bezoeken**
T-shirt	**T-shirt** (n)	vomit	**braaksel** (n);
Tuesday	**dinsdag** (c)		**overgeven**
turn	**draaien, keren**	wait (for)	**wachten (op)**
turn on	**aandoen**	wake	**wekken**
twelve	**twaalf**	walk	**wandeling** (c);
twenty	**twintig**		**lopen**
two	**twee**	walk around	**rondlopen**
typewriter	**schrijfmachine**	wall	**muur** (c)
	(c)	wallet	**portefeuille** (c)
typical	**normaal,**	Walloon	**Waal** (c)
	typisch	want to	**willen**
ugly	**lelijk**	war	**oorlog** (c)
umbrella	**paraplu** (c)	warm	**warm**
unbearable	**onuitstaanbaar**	warn	**waarschuwen**
uncle	**oom** (c)	wash	**wassen**
under	**onder**	wash up	**afwassen**
understand	**verstaan**	washing-up	**afwas** (c)
undress	**zich uitkleden**	watch	**horloge** (n)

watch	**kijken naar**	willingly	**graag**
watch	**televisie**	win	**winnen**
television	**kijken**	window	**raam** (n)
water	**water** (n)	wine	**wijn** (c)
wave	**golf** (c)	winter	**winter** (c)
way	**weg** (c)	wish	**wens** (c), **wensen**
we	**wij, we**	with	**met**
wear	**dragen**	within	**binnen**
weather	**weer** (n)	without	**zonder**
weather chart	**weerkaart** (c)	woman	**vrouw** (c)
weather report	**weerbericht** (n)	wonderful	**heerlijk,**
Wednesday	**woensdag** (c)		**verrukkelijk**
weekend	**weekend** (n)	wool	**wol** (c)
Have a nice	**Prettig**	work	**werk** (n),
weekend!	**weekend!**		**werken**
well-behaved	**braaf**	worth	**waard**
well-known	**bekend**	write	**schrijven**
west	**westen** (n)	wrong	**verkeerd**
western	**westelijk**	year	**jaar** (n)
wet	**nat**	for years	**jarenlang**
what	**wat**	yellow	**geel**
wheel	**wiel** (n)	yes	**ja, jawel**
wheelchair	**rolstoel** (c)	yesterday	**gisteren**
when	**als, toen,**	yesterday	**gistermiddag**
	wanneer	afternoon	
where	**waar**	yesterday	**gisteravond**
where ...	**waar ...**	evening	
from	**vandaan**	yesterday	**gisterochtend**
where ... to	**waar ...**	morning	
	naartoe	you	**jij, je, jou, jullie,**
whether	**of**		**u**
which	**welk; die, dat, wat**	young	**jong**
while	**terwijl**	your	**jouw, uw**
white	**wit**	yourself	**je, jou, u, zich;**
who	**wie; die**		**zelf**
whose	**van wie**	yourselves	**jullie, je; zelf**
why	**waarom**	yuck!	**ged verdemme!,**
wide	**breed**		**jasses!**
wife	**vrouw** (c)	yucky	**akelig**
will (verb used	**zullen**	yummy	**lekker**
for future		zero	**nul**
tense)			

Dutch–English glossary

aaien — to pat, pet, stroke

aan — on (vertical), at, to

aanbevelen (beval aan/ bevalen aan, aanbevolen) — to recommend

aandoen (deed aan/deden aan, aangedaan) — to turn on

aanhouden (hield aan/ hielden aan, aangehouden) — to stop/hail a car

aankleden (zich) — to get dressed

aankomen (kwam aan/ kwamen aan, is aangekomen) — to arrive

aannemen (nam aan/ namen aan, aangenomen) — to accept; to assume

aanpassen — to try on

aanrecht (n) — sink

aanstaande — next

aansteken (stak aan/ staken aan, aangestoken) — to light

aantrekken (trok aan/ trokken aan, aangetrokken) — to put on

aap (c) — monkey

aardappel (c) — potato

aardbeving (c) — earthquake

aardig — friendly

aardig vinden — to like (a person)

acht — eight

achter — behind

achterklein-dochter (c) — great-grand-daughter

achterkleinkind (n) — great-grandchild

achterkleinzoon (c) — great-grandson

achternaam (c) — surname

achterop — on the back

achtertuin (c) — back garden

achttien — eighteen

adres (n) — address

af en toe — now and then

afdrogen — to dry the dishes

afgelopen — last

afhangen (hing af/ hingen af, afgehangen) — to depend

Afsluitdijk (c)	Great Enclosing Dam	**Australiër** (c)	Australian (male)
afstand (c)	distance	**Australisch**	Australian (adj)
afstand doen	to abdicate	**auto** (c)	car
afwas (c)	washing-up	**autoweg** (c)	highway, freeway
afwasmiddel (n)	dishwashing liquid	**avond** (c)	evening
		avondeten (n)	evening meal
afwassen	to wash up	**baard** (c)	beard
(waste af/		**bad** (n)	bath
wasten af,		**bakken (bakte/**	to bake
afgewassen)		**bakten,**	
afzender (c)	sender	**gebakken)**	
akelig	yucky	**bakker** (c)	baker
al	already; all	**bakmeel** (n)	flour
allebei	both	**bal** (c)	ball
alledaags	everyday	**banaan** (c)	banana
alleen	alone	**bank** (c)	bank
alleen maar	only	**bank** (c)	bench, couch
allemaal	all	**bankbediende** (c)	bank teller
alles	everything, all	**bankstel** (n)	lounge suite
als	as; when, if	**bed** (n)	bed
alsjeblieft	please	**bedanken**	to thank
alsof	as if	**bedankt**	thanks
alstublieft	please	**bediende** (c)	assistant
Amerika	America	**bedoelen**	to mean
Amerikaans	American	**been** (n)	leg; bone
ananas (c)	pineapple	**beetje** (n)	bit
ander	other	**begeven (zich)**	to go onto/into
anderhalf	one and a half	**(begaf/**	
anders	otherwise	**begaven,**	
antwoord (n)	answer	**begeven)**	
antwoorden	to answer	**beginnen**	to begin
appel (c)	apple	**(begon/**	
april (c)	April	**begonnen,**	
arbeider (c)	labourer	**is begonnen)**	
arm	poor	**beha** (c)	bra
arm (c)	arm	**behalve**	except (for)
artikel (n)	article	**beide**	both
Atlantische	Atlantic	**bek** (c)	mouth (slang)
Oceaan		**hou je mond**	shut up!
augustus (c)	August	**bekend**	well-known
Australië	Australia		

bel (c)	bell
belachelijk	ridiculous
belanden (is	to land, end up
beland)	
belangrijk	important
beleg (n)	topping (for bread)
belegen	mature (of cheese)
Belg (c)	Belgian (male)
België	Belgium
Belgisch	Belgian (adj)
bellen	to ring
beloven	to promise
berg (c)	mountain
berichten	to report
beroep (n)	occupation; appeal
beslag (n)	batter
beslist	certainly
besluiten	to decide
(besloot/	
besloten,	
besloten)	
bestaan	to exist
(bestond/	
bestonden,	
bestaan)	
bestaan uit	to consist of
beste	dear (in letters)
besteden	to spend, pass (time)
betaalbaar	affordable
betalen	to pay
betekenen	to mean
beterschap!	get well soon!
betovergroot-	great-great-
moeder (c)	grandmother
betovergroot-	great-great-
vader (c)	grandfather
betrouwbaar	reliable
beurt (c)	turn, occasion
bevallen (beviel/	to please
bevielen,	
bevallen)	
bevinden (zich)	to be, to be
(bevond/	situated
bevonden,	
bevonden)	
bevrijden	to liberate
bevrijdingsdag	Liberation Day
(c)	
bewaken	to guard
bewaren	to keep, preserve
bewolking (c)	cloud cover
bewolkt	cloudy
bewoonbaar	inhabitable
bezem (c)	broom
bezetting (c)	occupation
bezig	busy
bezitten (bezat/	to own, possess
bezaten,	
bezeten)	
bezitting (c)	possession
bezoek (n)	visit
bezoeken	to visit
(bezocht/	
bezochten,	
bezocht)	
bier (n)	beer
bij	near, by, at; at the house of
bijna	almost, nearly
bijten (beet/	to bite
beten, gebeten)	
bijvoorbeeld	for example
biljet (n)	note; ticket
binnen	within, in(side)
binnenkomen	to come in
(kwam binnen/	
kwamen	
binnen, is	
binnengekomen)	

binnenland (n)	interior of a country	**braaf**	well-behaved
bioscoop (c)	movies, cinema	**braaksel** (n)	vomit
blad (n)	leaf	**branden**	to burn
blaffen (tegen)	to bark (at)	**breed**	wide
blauw	blue	**breken (brak/**	to break
blijven (bleef/	to stay, remain	**braken,**	
bleven, is		**gebroken)**	
gebleven)		**brengen (bracht/**	to bring
bliksem (c)	lightning	**brachten,**	
bliksemen	to have an	**gebracht)**	
	electrical	**brief** (c)	letter
	storm	**briefje** (n)	note
bloem (c)	flower	**broek** (c)	trousers
blozen	to blush	**broer** (c)	brother
blut	broke, skint	**brood** (n)	bread, loaf of
boek (n)	book		bread
boekenkast (c)	book case	**brouwen**	to trill one's 'r'
boffen	to be lucky		in the throat
Wat heeft zij	Wasn't she	**brug** (c)	bridge
geboft!	lucky!	**bruin**	brown
bol (c)	bulb	**buik** (c)	stomach
Bondsrepubliek	Federal Republic	**buiten**	out(side)
(c)	of Germany	**buitenland** (n)	abroad, overseas
boodschap (c)	message, errand	**bus** (c)	bus; letterbox
boodschappen	to go	**buur** (c)	neighbour
doen	shopping	**buurman** (c)	man next door,
boom (c)	tree		neighbour
boos	cross, angry	**buurvrouw** (c)	woman next
boot (c)	boat		door,
bord (n)	plate; sign		neighbour
borrel (c)	tot (e.g. of gin)	**buurt** (c)	neighbourhood
borst (c)	chest, breast	**cadeau** (n)	present, gift
borstel (c)	brush	**cadeau geven**	to give (as a
bos (n)	forest		present)
boter (c)	butter	**café** (n)	pub
bouw (c)	construction	**cent** (c)	cent
boven	above, over;	**chocola** (c)	chocolate
	upstairs	**colbert** (n)	jacket, suit coat
bovendien	in addition,	**computer** (c)	computer
	moreover	**Concertgebouw**	The Concert-
bovenzijde (c)	top	(n)	gebouw
			(concert hall)

controle (c)	control, surveillance	**die**	that, those; who, which; he, she, it, they
coupé (c)	compartment		
dáág	bye	**dienen**	to serve; to have to
daar	there		
daarnaast	in addition	**diens**	his (formal)
daarom	therefore, for that reason	**dienst** (c)	service
		dier (n)	animal
dag (c)	day	**dijk** (c)	dike
dagelijks	daily	**dijkwacht** (c)	dike watch
dagretour (n)	day return ticket	**dik**	fat
dagschotel (c)	meal of the day	**dikwijls**	often
dak (n)	roof	**ding** (n)	thing
Dam (c)	The Dam (square in Amsterdam)	**dinsdag** (c)	Tuesday
		directeur (c)	director, manager
dan	than; then	**dit**	this
dank je wel	thank you	**dochter** (c)	daughter
dank u wel	thank you	**doden**	to kill
dansen	to dance	**doen (deed/**	to do
das (c)	tie	**deden,**	
das (c)	badger	**gedaan)**	
dat	that, which	**donder** (c)	thunder
de	the	**donderdag** (c)	Thursday
december (c)	December	**donderen**	to thunder
deeg (n)	dough	**donker** (n)	dark
deel (n)	part	**dood**	dead
deken (c)	blanket	**doof**	deaf
denken aan	to think of	**doos** (c)	box
(dacht/		**dorp** (n)	village
dachten,		**dorst**	thirst
gedacht)		**dorst hebben**	to be thirsty
dertien	thirteen	**doven**	to extinguish
dertig	thirty	**draaien**	to turn, dial
deur (c)	door	**dragen (droeg/**	to wear
deze	this, these	**droegen,**	
dezelfde	the same	**gedragen)**	
dialect (n)	dialect	**drie**	three
dichtdoen	to close	**dringend**	urgent
(deed dicht/		**drinken (dronk/**	to drink
deden dicht,		**dronken,**	
dichtgedaan)		**gedronken)**	

droog	dry	**Engelse** (c)	English woman
droogleggen	to reclaim	**Engelsman** (c)	Englishman
druif (c)	grape	**enkel**	single
dubbeltje (n)	10 cents	een enkele	a single
duif (c)	dove, pigeon	reis	ticket/journey
Duits	German (adj)	**er**	there
Duitser (c)	German (male)	**erg**	very, terribly
Duitsland	Germany	**ergens**	somewhere
duizend	(a) thousand	**erven**	to inherit
dun	thin	**erwt** (c)	pea
duren	to last	**erwtensoep** (c)	peasoup
durven	to dare	**eten (at/aten,**	to eat
dus	so, thus	**gegeten)**	
duur	expensive	**eten** (n)	food
echt	real, true	**evangelisch**	evangelical
echtpaar (c)	married couple	**even**	just, a moment
economisch	economic	**eveneens**	also, as well
eekhoorn (c)	squirrel	**familie** (c)	(extended)
een	a, an		family
één	one	**familienaam** (c)	surname
eend (c)	duck	**fantastisch**	fantastic
eens	just	**februari** (c)	February
eenvoudig	simple	**feest(je)** (n)	party
eergisteren	the day before	**feit** (n)	fact
	yesterday	in feite	in fact
eetcafé (n)	café	**feliciteren**	to congratulate
eeuw (c)	century; age, era	**fiets** (c)	bicycle
egel (c)	hedgehog	**fietsen (is/heeft**	to cycle
ei (n)	egg	**gefietst)**	
eigenlijk	actually	**fietsenrek** (c)	bicycle stand
eik (c)	oak	**fietsenstalling** (c)	bicycle garage
eiland (n)	island	**fietspad** (n)	bicycle path
einde (n)	end	**film** (c)	film
eindelijk	finally	**firma** (c)	firm
elf	eleven	**flat** (c)	flat, apartment
elk	each, every	**fornuis** (n)	stove, cooker
elkaar	each other	**Française** (c)	French woman
elleboog (c)	elbow	**frank** (c)	(Belgian) franc
en	and	**Frankrijk**	France
energie (c)	energy	**Frans** (n)	French
Engeland	England	**Fransman** (c)	Frenchman
Engels	English	**Fries** (c)	Frisian

Friesland	Frisia
frisdrank (c)	soft drink
fruit (n)	fruit
gaan (ging/	to go
gingen, is	
gegaan)	
gans (c)	goose
garage (c)	garage
gat (n)	hole
geachte	dear (in letters)
gebak (n)	pastries, cakes
	(collective)
gebeuren	to happen
geboren	born
gebouw (n)	building
gebruikelijk	common
gebruiken	to use
gecondoleerd!	condolences!
ged verdemme!	yuck!
gedragen (zich)	to behave
(gedroeg/	
gedroegen,	
gedragen)	
gedurende	during
geel	yellow
gefeliciteerd!	congratulations!
gehakt (n)	minced meat
gek	mad, crazy
gekkenhuis (n)	madhouse
geld (n)	money
geleden	ago
geloven (in)	to believe (in)
gelukkig	fortunately;
	happy
gemakkelijk	easy
gemiddeld	average
genoeg	enough
gescheiden	divorced
geschiedenis (c)	history
gesprek (n)	conversation
in gesprek	engaged, busy
getrouwd	married

gevaar (n)	danger
gevaarlijk	dangerous
geval (n)	situation, case;
	fact
geven (gaf/	to give
gaven,	
gegeven)	
gewoonlijk	usually
gewoonte (c)	habit
gezellig	cosy, nice,
	comfortable
gezelligheid (c)	cosiness
gezicht (n)	face
gezin (n)	(nuclear) family
gezond	healthy
gezondheid (c)	health
Gezondheid!	Bless you!
Op uw	To your
gezondheid!	health!
gisteravond	last night
gisteren	yesterday
gistermiddag	yesterday
	afternoon
gisterochtend	yesterday
	morning
glad	soft, smooth
glas (n)	glass
glimlachen	to smile (at)
(tegen/naar)	
god-	damn!
verdikkeme!	
godverdikkie!	damn!
godverdomme!	bloody hell!,
	bugger!
godverdorie!	damn!
God (c)	God
god!	Lord!
goed	good
goedkoop	cheap
goeie hemel!	good heavens!
goeie middag	good afternoon
goeie morgen	good morning

goeien avond	good evening
golf (c)	wave
graad (c)	degree
graag	willingly; please
gracht (c)	canal (in a city)
grappig	funny
gras (n)	grass
gratis	free
graven (groef/	to dig
groeven,	
gegraven)	
grens (c)	border
grijs	grey
groen	green
groente (c)	vegetables
groenteboer (c)	greengrocer
groet (c)	greeting
grond (c)	ground
groot	big, large
grootmoeder (c)	grandmother
grootouders (pl.)	grandparents
grootvader (c)	grandfather
gulden (c)	guilder
gulp (c)	fly (of trousers)
haar	her
haar (n)	hair
haast	haste, hurry
haast hebben	to be in a hurry
haasten (zich)	to hurry up
hagel (c)	hail
hagelen	to hail
halen	to fetch
half	half
ham (c)	ham
hamer (c)	hammer
hameren	to hammer
hand (c)	hand
handschoen (c)	glove
handtas (c)	handbag
hapje (n)	mouthful, bite
hard	fast; loud

hartelijk	heartily
hartstikke	extremely
haven (c)	harbour, port
havik (c)	hawk
hebben (had/	to have
hadden,	
gehad)	
hechten	to stitch; become attached to
heel	very; entirely
heerlijk	wonderful
heet	hot
heilig	holy
hek (n)	fence
hekel (c)	dislike, loathing
een hekel	to dislike,
hebben aan	loathe
helaas	unfortunately
heleboel (c)	a lot (of)
helemaal	entirely
helemaal niet	not at all
helpen (hielp/	to help
hielpen,	
geholpen)	
hem	him
hen	them
herdenken	to commemorate
(herdacht/	
herdachten,	
herdacht)	
herfst (c)	autumn
herhalen	to repeat
herhaling (c)	repeat
herinneren	to remember
(zich)	
herinneren	to remind (of)
(aan)	
herrie (c)	noise, din
herstellen	to repair, recover
Hervorming (c)	Reformation
het	the; it

heten (heette/	to be called	**huren**	to rent
heetten,		**ieder**	each, every
geheten)		**iedereen**	everyone
hetzelfde	the same	**iets**	something,
heuvel (c)	hill		anything
hier	here	**ijs** (n)	ice; icecream
hiernaast	next door	**ijsje** (n)	icecream
hij	he	**ik**	I
hoed (c)	hat	**ikke**	me, I
hoek (c)	corner	**in**	in, into
hoeveel	how many, how	**ingang** (c)	entrance
	much	**ingenieur** (c)	engineer
hoeven	to need to	**inktvis** (c)	octopus
hoewel	although	**inpakken**	to pack up
hogedrukgebied	high (pressure	**instappen (is**	to get in
(n)	area)	**ingestapt)**	
hoi	hi	**intelligent**	intelligent
hond (c)	dog	**interessant**	interesting
hondenlijn (c)	leash	**inwoner** (c)	inhabitant
honderd	(a) hundred	**Italië**	Italy
honger (c)	hunger	**ja**	yes
honger	to be hungry	**jaar** (n)	year
hebben		**januari** (c)	January
hoofd (n)	head	**jarenlang**	for years
hoofdpunt (n)	headline; main	**jarig**	
	point	**ik ben jarig**	it's my
hoofdstad (c)	capital city		birthday
hoofdstuk (n)	chapter	**jas** (c)	coat
hoog	high	**jasses!**	yuck!
hopen	to hope	**jawel**	yes (emphatic)
horen	to hear	**je**	you, your
horloge (n)	watch	**jee!**	Gee!
houden (hield/	to hold, keep	**jeetje!**	blast!
hielden,		**jij**	you
gehouden)		**jong**	young
houden van	to like, love	**jongen** (c)	boy
huilen	to cry	**jou**	you
huis (n)	house	**journaal** (n)	news (on TV)
huisvrouw (c)	housewife	**jouw**	your
huiswerk (n)	housework;	**juli** (c)	July
	homework	**jullie**	you
hun	them; their	**juni** (c)	June

jurk (c)	dress
kaal	bald
kaars (c)	candle
kaart (c)	map
kaartje (n)	ticket
kaas (c)	cheese
kalender (c)	calendar
kalf (n)	calf
kam (c)	comb
kamer (c)	room
kampen	to battle, struggle
kamperen	to camp
kanaal (n)	canal (in the country)
kans (c)	chance
kant (c)	direction, way
kantoor (n)	office
kapot	broken
kast (c)	cupboard
kat (c)	cat
katoen (n)	cotton
keer (c)	time
keizer (c)	emperor
kennen	to be acquainted with, know
kennis (c)	acquaintance
keren	to turn
kerk (c)	church
Kerstfeest (n)	Christmas season
Gelukkig Kerstfeest!	Merry Christmas!
Kerstmis (c)	Christmas
Eerste Kerstdag (c)	Christmas Day
Tweede Kerstdag (c)	Boxing Day
keuken (c)	kitchen
kies (c)	tooth, molar
kiezen	to choose
kijken (naar) (keek/keken, gekeken)	to look (at), watch
kilo (c)	kilogram
kind (n)	child
kip (c)	chicken
klaar	ready, finished
klaarmaken	to prepare
klant (c)	customer
klas	(school) class
klasse (c)	(social) class
klein	small
kleindochter (c)	granddaughter
kleingeld (n)	change (money)
kleinkind (n)	grandchild
kleinzoon (c)	grandson
kleren (pl.)	clothes
kloppen	to beat (e.g. an egg); to knock
dat klopt	that's right
knippen	to cut, clip
knoflook (c)	garlic
knoop (c)	button
koekenpan (c)	frying pan
koekje (n)	biscuit
koekjes-trommel (c)	biscuit barrel
koelkast (c)	refrigerator
koffie (c)	coffee
koffiepot (c)	coffeepot
koken	to cook
kolonie (c)	colony
kom (c)	bowl
komen (kwam/ kwamen, is gekomen)	to come
konijn (n)	rabbit
koning (c)	king
koningin (c)	queen
Koninginnedag (c)	Queen's Birthday
koninkrijk (n)	kingdom, monarchy

kopen (kocht/	to buy	laag	low
kochten,		laars (c)	boot
gekocht)		(pl. laarzen)	
te koop	for sale	lachen	to laugh
kopje (n)	cup	ladder (c)	ladder
kosten	to cost	ladenkast (c)	chest of drawers
koud	cold	lagedrukgebied	low (pressure
kous (c)	stocking	(n)	area)
kraag (c)	collar	lam (n)	lamb
kraai (c)	crow	lamp (c)	light, lamp
kraan (c)	tap	land (n)	land, country
krabben	to scratch	landbouw (c)	agriculture
krant (c)	newspaper	landelijk	rural
krijgen (kreeg/	to get, receive	lang	long; high
kregen,		langs	along, past
gekregen)		langzaam	slow
kroeg (c)	pub	lastig	irritating
kroket (c)	croquette	laten (liet/	to let, leave
kroon (c)	crown	lieten, gelaten)	
kruid (n)	spice, herb	later	later
kruispunt (n)	crossroad	leeftijd (c)	age
kunnen (kon/	to be able to/can	leggen	to lay, put
konden,		lekker	delicious,
gekund)			yummy
kunst (c)	art	lelijk	ugly
kus (c)	kiss	lenen	to loan, lend,
kussen	to kiss		borrow
kussen (n)	cushion	lengte (c)	height; length
kust (c)	coast	lente (c)	spring
kwalijk nemen	to blame	lepel (c)	spoon
(nam kwalijk/		leraar (c)	teacher
namen kwalijk,		leren	to learn
kwalijk		lesgeven (gaf	to teach
genomen)		les/gaven les,	
Neem me	I'm sorry,	lesgegeven)	
niet kwalijk	forgive me	leuk	nice, fun
kwart (c)	quarter	leven	to live
kwartier (n)	quarter of an	leven (n)	life
	hour	lezen (las/lazen,	to read
kwartje (n)	25 cents	gelezen)	
kwast (c)	paintbrush	licht (n)	light
la (c)	drawer	lief	sweet, cute

liefje (n)	sweetie	**meebrengen**	to bring along
lieve	dear (in letters)	**(bracht mee/**	
lieveling	darling	**brachten mee,**	
lievelings-	favourite	**meegebracht)**	
lieverd	darling, dear	**meekomen**	to come along
liggen (lag/	to lie	**(kwam mee/**	
lagen, heeft		**kwamen mee, is**	
gelegen)		**meegekomen)**	
lijken (leek/	to seem	**meel** (n)	flour
leken, geleken)		**meer**	more
lijken op	to look like	**meest**	most
lijst (c)	list	**meestal**	mostly
linkerkant (c)	left-hand side	**mei** (c)	May
links	left	**meisje** (n)	girl
linksaf	to the left	**mekaar**	each other (coll.)
logeren	to stay, lodge	**melk** (c)	milk
loop (c)	course	**men**	one (pronoun)
lopen (liep/	to walk	**meneer** (c)	Mr, sir
liepen, is/		**menen**	to be of the
heeft gelopen)			opinion
lottokaartje (n)	lottery ticket	**menigte** (c)	crowd, multitude
lucifer (c)	match	**mens** (c)	person; human
luisteren (naar)	to listen (to)	**menu** (n)	menu
lusten	to have an	**mes** (n)	knife
	appetite for	**met**	with, by
maaien	to mow	**mevrouw** (c)	Mrs, madam
maaltijd (c)	meal	**middag** (c)	afternoon
maand (c)	month	**middel** (n)	middle
maandag (c)	Monday	**middelbaar**	secondary
maar	but		(school)
maart (c)	March	**middeleeuwen** (c)	Middle Ages
Maas (c)	the Meuse	**midden** (n)	middle
maat (c)	size	**in het**	in the middle
maken	to make	**midden van**	of
makkelijk	easy	**mij**	me
man (c)	man; husband	**mijn**	my
manager (c)	manager	**miljoen** (n)	million
mannelijk	male, masculine	**minder**	less
marmot (c)	guinea pig	**misschien**	perhaps
me	me; myself	**mist** (c)	fog, mist
medelijden (n)	sympathy,	**modern**	modern
	pity	**moe**	mum

moe	tired	**nauwelijks**	hardly, scarcely
moeder (c)	mother	**Nederland**	the Netherlands
moedertaal (c)	native language	**Nederlander** (c)	Dutchman
moeilijk	difficult	**Nederlands**	Dutch
moeite (c)	difficulty, trouble	**Nederlandse** (c)	Dutch woman
moeten (moest/	to have to/must	**Nederlandstalig**	Dutch-speaking
moesten,		**neef** (c)	male cousin;
gemoeten)			nephew
mogelijk	possible	**negen**	nine
mogen (mocht/	to be allowed	**negentien**	nineteen
mochten,	to/may	**negentig**	ninety
gemogen)		**nemen (nam/**	to take
mond (c)	mouth	**namen,**	
morgen (c)	morning;	**genomen)**	
	tomorrow	**nergens**	nowhere
morgenavond	tomorrow	**nest** (c)	nest
	evening	**net**	just
morgenmiddag	tomorrow	**net zo(als)**	just like, just
	afternoon		as
morgenochtend	tomorrow	**net** (n)	television
	morning		channel
muis (c)	mouse	**netjes**	neat
munt (c)	coin	**neus** (c)	nose
mus (c)	sparrow	**neushoorn** (c)	rhinoceros
muts (c)	cap	**nicht** (c)	female cousin;
muur (c)	wall		niece
muziek (c)	music	**niemand**	no one
na	after	**niet**	not
naaien	to sew	**niet per se**	not necessarily
naald (c)	needle	**niets**	nothing
naam	name; surname	**nieuw**	new
naar	to	**Nieuwjaarsdag**	New Year's Day
naast	next to	**(c)**	
nacht (c)	night	**Gelukkig**	Happy New
nadat	after	**Nieuwjaar!**	Year!
nadenken (over)	to think (about)	**nieuws** (n)	news
namelijk	you see, of	**nijlpaard** (n)	hippopotamus
	course	**nodig**	necessary
nat	wet	**nodig hebben**	to need
nationaliteit (c)	nationality	**(had nodig/**	
natuurlijk	naturally, of	**hadden nodig,**	
	course	**nodig gehad)**	

noemen	to call	**ongeveer**	approximately,
nogal	rather		about
nooit	never	**onmiddellijk**	immediate(ly)
noordelijk	northern	**onoplettend**	unobservant
noorden (n)	north	**ons**	us; our
ten noorden	to the north	**ons** (n)	'ounce',
van	of		100 grams
Noordzee (c)	the North Sea	**ontbijt** (n)	breakfast
noot (c)	nut	**ontbijten**	to breakfast
notenboom (c)	walnut tree	**(ontbeet/**	
nou	now	**ontbeten,**	
november (c)	November	**ontbeten)**	
NS (c)	Dutch Railways	**ontmoeten**	to meet
nu	now	**ontvangen**	to receive
nul	zero	**(ontving/**	
nummer (n)	number	**ontvingen,**	
nuttig	necessary,	**ontvangen)**	
	useful	**onuitstaanbaar**	unbearable
(nylon)kous (c)	stocking	**onweer** (n)	storm
oceaan (c)	ocean	**onweren**	to storm
ochtend (c)	morning	**onze**	our
of	whether, if; or	**onzin** (c)	nonsense
ogen	eyes	**oog** (n)	eye
ogenblik (n)	moment	**ooit**	ever
oktober (c)	October	**ook**	also, too
olifant (c)	elephant	**oom** (c)	uncle
om	around	**oor** (n)	ear
om ... te	(in order) to	**oorlog** (c)	war
oma (c)	grandma	**oostelijk**	eastern
omdat	because	**oosten** (n)	east
omkleden (zich)	to get changed	**ten oosten**	to the east of
omroep (c)	broadcasting	**van**	
	association	**op**	on (horizontal),
omtrent	circa, about		at
omvallen (viel	to fall over,	**opa** (c)	grandpa
om/vielen om,	topple over	**opbellen**	to ring up
is omgevallen)		**opdagen**	to appear, turn
onbetrouwbaar	unreliable		up
ondanks	in spite of,	**opdrinken**	to drink up
	despite	**(dronk op/**	
onder	under	**dronken op,**	
ongeluk (n)	accident	**opgedronken)**	

openbaar	public	**over**	about, over
het openbaar	public	**overal**	everywhere
vervoer	transport	**overgroot-**	great-
opendoen (**deed**	to open	**moeder** (c)	grandmother
open/deden		**overgrootvader**	great-
open,		(c)	grandfather
opengedaan)		**overhemd** (n)	shirt
openen	to open	**overleven**	to survive
operatie (c)	operation	**overlijden**	to pass away
opeten (**at op/**	to eat up	(**overleed/**	
aten op,		**overleden,**	
opgegeten)		**is overleden**)	
ophalen	to pick up,	**overloop** (c)	landing
	collect	**overmorgen**	the day after
ophangen	to hang up		tomorrow
(**hing op/**		**overstappen**	to change (e.g.
hingen op,		(**is overgestapt**)	trains)
opgehangen)		**overstromen**	to flood
opklaren	to clear up	**pa**	dad
opletten	to look out; to	**paar** (c)	couple
	pay attention	**een paar**	a few
oplopen	to rise	**paars**	purple
oploskoffie (c)	instant coffee	**pad** (n)	path
opmaken	to make, make	**pak** (n)	suit
	up	**paleis** (n)	palace
opnemen (**nam**	to pick up	**pan** (c)	pot, pan
op/namen op,		**pannenkoek** (c)	pancake
opgenomen)		**papegaai** (c)	parrot
oppassen	to look out; to	**paraplu** (c)	umbrella
	look after	**pardon!**	excuse me!
opruimen	to clean up, tidy	**Parijs**	Paris
opstaan (**stond**	to get up, stand	**park** (n)	park
op/stonden	up	**parkeerterrein**	car park
op, is		(n)	
opgestaan)		**parkeren**	to park
opstandig	rebellious	**parkiet** (c)	budgerigar
opstel (n)	essay	**pas**	not until
opzicht (n)	view, respect	**Pasen** (c)	Easter
in dit opzicht	in this respect	**paspoort** (n)	passport
oranje	orange	**passen**	to fit
oud	old	**pastoor** (c)	priest, minister
ouders (pl.)	parents	**patat** (c) (pl.)	(hot) chips

pauw (c)	peacock	**praktisch**	practical
peer (c)	pear	**praten**	to talk
pen (c)	pen	**precies**	exactly
perenboom (c)	pear tree	**prettig**	nice
per se	necessarily	**prima**	great
veroorloven	to afford	**prins** (c)	prince
(zich)		**prinses** (c)	princess
perron (n)	platform	**proberen**	to try
persje (n)	Persian rug	**proeven**	to taste
pet (c)	cap	**programma** (n)	programme
piepklein	tiny	**proost!**	cheers!
pijn (c)	pain	**provincie** (c)	province
pijp (c)	pipe	**pruim** (c)	plum
pils (c)	beer	**puinhoop** (c)	mess
pilsje (n)	a glass of beer	**purper**	purple
Pinksteren (c)	Pentecost,	**raam** (n)	window
	Whitsuntide	**radio** (c)	radio
plaats (c)	place; room,	**raken**	to become, get
	space	**rand** (c)	edge, rim
in plaats van	instead of	**rechtdoor**	direct, straight
platteland (n)	countryside,		ahead
	rural areas	**rechterhand** (c)	right-hand
plezier (n)	enjoyment	**rechts**	right
Veel plezier!	Enjoy	**rechtsaf**	to the right
	yourself!	**rechtstreeks**	directly
plukken	to pick, pluck	**regen** (c)	rain
poetsen	to polish, clean	**regenen**	to rain
polder (c)	polder	**regeren**	to govern
politiek	political	**regering** (c)	government
pond (n)	'pound',	**reiger** (c)	heron
	500 grams	**reis** (c)	journey
pont (c)	ferry	**reisbureau** (n)	travel agency
pontveer (n)	ferry	**reischeque** (c)	traveller's
pop (c)	doll		cheque
populair	popular	**reizen (is/heeft**	to travel
portefeuille (c)	wallet	**gereisd)**	
portemonnaie	purse	**rekening** (c)	bill
(c)		**rennen**	to run
postkantoor (n)	post-office	**repareren**	to repair
postzegel (c)	stamp	**reserveren**	to book
potlood (n)	pencil	**rest** (c)	rest, remainder
prachtig	fabulous	**restaurant** (n)	restaurant

retour (n)	return ticket	**schamen (zich)**	to be ashamed
reuze	gigantic	**schat**	dear, darling
rib (c)	rib	**scheiden**	to separate
riem (c)	belt	**scheiding** (c)	separation;
rijbewijs (n)	driver's licence		parting (in
rijden (reed/	to ride, drive		hair)
reden, is/		**schenken**	to pour
heeft gereden)		**(schonk/**	
rijk	rich	**schonken,**	
rijksdaalder (c)	2 guilders	**geschonken)**	
	50 cents	**scheren (schoor/**	to shave
Rijn (c)	the Rhine	**schoren,**	
rijp	ripe	**geschoren)**	
rijst (c)	rice	**scherp**	sharp
rijsttafel (c)	Indonesian rice	**schijfje** (n)	slice; floppy disk
	banquet	**schijnen**	to seem, appear
rijtjeshuis (n)	terrace house	**(scheen/**	
rivier (c)	river	**schenen,**	
roepnaam (c)	name you are	**geschenen)**	
	called by	**schilderen**	to paint
roeren	to stir	**schillen**	to peel
rok (c)	skirt	**schip** (n)	ship
roken	to smoke	**schoen** (c)	shoe
rolstoel (c)	wheelchair	**school** (c)	school
Romeins	Roman	**schoon**	clean
rommel (c)	junk	**schoondochter**	daughter-in-law
rond	round	(c)	
rondlopen (liep	to walk around	**schoonmaken**	to clean
rond/liepen		**schoonmoeder**	mother-in-law
rond,		(c)	
rondgelopen)		**schoonouders**	parents-in-law
rood	red	(pl.)	
roomboter (c)	butter	**schoonvader** (c)	father-in-law
rose	pink	**schoonzoon** (c)	son-in-law
rubber (c)	rubber	**schoonzuster** (c)	sister-in-law
rund (n)	cattle	**schop** (c)	shovel
Rusland	Russia	**schouwburg** (c)	theatre
ruzie (c)	argument	**schrijfmachine** (c)	typewriter
samen	together	**schrijven**	to write
saus (c)	sauce	**(schreef/**	
schaap (n)	sheep	**schreven,**	
schaar (c)	scissors	**geschreven)**	

schuld (c)	blame, guilt	**snel**	quick
schurk (c)	scoundrel	**snijden (sneed/**	to cut, slice
schuur (c)	shed	**sneden,**	
secretaresse (c)	secretary	**gesneden)**	
september (c)	September	**snoep** (c)	confectionery,
sfeer (c)	atmosphere		candy
sigaar (c)	cigar	**snufje** (n)	pinch
sigaret (c)	cigarette	**een snufje**	a pinch of salt
sinds	since	**zout**	
sjaal (c)	scarf	**soep** (c)	soup
sjekkie (n)	roll-your-own	**sofa** (c)	sofa
	cigarette	**sok** (c)	sock
sla (c)	salad, lettuce	**soms**	sometimes;
slaan (sloeg/	to hit		perhaps
sloegen,		**soort** (n)	sort, kind
geslagen)		**sorry**	sorry, excuse me
slaapkamer (c)	bedroom	**spaarboekje** (n)	savings book
slapen (sliep/	to sleep	**spaarpotje** (n)	piggy bank
sliepen,		**Spanje**	Spain
geslapen)		**spannend**	exciting
slaap hebben	to be sleepy	**sparen**	to save
slecht	bad	**speciaal**	special
sleutel (c)	key	**speculaas** (c)	spicy biscuit
slipje (n)	panties	**speelfilm** (c)	feature film;
sloop (c)	cover		movie
slot (n)	lock	**speelgoed** (n)	toys
sluiten (sloot/	to shut	**spelen**	to play
sloten,		**spellen**	to spell
gesloten)		**spelling** (c)	spelling
smakelijk	tasty	**spijker** (c)	nail
Eet	Bon appétit!	**spijkerbroek** (c)	jeans
smakelijk!/		**spijten (speet/**	to regret
Smakelijk eten!		**speten,**	
smaken	to taste; to like	**gespeten)**	
	(food)	**het spijt me**	I'm sorry
smal	narrow	**splinternieuw**	brand new
smelten (smolt/	to melt	**spoor** (n)	line, platform
smolten,		**spoorboekje** (n)	railway
gesmolten)			timetable book
snee (c)	slice	**spoorweg** (c)	railway
sneeuw (c)	snow	**spoorwegnet** (n)	railway network
sneeuwen	to snow	**spreeuw** (c)	starling

spreken (sprak/	to speak
spraken,	
gesproken)	
staan (stond/	to stand
stonden,	
gestaan)	
stad (c)	city, town
stadhuis (n)	town hall
staking (c)	strike
stap (c)	step
op stap	travelling
station (n)	station
status (c)	status
ster (c)	star
Sterkte!	Chin up! Keep at it!
sterven (stierf/	to die
stierven, is	
gestorven)	
stil	quiet
stom	dumb, stupid
stoppen	to put in; to stop
storm (n)	storm
stout	naughty
straat (c)	street
strak	tight
straks	soon
strijken (streek/	to iron
streken,	
gestreken)	
strippenkaart (c)	strip ticket
strooien	to scatter, strew
(strop)das (c)	tie
struisvogel (c)	ostrich
studeren	to study
stuiver (c)	5 cents
stuk	broken
stuk (n)	piece
sturen	to send
succesvol	successful
suiker (c)	sugar

supermarkt (c)	supermarket
taal (c)	language
tachtig	eighty
tafel (c)	table
tand (c)	tooth
tante (c)	aunt
taxi (c)	taxi
te	to; too
teddybeer (c)	teddybear
teen (c)	toe
tegen	against
tegenover	opposite
tegenwoordig	these days
tekenen	to sign; to draw
tekening (c)	drawing
telefoon (c)	telephone
telefoonkaart (c)	telephone card
televisie (c)	television
televisie kijken	to watch television
tellen	to count
temperatuur (c)	temperature
tenslotte	after all
terrein (n)	ground, field
terug	back
teruggaan	to return, go back
(ging terug/	
gingen terug,	
is teruggegaan)	
terwijl	while
thee (c)	tea
thuis	home, at home
thuiskomen	to come home
(kwam thuis/	
kwamen thuis, is	
thuisgekomen)	
ticket (n)	ticket
tien	ten
tientje (n)	ten guilder note
tijd (c)	time
op tijd	on time
tijdens	during

tijdschrift (n)	magazine	uitgeven (gaf	to give out, to
toegang (c)	entrance	uit/gaven uit,	spend; to
toelaten (liet	to permit, allow	uitgegeven)	publish
toe/lieten toe,		uitkleden (zich)	to get undressed
toegelaten)		uitnodigen	to invite
toen	when; then	uitsmijter (c)	bread with fried
tomaat (c)	tomato		egg, cheese
tong (c)	tongue		etc.
tot	until	uitstappen (is	to get out
tot ziens	goodbye	uitgestapt)	
traditioneel	traditional	uitstekend	excellent
tram (c)	tram	uittrekken (trok	to take off
trap (c)	staircase	uit/trokken uit,	
trein (c)	train	uitgetrokken)	
treinstel (n)	train set	uitvallen (viel	to fall out, turn
trek	appetite	uit/vielen uit,	out
trek hebben	to feel like	is uitgevallen)	
in	(eating)	uitzenden (zond	to transmit
troon (c)	throne	uit/zonden uit,	
trots (op)	proud (of)	uitgezonden)	
trouwen (met)	to get married	uniek	unique
	(to)	urenlang	for hours
trui (c)	jumper, top,	uur (n)	hour
	pullover	uw	your
T-shirt (n)	T-shirt	vaak	often
tuin (c)	garden	vaas (c)	vase
tuinieren	to garden	vader (c)	father
tussen	between	vakantie (c)	vacation,
twaalf	twelve		holidays
twee	two	Prettige	Have a nice
tweetalig	bilingual	vakantie!	holiday!
twintig	twenty	vallen (viel/	to fall
typisch	typical	vielen, is	
u	you	gevallen)	
ui (c)	onion	van	from; of, off
uit	out (of), from	vanaf	from ... on
uitbreken (brak	to break out	vanavond	this evening
uit/braken uit,		vandaag	today
uitgebroken)		vanmiddag	this afternoon
uitdoen (deed	to switch off	vanmorgen	this morning
uit/deden uit,		vannacht	last night;
uitgedaan)			tonight

vanochtend	this morning
vanwege	on account of, because of
varen (voer/ voeren, is/ heeft gevaren)	to sail, go by boat
vasteland (n)	mainland
veertien	fourteen
veertig	forty
vegen	to sweep
vegetariër (c)	vegetarian
veld (n)	field
vent (c)	fellow, guy
ver	far
veranderen (is veranderd)	to change
verbergen (verborg/ verborgen, verborgen)	to hide
verbieden (verbood/ verboden, verboden)	to forbid
verbinden (verbond/ verbonden, verbonden)	to connect
verbranden	to burn
verdedigen	to defend
verdediging (c)	defence
verdelen	to divide
verdienen	to earn
verdikkeme!	damn!
verdikkie!	damn!
verdomme!	bloody hell!, bugger!
verdorie!	damn!
verdwijnen (verdween/ verdwenen, is verdwenen)	to disappear

vergadering (c)	meeting
vergemakke- lijken	to simplify, make easier
vergeten (vergat/ vergaten, is/heeft vergeten)	to forget
vergissen (zich)	to be mistaken
verheugen (op) (zich)	to look forward (to)
verhogen	to raise
verhuizen (is verhuisd)	to move house
verjaardag (c)	birthday
verjaardags- kalender (c)	birthday calender
verkeer (n)	traffic
verkeerd	wrong
u bent	you have the
verkeerd verbonden	wrong number
verkeerslicht (n)	traffic light
verkiezen (boven) (verkoos/ verkozen, verkozen)	to prefer (to)
verkopen (verkocht/ verkochten, verkocht)	to sell
verlaten (verliet/ verlieten, verlaten)	to leave
verleden	last
verliezen (verloor/ verloren, verloren)	to lose
verrukkelijk	wonderful
vers	fresh

verschillend	different	**vis** (c)	fish
verslapen (zich)	to oversleep,	**visite** (c)	visit
(**versliep/**	sleep in	**Vlaams**	Flemish
versliepen,		**Vlaanderen**	Flanders
verslapen)		**vlag** (c)	flag
verstaan	understand	**vlak**	flat, even
(**verstond/**		**Vlaming** (c)	Fleming (male)
verstonden,		**vlees** (n)	meat
verstaan)		**vliegen (vloog/**	to fly
verstandig	sensible	**vlogen, is/**	
vertalen	to translate	**heeft gevlogen)**	
vertellen	to tell	**vliegtuig** (n)	aeroplane
vertragen	to delay	**vliering** (c)	attic
vertraging (c)	delay	**vlinder** (c)	butterfly
vertrekken	to depart, leave	**vloer** (c)	floor
(**vertrok/**		**vlug**	fast
vertrokken,		**voeden**	to feed
is vertrokken)		**voelen**	to feel
vertrouwen	to trust	**voet** (c)	foot
vervelen (zich)	to be bored	**vogel** (c)	bird
verven	to paint	**vol**	full
vervoer (n)	transport	**volgend**	next
het openbaar	public	**volgens**	according to
vervoer	transport	**voor**	for
vervoermiddel	means/mode of	**vóór**	in front of, before
(n)	transport	**voorbeeld** (n)	example
verwachten	to expect	**bijvoorbeeld**	for example
verwennen	to spoil	**voordat**	before
veter (c)	shoelace	**voorkomen**	to occur
Victoriaans	Victorian	(**kwam voor/**	
vier	four	**kwamen voor,**	
vies	dirty	**is**	
vijand (c)	enemy	**voorgekomen)**	
vijf	five	**voorlezen (las**	to read aloud
vijftien	fifteen	**voor/lazen**	
vijftig	fifty	**voor,**	
villa (c)	detached house	**voorgelezen)**	
vinden (vond/	to find	**voornaam** (c)	first name
vonden,		**voorop**	on the front
gevonden)		**voorrang** (c)	right-of-way
vinger (c)	finger	**voorstellen**	to suggest; to
viool (c)	violin		introduce

voortaan	in future; from now on	**wang** (c)	cheek
		wanhopig	desperate
voortuin (c)	front garden	**wanneer**	when
vorig	last	**want**	because
vork (c)	fork	**warm**	warm, hot
vragen (om)	to ask (for)	**wassen (waste/**	to wash
(vroeg/		**wasten,**	
vroegen,		**gewassen)**	
gevraagd)		**wat**	what; that, which;
vreselijk	terrible		some(what)
vriend (c)	friend	**wat voor**	what sort of a
vriendelijk	friendly	**een ...**	...
vriespunt (n)	freezing point	**water** (n)	water
vriesvak (n)	freezer compartment	**wc** (c)	toilet
		we	we
vriezen (vroor/	to freeze	**weekend** (n)	weekend
vroren,		**Prettig**	Have a nice
gevroren)		**weekend!**	weekend!
vrij	free; rather	**weer**	again
vrijdag (c)	Friday	**weer** (n)	weather
vrijgezel (c)	bachelor	**weerbericht** (n)	weather report
vroeg	early	**weerkaart** (c)	weather chart
vrouw (c)	woman; wife	**weersver-**	weather forecast
vrouwelijk	female, feminine	**wachting** (c)	
vulpen (c)	fountain pen	**wees!**	be!
vuur (n)	fire; 'a light'	**weg** (c)	way; road
VVV (c)	tourist bureau	**wegdoen (deed**	to get rid of,
Waal (c)	Waal (a river)	**weg/deden**	clear away
Waal (c)	Walloon	**weg,**	
waar	true	**weggedaan)**	
waar	where	**wegennet** (n)	road network
waar ...	where ...	**weggaan (ging**	to go away
vandaan	from	**weg/gingen**	
waar ...	where ... to	**weg, is**	
naartoe		**weggegaan)**	
waard	worth	**weggooien**	to throw away
waarom	why	**weinig**	few
waarschijnlijk	probable(-ly)	**wekken**	to wake
waarschuwen	to warn	**welterusten**	good night
wachten (op)	to wait (for)	**wel**	(used to
wakker	awake		contradict a
wandeling (c)	walk		negative)

welk	which	**wreed**	cruel
wensen	to wish, want to	**zaag** (c)	saw
werk (n)	work	**zacht**	soft
werken	to work	**zagen**	to saw
westelijk	western	**zak** (c)	pocket
westen (n)	west	**zakdoek** (c)	handkerchief
ten westen van	to the west of	**zanger** (c)	singer
weten (wist/	to know	**zaterdag** (c)	Saturday
wisten,		**ze**	she; they; them
geweten)		**zee** (c)	sea
wie	who	**zeep** (c)	soap
van wie	whose	**zeer** (n)	pain
wieg (c)	cradle	**zeer**	very
in de wieg	to be made	**zeggen (tegen)**	to say (to)
gelegd zijn	for/cut out for	**(zei/zeiden,**	
wiel (n)	wheel	**gezegd)**	
wij	we	**zeker**	of course,
wijn (c)	wine		certainly
willen (wou,	to want to	**zelf**	self; myself,
wilde/wilden,			yourself,
gewild)			himself,
winkel (c)	shop		herself, itself,
winnen (won/	to win		ourselves,
wonnen,			themselves
gewonnen)		**zelfrijzend**	self-raising
winter (c)	winter	**zelfs**	even
wisselen	to change (e.g.	**zes**	six
	money)	**zestien**	sixteen
wisselkantoor	exchange bureau	**zestig**	sixty
(n)		**zetel** (c)	seat (figurative)
wisselkoers (c)	exchange rate	**zetten**	to put
wit	white	**zeven**	seven
woensdag (c)	Wednesday	**zeventien**	seventeen
wol (c)	wool	**zeventig**	seventy
wolk (c)	cloud	**zich**	himself, herself,
wonen	to live		itself, them-
woonkamer (c)	lounge		selves
worden (werd/	to become	**ziek**	sick
werden, is		**ziekenhuis** (n)	hospital
geworden)		**zien (zag/zagen,**	to see
(rook)worst (c)	(smoked)	**gezien)**	
	sausage	**zij**	she; they

zijn	his, its	**zoon** (c)	son
zijn (was/waren,	to be	**zout** (n)	salt
is geweest)		**zuidelijk**	southern
zin (c)	interest	**zuiden** (n)	south
zin hebben	to be	**ten zuiden**	to the south
in	interested in	**van**	of
zingen (zong/	to sing	**zulk**	such
zongen,		**zullen (zou/**	'will', verb used
gezongen)		**zouden)**	for future
zitplaats (c)	seat		tense
zitten (zat/	to sit	**zus(ter)** (c)	sister
zaten, gezeten)		**zwaan** (c)	swan
zo	so; as	**zwager** (c)	brother-in-law
zodat	so that	**zwaluw** (c)	swallow
zodra	as soon as	**zwart**	black
zoeken (zocht/	to look for	**Zweden**	Sweden
zochten,		**Zweed** (c)	Swede
gezocht)		**Zweeds**	Swedish
zogenaamd	so-called	**Zweedse** (c)	Swedish woman
zolder (c)	attic	**zwembad** (n)	swimming pool
zomer (c)	summer	**zwemmen**	to swim
zondag (c)	Sunday	**(zwom/**	
zonder	without	**zwommen,**	
zonneschijn (c)	sunshine	**is/heeft**	
zonnig	sunny	**gezwommen)**	

Index

The numbers refer to lesson numbers unless otherwise indicated.